ENTERPRISE MONOPOLY IN THE
UNITED STATES: 1899–1958

Enterprise Monopoly in the United States: 1899-1958

G. WARREN NUTTER

and

HENRY ADLER EINHORN

COLUMBIA UNIVERSITY PRESS

New York and London

1969

Copyright © 1969 Columbia University Press
Library of Congress Catalog Number: 69–15570
Printed in the United States of America

Preface

This book is best viewed as a composite rather than a joint product. In essence, it brings together under one cover two separate studies of the extent of monopoly in the United States: mine covering the period 1899–1939 and completed almost two decades ago; and Dr. Einhorn's covering the period 1939–1958 and completed recently. Both have the common feature of having appeared first as doctoral dissertations.

My own work is reproduced here as it was originally published in 1951 except for revisions and additions in the introductory chapter, stylistic changes, correction of errors, and condensation of appendix materials. In particular, I am responsible for Chapters 1 through 3 and Appendixes A and B, whereas Einhorn has contributed Chapters 4 through 6 and Appendixes C and D. The summary, Chapter 7, results from our joint efforts.

No doubt this book could have been improved if the two studies had been carefully integrated and if my earlier work had been revised, but I did not feel up to this task, having been out of touch with the field of industrial organization for so long.

We hope that, despite its obvious weaknesses, this study may shed some additional light on an issue that continues to command attention. And perhaps some future historian of thought may find it interesting to compare two empirical studies of the same subject conducted fifteen years apart.

G. Warren Nutter

University of Virginia, July 1, 1968

Acknowledgments

The study covering the period 1899–1939, which originally appeared as a doctoral dissertation, is the result of research begun in 1947–1948 as a part of the Free Market Study at the University of Chicago and continued in 1948–1949 under a Research Training Fellowship granted by the Social Science Research Council. I am extremely grateful to both these sources for their generous financial assistance.

The reader is entitled to a preview of an author's general outlook. This outlook is perhaps best revealed through the names of those selected for special acknowledgment. Permit me to express, first, an inestimable debt to two great teachers and scholars: the late Professor Henry C. Simons and Professor Frank H. Knight. Their influence on my thinking about economics and political economy has been so pervasive as to defy specification. Special recognition is also due three men who guided this study: Professors O. H. Brownlee, Aaron Director, and Milton Friedman. Their continual insistence on scientific inquiry, relevance of argument, and clarity of expression is largely responsible for whatever merit this study may have. All arguments, statements, and data are, of course, mine alone. No one else can be held accountable for them.

G. Warren Nutter

Yale University, March 30, 1951

The study covering the period 1939–1958, also originally written as a dissertation, was begun in Washington, D.C., during the fall of 1960 and was completed in Rotterdam in early 1963. I was particularly fortunate in receiving encouragement and aid from many individuals and organizations. Foremost of those to whom thanks are due is Professor Donald Dewey of Columbia University, who first suggested that the study be attempted, and who since provided invaluable comments on the preliminary drafts and assistance in obtaining institutional support for the project.

Most of the work was completed during the 1961–1962 academic year when I was at Columbia on a Watson Laboratories Fellowship. At this time I was engaged in a related project comparing measures of industrial concentration; although this other project has not yet been completed, several results have been used in this dissertation. Thus thanks are expressed to the National Bureau of Economic Research, Inc., through the very kind auspices of Dr. Gerhard Bry and Mrs. Lottie Boschan, for the use of a very comprehensive frequency distribution analysis program which was prepared by Miss Juanita Johnson for use on the IBM 704 and 7090 electronic computers. Gratitude must also be expressed to Mr. Louis de Groot of IBM, who provided invaluable help. The dissertation was completed during the 1962–1963 academic year, when I was Edward W. Box Fellow at the Netherlands School of Economics. I am grateful to the school for providing very helpful research facilities.

Professor Harold Barger, chairman of the Graduate Department of Economics at Columbia University, was very helpful in securing Watson, Bok, and Fulbright grants. Dr. Albert Neisser provided valuable comments during the early stages of research and writing. Finally, to my parents and sister for their understanding and encouragement, this dissertation is dedicated.

Henry Adler Einhorn

Rotterdam, April 4, 1963

Both of us are indebted to Donald Dewey for his initial suggestion that the two studies be combined and for his subsequent advice and encouragement. The book could not have been prepared without the secretarial assistance of Anita L. Swint, Irene Grodzienski, Judy Sigall, and Cecelia Brown. We are also grateful to Marie-Christine MacAndrew for critical editorial work and to Coleman Nutter for preparing the index.

G. Warren Nutter

Henry Adler Einhorn

July 1, 1968

Contents

LIST OF TABLES

ENTERPRISE MONOPOLY IN THE
UNITED STATES: 1899–1958

CHAPTER 1

Issues, Problems, and Definitions

That competition is a virtue, at least as far as enterprises are concerned, has been a basic article of faith in the American tradition, and a vigorous antitrust policy has long been regarded as both beneficial and necessary, not only to extend competitive forces into new regions but also to preserve them where they may be flourishing at the moment. The traditional policy of free enterprise has not meant that every enterprise is free to do whatever it wishes, but rather that every person is free to engage in whatever line of business he may wish to enter. More than that, it has meant that the state has an obligation to enforce competition everywhere except in areas in which monopoly is "natural" —and at times even there.

To say that such policy has been traditional is certainly not to imply that it has been universally endorsed by scholars or the public at large. For example, some economists, like Schumpeter, have argued that monopolistic enterprises comprise one of the more powerful engines of progress in a market economy and that rigorous enforcement of competition is likely to do more harm than good.[1]* Others, some agreeing with Schumpeter and some not, have condemned traditional policy as futile in any event, on the grounds that monopolistic elements are too deeply rooted, too widespread, and too expansive to be eliminated or contained. At one extreme is the view, sometimes derived from the Marxian dialectic but more frequently not, that the American economy has steadily become less competitive and more monopolistic, and must continue to follow this trend.[2]

Of course, many voices have spoken for opposing views that support traditional policy in varying degrees, and the debate has waxed and

* Notes referred to by superior numbers will be found, arranged by chapters, in the section beginning on p. 231.

waned from time to time. The relatively dormant state of controversy today reflects, perhaps, the fact that the volume of empirical evidence accumulated over the last three decades has either settled old disputes or caused them to be reformulated. Part of that evidence will be presented here, some of it—covering the period from 1899 through 1939—reprinted from a work that was completed almost two decades ago but seems to have remained valid.

PROBLEMS AND DEFINITIONS

Much of the argument over the extent and growth of monopoly has arisen from confusion of two separable issues: what monopoly is, on the one hand, and how widespread it is, on the other. Basic agreement on a measure of extent can be obscured by an irrelevant dispute over what is being measured, or vice versa. There is no point in arguing, for instance, about the meaning of monopoly if measures of its extent are not significantly changed by substantial variations in its definition. In brief, the best way to eliminate disagreement on questions of fact is to attack the issues of definition and measurement separately.

This study has little to contribute on the issue of definition. Its primary purpose is to develop a meaningful quantitative index of the extent and growth of monopoly as defined by a particular set of criteria and to indicate how sensitive that index is to changes in those criteria. Discussion of definitional problems will be limited mainly to pointing out some of the major difficulties involved.

Definition of Monopoly. To define monopoly, we must set forth, first, what we are looking for and, second, how to find it. The first is a problem of concept; and the second, one of identification or operational definition. The conceptual meaning to be attached to monopoly must be delimited as clearly as possible, and it will depend primarily on the particular set of social problems that the investigator is interested in. Once the concept is determined, the problem shifts to outlining, as specifically as practicable, the objective criteria that will indicate the presence of monopoly.

The problem of definition is one of drawing lines that nature has omitted: "nature makes no leap." Hence some arbitrariness is involved in all definition. The primary objectives of a particular enquiry will dictate the way in which lines should be drawn. On the basis of these objectives, the number of lines will be held to a minimum and will be drawn in such a way that "considerable" movement in any direction will produce only "negligible" effects.

It is important to distinguish at the outset the "political" and "economic" aspects of monopoly. In a political sense, monopoly may refer to situations that provide a concentration of privileges or advantages in making and enforcing the effective rules of society. In an economic sense, monopoly refers to situations in the market that, within the existing effective framework of rules, lead to a particular kind of pricing process. The frequent use of the terms "concentration of economic power," "economic concentration," and "concentration of output" as interchangeable synonyms in the literature on monopoly reflects confusion of these fundamentally different concepts.

Many writers identify market monopoly with "big business," and big business in turn with political power. The identification is only partly correct and is more misleading than informative. Strong political pressure emanates from many industrial sectors not at all typified by big business. Witness the power of the farm bloc, of labor unions, and of local industries like the building trades in most regions. Moreover, not all big business possesses market monopoly. Large firms in the distributive trades, such as Sears, Roebuck, Woolworth, and the A & P, actually extend the range of services offered to consumers and thereby widen the scope of competition. Firms like General Motors and General Electric have only extremely limited, if any, monopolistic advantages in some product markets, such as home appliances. To complete the argument, we can observe that many relatively small firms are extremely monopolistic.

Economic power may, of course, exert itself in many ways other than through political influence or market monopoly. From this broader view, it is more difficult to make reasonable generalizations. In some aspects, the problems connected with corporate giantism may be subsumed under the general question of the desirable distribution of control over wealth, if there is any meaning to the distinction between ownership and control. In other aspects, the problems are merely another reflection of the rise of mass society. Business enterprises, like government and many social groups, have steadily grown in size, whereas the individual and the family, which remain the basic units in a democratic system, have stayed the same. The rise of mass society raises many significant and troublesome issues, but most of these lie outside the area of market monopoly.

The present study is concerned with monopoly in the market place. For that reason, no attempt will be made to analyze the findings and implications of studies of the "concentration of economic power" in any other sense.

There is no single meaning of market monopoly that will serve equally well for all purposes. For this study it seems appropriate to focus on enterprise monopoly as opposed to labor monopoly, but this choice should not be taken as implying that there are fundamental differences between the results of the two types. It is simply irrelevant here whether such differences do or do not exist.

Some monopolistic enterprises whose products are imported into American markets have developed outside the jurisdiction of the United States. These monopolies will not be considered, since neither their development nor their elimination can be considered as a direct consequence of economic conditions or public policy within the United States.

Enterprise monopoly will be considered to include many situations that might go by different names elsewhere. It seems relevant and sufficient in this study to divide all possible types of enterprise into three categories: monopolistic, competitive, and governmentally supervised. Some may object to such a broad concept of monopoly, preferring to distinguish a variety of cases and, in particular, to use the generic term "oligopoly." But in ordinary usage no one concept seems to enjoy a monopoly in the use of the term "monopoly." The typical case is to let the nature of the discussion rule the meaning of the word.[3]

Theoretical constructs are indispensable to the process of definition, but they must be severely modified to be relevant to an empirical study. For instance, the notion of "workable" competition must be substituted for that of "perfect" or "pure" competition, with differences in both preconditions and results. Workable results are those that approach the ones predicted for pure competition as closely as can be expected or closely enough for "all practical purposes"; workable preconditions are those that can be expected to lead to workable results. It is extremely difficult to make statements more precise or meaningful than these.

The structure of the theory of perfect, or even pure, competition offers few clues useful for defining workable competition. It is particularly misleading to judge market conditions by the presence or absence of the basic formal assumptions of perfect competition. Since the theory of perfect competition, like all theories, is an artificial system constructed for the purpose of analysis and prediction, the simplest set of assumptions has been chosen that is consistent with the processes and results of that system. It is always possible to construct alternative sets of assumptions, with any desired degree of complexity, equally consistent.[4] The purpose of simplification is to facilitate analysis, not to approximate reality.

One useful point of departure from theory is provided by the distinction between long-run demand conditions facing monopolistic and competitive firms. The essential precondition of competition (monopoly) is the fact that a firm will not (will) significantly affect price through relatively moderate variations in its output. The essential precondition of cartel-like behavior is the fact that an existing collusive group of firms will significantly affect price but that any one member-firm, acting by itself, will not.

It may be misleading, however, to concentrate on demand conditions in defining monopoly. Monopoly is of concern because of its effects, primarily on resource allocation. Monopoly is presumed to lead to a misallocation of resources because monopolistic firms are assumed to set output so that marginal costs persistently tend to differ from price. Such a policy implies an elasticity of demand significantly below infinity, but the converse need not hold: less than infinite elasticity of demand is a necessary, but not a sufficient, condition for monopolistic results.[5] Looked at the other way, infinite elasticity of demand is a sufficient, but not a necessary, condition for competitive results. A concept of monopoly that is to be relevant to social issues should be outlined in terms of kinds of behavior, not in terms of a framework of conditions. The distinction between preconditions and results is unimportant only in the rigorously controlled environment of economic theory.

The best method of identifying workably competitive (effectively monopolistic) situations would seem to be to discover behavior uniquely consistent with the theory of competition (monopoly), but such an approach would encounter at least two major problems. First, the required large-scale research would be prohibitively expensive. Second, the behavior of a firm or industry over a specified period of time may by no means be uniformly competitive or monopolistic. It may act as if it were competitive in some respects and not in others. For some purposes it is sufficient to know that responses will be competitive to certain changes but monopolistic to others. However, if we are trying to estimate the extent of monopoly and competition in the economy, it becomes necessary to characterize the nature of responses "in general."

Hence, we are forced to rely on less satisfactory indicators of monopoly and competition—in particular, on estimates of long-run elasticity of demand for individual firms. As pointed out, demand elasticity provides an asymmetrical test: high elasticity, in the absence of effective collusion, is a sufficient condition for competitive behavior; low elasticity is a necessary, but not a sufficient, condition for monopolistic behavior. The decision about how low elasticity must be to make monopolistic behavior probable is essentially arbitrary, involving implicit judgments on how much deviation from the "ideal" results of competition can be tolerated and how low elasticity of demand must be before behavior beyond tolerable limits can be expected to occur "in general." It is not enough that no precise judgments can be made; accurate measurement of long-run elasticity of demand is impossible in any case.

Elasticity of demand may be estimated directly or indirectly, and it is not clear that either method possesses a distinct advantage over the other. Direct measurement yields a more precise, but not necessarily more accurate, estimate. Measured elasticities are likely to be particularly misleading in themselves because, without elaborate data that are generally unavailable, they cannot reflect long-run demand conditions. In any case, little progress has been made in direct measurement of elasticities, so that the investigator has few such estimates at his disposal. He must rely instead on indirect evidence such as that provided by studies of the structure of industries—in terms of number of firms, concentration of output, and so on.

It should be clear that the development of operational definitions of workable competition and effective monopoly must take place outside the realm of formal mathematical precision and elegance. The element of "practical judgment" must pervade the entire analysis. Any decision on empirical criteria of monopoly involves hidden and indefinite answers to a host of hidden and indefinite questions about the nature and pre-conditions of effective monopoly. The validity of criteria can be determined only by submitting them to critical evaluation by the economic profession. Substantiation of practical judgments comes ultimately from agreement by respected economists that the judgments are as reasonable as can be expected, that is, that these experts would expect to make the same decisions in independently conducted research.

As stated earlier, this study does not pretend to resolve the problem of devising satisfactory operational definitions of competition and monopoly. In the absence of definitive studies of this problem and general agreement on conclusions, some arbitrariness in definitions is unavoidable. The particular choice here is to classify industries wherever possible on the basis of structural criteria, primarily in terms of concentration of output, unless other types of evidence strongly contradict the structural classification. This choice is made for two reasons: first, data on concentration of output constitute the only pertinent evidence on monopoly for broad sectors of the economy; and, second, those who disagree about the extent and growth of mo-nopoly seem most frequently to conceive of monopoly in terms of high output concentration. At least, they usually cite concentrated output as evidence that monopoly exists.

On the basis of structural evidence, an industry can be considered workably competitive if no firm produces more than a small pro-portion of total output, provided that there are no effective collusive arrangements among firms producing a substantial proportion. With such collusion, the industry can be considered effectively cartelized. If any one firm produces a substantial proportion of total output, the industry can be considered effectively monopolistic. Classification as monopolistic could be contradicted if independent evidence strongly indicates that long-run demand for the large firms is highly elastic or that pricing behavior is essentially in accord with behavior predictable only under the competitive abstraction.

The task of classifying all industries into these categories was considered much too imposing for the present study. Limited data and serious conceptual difficulties make it impossible to devise mutually exclusive operational definitions that will cause every industry to be included in a single category—unless the problem is defined away by setting up one classification to contain all industries that do not fall elsewhere. That is the procedure that we have followed: only the effectively monopolistic industries have been independently classified; the residual industries are taken as workably competitive. It was considered beyond the scope of this study to differentiate further between effectively cartelized and workably competitive industries, so that some of the former may be included among the latter.

A discussion of the many problems connected with the proper definition of industries and the determination of critical degrees of output concentration is presented in Chapter 2. It is impossible adequately to summarize the decisions made. The general tenor of this introductory discussion should make it clear that answers to these problems can be given only in the process of analyzing the concrete data available. Generalized statements have little meaning outside the context of the concrete situations.

Measurement of the Extent of Monopoly.   Sound appraisal of the extent of monopoly depends as much on adequate methods of measurement as on proper definition. Economists seem, indeed, to disagree more about the significance of monopolistic industries in the economy than about the identification of those industries.

Information on monopoly and competition is often summarized by verbal description or by counting up the number of industries in each category. Both methods are misleading. Clair Wilcox, in his important study of monopoly and competition in the United States,[6] devotes five times as many pages to monopolistic industries as to competitive industries, but it would be a mistake to conclude that monopoly is in any relevant sense five times as prevalent as competition. Verbal description overemphasizes the significance of monopoly; there is simply much more to say about the devious and often ingenious ways of monopoly than about the comparatively dull and uninteresting ways of competition.

Lists of industries can be equally misleading, since the number in a list can be increased or decreased almost at will by appropriately redefining industries. Regardless of how industries are defined, it is difficult to conceive of any useful purpose served by an index of extent with the industry as the unit of measurement. To add industries together is to add oranges and apples.

We should like to estimate the significance of monopoly and its change over time. The significance depends on how much monopoly there is in some relevant sense and on how much difference the existence of that much monopoly makes. We can find a meaningful quantitative answer to the first question, which concerns the extent of monopoly, but not to the second, which involves its importance.

A good index of extent should be based on a common denominator with the same meaning over time and in all sectors of the economy and should show the relation of the part estimated to the whole economy. The fraction of national income originating in monopolistic industries seems to be a satisfactory measure in these two respects. Like all major economic magnitudes, national income is subject to serious accounting and conceptual deficiencies. However, in view of recent developments in income accounting, these deficiencies are probably less serious than those for other magnitudes, certainly than for capital (i.e., wealth) accounts.

It is clear that estimates of extent, so defined, do not provide direct estimates of importance. In the relevant sense the importance of monopoly depends on the proportion by which real national income would change if monopolistic pricing could be everywhere replaced by competitive pricing. The proposed index of extent contributes little direct evidence on that question. If the fraction of national income originating in monopolistic industries were identical for two widely separated years, this identity could not be taken as meaning in itself that monopoly was equally important in both years.

This difficulty does not destroy the usefulness of such an index of extent. Provided that certain other relevant factors remain unchanged, the larger the fraction of national income originating in monopolistic industries, the greater is the importance of monopoly. If we insist that the index is useless because it does not reflect changes in the other relevant factors, we are indulging in foolish perfectionism. It is never possible to construct an economic measure that conforms in all important respects with the best measure that can be conceived. All we can hope for is a measure that is the best of those that can be constructed, and it is then up to us to interpret this measure with care.

THE EVIDENCE

The aims of this study are modest; consequently, the findings are of restricted usefulness. We are trying to summarize evidence that may help to resolve a basic disagreement about appropriate antimonopoly policy, a disagreement that seems to center on conflicting interpretations of the pervasiveness and expansive tendencies of economies of large size as a cause of monopoly. The evidence to be presented attacks the latter issue only obliquely by indicating, in quantitative form, the extent and growth of that enterprise monopoly which might conceivably be the result of economies of large size. No exhaustive survey is made of the probable causes of monopoly.

Since the core of this study, covering the period 1899–1939, was originally published sixteen years ago, enough time has passed for careful professional review of both methods and findings. The general reaction has been favorable, and corroborative evidence has emerged from other studies. But some specific criticisms warrant consideration.

In the fifth of his London lectures,[7] George J. Stigler presented his own estimates on the extent of monopoly in 1939 and its growth since 1900. On the surface Stigler's findings seem fully consistent with our own, but in a joint review of the two studies[8] Solomon Fabricant reveals important differences between the two and raises valid questions about both. One significant difference arises from Stigler's procedure of independently classifying industries into three categories—competition, compulsory cartel, and monopoly—and assigning those not classifiable to an unallocable category accounting for 18 per cent of national income in 1939. Moreover, some of Stigler's judgments on classification of industries differ from ours. Hence, as Fabricant points out,[9] our "estimate of degree of monopoly for 1939 is 23 per cent (the same as for 1937); Stigler's is 27 per cent (not including any monopolistic industries lost in the 'not allocable' group);[10] the estimate drawing on both [i.e., based on industries classified in either case as monopolistic] is 33 per cent."

After reviewing the shortcomings of these two studies, Fabricant comments[11] that nevertheless

... the essential validity of their conclusion must stand. All the doubts that can be raised do not destroy, rather they support, the conclusion that there is no basis for believing that the economy of the United States is largely monopolistic and has been growing more monopolistic.

Morris A. Adelman also endorsed this conclusion in his well-known article analyzing broader trends in economic concentration up to 1947.[12] In the ensuing discussion generated by this article,[13] Corwin D. Edwards objected[14] to some of the identifications of monopolistic industries for 1899, but Adelman pointed out[15] that the objections were based largely on a misinterpretation of the data.

Perhaps the sharpest criticism of the original study, aimed in part at the evidence for 1899 and in part at the treatment of railroads for 1939, was expressed in a brief journal note by Stanley Lebergott in 1953.[16] In effect, he argued that the evidence, properly revised, would demonstrate a clear and significant rise in the extent of monopoly between 1899 and 1939, contrary to the conclusion of our study. Lebergott's criticism was rejoined point by point in the same journal issue,[17] and it seems not to have been revived or supported since.

Meanwhile, a number of increasingly refined studies of industrial concentration (usually limited to mining and manufacturing) have appeared, using more sophisticated techniques for describing concentration and analyzing causal relations.[18] The question arises as to whether some of these newer techniques should be substituted for the cruder counterparts used in the original core of the present study and retained for its extension. We have concluded that these newer techniques as yet offer little promise for improved analysis of the problem at hand.

Consider, for example, the growing practice of fitting observed data on the size of firms within an industry to such standard frequency distributions, generated by various stochastic processes, as the log-normal, Yule, Pareto, and similar types.[19] If the fits are good, this procedure has the important advantages of permitting, among other things, formal statistical analysis of the phenomenon of concentration and derivation of the details of concentration in any given industry from the estimated parameters of the distribution function plus the number of firms. However, no systematic theory of industrial structure implying and rationalizing appropriate statistical distributions of firm size has emerged from empirical studies so far, and even if it does in the future there remains the task of linking the statistical parameters of such distributions to the expected monopolistic or competitive behavior of industries.

In brief there do not seem to be any broad substitutes as yet for the simple and conventional concentration ratios, calculated from census data in accord with disclosure rules, as generalized indicators of structural characteristics of industries. In response to continuing interest in antitrust and related problems on the part of various governmental agencies and congressional committees, concentration ratios have been periodically calculated in recent years on a comprehensive scale, at least for manufacturing. Hence the groundwork has been laid for studying the extent and growth of monopoly to as late, at this moment, as 1958.

We present in the following pages the results of such a study.

CHAPTER 2

Extent of Monopoly: 1937 and 1939

A CRITIQUE OF EARLIER STUDIES

A substantial revival of interest in the problems of market monopoly occurred in the United States during the 1930's. The renewed interest was reflected in the enthusiastic reception accorded the Robinson and Chamberlin works on imperfect and monopolistic competition. It was also reflected in the increased vigor of antimonopoly policy under the direction of Thurman Arnold. Developments in theory and anti-monopoly policy plus searches for explanations of the depression stimulated the output of empirical research. The climax came with the governmentally sponsored statistical studies of the National Resources Committee and the Temporary National Economic Committee.

The principal comprehensive investigations of industrial monopoly sponsored by these committees were (1) *The Structure of the American Economy*, written under the supervision of Gardiner C. Means; (2) *The Structure of Industry*, written under the joint supervision of Willard L. Thorp and Walter F. Crowder; and (3) *Competition and Monopoly in American Industry*, written under the supervision of Clair Wilcox.[1] The Means report and the Thorp and Crowder monograph exploited primary sources of data. The Wilcox work is essentially a comprehensive summary of many primary investigations.

THE MEANS AND CROWDER STUDIES

Only parts of the Means report and of the Thorp and Crowder monograph are concerned with the extent of market monopoly in the 1930's. Chapter vii and Appendixes 7 and 8 contain the pertinent materials in the Means report;[2] the bulk of Part V, written by Crowder, contains the pertinent materials in the Thorp and Crowder monograph. These are the parts which will be examined. They will be referred to as the "Means study" and the "Crowder study."

The purpose of our discussion is to determine what can and what cannot be inferred from these two studies about the extent of monopoly in the United States in the 1930's. We shall examine separately the matters of identifying monopoly and of estimating its extent.

The Identification of Monopoly. The Means and Crowder studies were both limited almost exclusively to manufacturing industries.[3] They differ significantly only in the care with which the investigations were conducted and in the methods used for defining industries. Crowder's study is the more scholarly and studiously avoids drawing tenuous conclusions about the importance of monopoly from data on concentration.[4] On the other hand, Crowder's definition of industries is not clearly an improvement over the approach in the Means study.

Since the studies were limited to manufacturing, they are useful for identifying monopoly in that area only. Moreover, the evidence on monopoly is in the form of output concentration, which is not by itself a completely reliable indicator of monopoly, even if industries and market areas are properly defined. In the first place, "high" output concentration means at best "low" elasticity of demand for the largest firms; and "low" elasticity of demand, for reasons pointed out in Chapter 1, is not a sufficient condition for monopolistic behavior. In the second place, long-run elasticity of demand for the largest firms does not depend only on their proportional shares of output; it depends also on the elasticity of market demand over the relevant range of prices and on the cost conditions for actual or potential competing firms. There is considerable merit in the old, and now unpopular, notion of "potential competition," if it is properly interpreted. The size of firms may be a matter of indifference within rather wide limits because of locational factors, possible variation in decentralization of management and of control over policy, the offsetting of apparent economies of scale by other important diseconomies, and so on. This interpretation seems consistent with industries that have a few dominant firms and a large number of small firms. Many contemporary economists have moved too far in the direction of assuming that prevailing industry patterns are exceedingly stable within very wide ranges of price and cost fluctuations. Although much can be said for using concentration of output as the basic test of monopoly, results obtained by this method should be qualified in the light of other evidence.

Concentration of output becomes a more tenuous indication of monopoly if industries are poorly defined in terms of either product group or market area. Consider, first, the case in which market area is not in serious doubt. Then an industry may be either too loosely or too specifically defined in terms of products. The definition is too loose if obviously wide gaps in substitutability or complementarity exist among the products; the definition is too specific if scarcely any gaps exist and very closely related commodities are not included. Whereas the Means study seems to err in the direction of looseness, the Crowder study, in attempting to correct the situation, errs seriously in the opposite direction.

Both used the industrial classification system of the *Census of Manufactures* as the source of data. The census classificatory system has been developed over a number of years and undergoes periodic revision. Commodities are grouped together in accordance with several criteria other than substitutability or complementarity in the market. Some groupings are made on the basis of use of a common raw material; others on the basis of manufacture in the same establishment; still others on the basis of a common technique of manufacture.

The system ranges from narrowest to broadest categories. The narrowest category is the "product"; the broadest, the "major industry group." Intermediate are the "industry," the "industry sub-group," and the "industry group." An example of the system in the 1939 Census is the following:

> Product: innerspring mattresses.
> Industry: mattresses and bedsprings.
> Industry subgroup: household furniture.
> Industry group: furniture.
> Major industry group: furniture and finished lumber
> products.

The extremes in this system are least likely, in general, to provide useful industry definitions for the purpose of monopoly investigations. The one is too narrow and specific; the other too broad and heterogeneous. Moreover, the same objections may apply to any particular item, regardless of its position in the general schema. That is, some "products" may be too heterogeneous; some "industries" too specific; and so on. As in so many cases, we are faced with an insoluble problem of classification which must somehow be solved within reasonably exact limits.

If the definition of industries on the basis of cross-elasticities of demand is discarded as not practicable, three alternatives remain. One consists in selecting one of the classificatory categories, such as the census industry, and confining study to it. That category would be chosen which provides, loosely speaking, the smallest number of improperly defined industries or, more accurately, the smallest amount of national income originating in improperly defined industries. A second alternative consists in judging each census item separately, regardless of category. This method would mean essentially the construction of an entirely new classificatory system. A third alternative would be some combination of the other two. Of the three possibilities, the second is most costly. At the same time, the results might not be significantly different from those yielded by a skilful application of the third procedure. In any event, the second alternative has not yet been extensively explored.

Both Means and Crowder adopted the first procedure. The former investigated the concentration of output in census industries; the latter, the concentration in census products. Means argued that the use of census industries caused an understatement of concentration ratios. (The "concentration ratio" is defined in the Means and Crowder studies as the proportion of total value of output in an industry which is produced by the four largest firms.) He maintained, "If the manufacture of each major product were taken separately, a very much greater degree of concentration would be shown."[5]

The argument is misleading. The concentration ratios which Crowder computed for census products were, in general, larger than those for census industries.[6] But the two sets of ratios are not directly comparable if the increase in ratios has been accomplished through a redefinition of industries that leads to a marked general increase in the elasticities of market demand. Crowder explicitly recognized the difficulty here but resolved it most peculiarly by stating, "In general, however, one is warranted in assuming that Census product differentiations do reflect in varying degrees significant economic functional differences, since they represent largely the cumulative result of suggestions and requests made through the years by manufacturers and their trade associations."[7] This statement notwithstanding, the use of census products does lead in many instances to ridiculous degrees of commodity differentiation. "Boys' suits" was a census industry in 1937. This industry was broken down into the following seven products: (1) boys' suits, cotton; (2) boys' suits, mohair, silk, linen, etc.; (3) boys' suits, 1-pants (knickers); (4) boys' suits, 1-pants (not knickers); (5) boys' suits, 2-pants (knickers); (6) boys' suits, 2-pants (not knickers); and (7) boys' suits, 2-pants (1 long pants, 1 knickers). In addition, "boys' separate garments" was listed as a different industry, including the following four products: (1) pants and knickers, cotton; (2) pants and knickers, wholly or partly wool; (3) coats; and (4) overcoats. These "products" obviously have very high elasticities of substitution as far as both demand and supply are concerned. By disregarding such considerations, concentration ratios up to 100 per cent could be produced at will. But they would provide little useful information on monopoly.

Examples of excessively narrow product definitions can be easily proliferated. For instance, among census products with concentration ratios of 3/4 or larger are the following:[8]

1. Canned meats other than vacuum-cooked.
2. Wool, in meat-packing establishments.
3. Mixtures of corn and other syrups.
4. Men's-wear suitings and pantings, other worsted (except all-wool).
5. Machine-finished book paper containing ground wood.
6. Men's work shoes, wood or metal fastened.
7. Radio receiving sets, extending beyond standard broadcast band, socket-power-operated, over $45 but not over $65.
8. Tractors, wheel type, except "all-purpose," 30 belt horsepower and over.
9. Tractors, wheel type, "all-purpose," under 30 belt horsepower, steel tires.

10. Tractors, wheel type, "all-purpose," under 30 belt horsepower, rubber tires.
11. Domestic refrigerators, electric, 6 cubic feet or more but under 10.
12. Refrigerating systems, complete without cabinets.
13. Refrigerator cabinets, domestic.

Of course, not all census products are too narrowly defined for study of monopoly, and this consideration cannot be taken as completely invalidating the Crowder study. Objections can also be raised to the use of census industries on the grounds that they are frequently too broadly defined. In making judgments on the location of monopoly, we should utilize the findings from both approaches. In doing so, we must keep in mind that the particular height of a concentration ratio has little meaning unless the nature of industry definitions is also taken into account. The important problem is the determination of critical values for concentration ratios, that is, the determination of values which are considered to be high enough to make workable competition improbable. In general, these critical values should be higher for census products than for census industries.

Up to this point it has been assumed that market areas were not in doubt. Let us now consider that problem, supposing that industries are otherwise properly defined.

Concentration ratios were computed on a national basis. This procedure makes no allowance for markets which are, on the one side, regional and, on the other, international in scope. Failure to take account of these factors means that some ratios overstate and others understate the degree of concentration. Both Means and Crowder explicitly recognized the understatement for regional industries,[9] but neither considered the likelihood of overstatement for international industries.

There is no doubt that concentration ratios would be more meaningful if computed on the basis of actual market areas. At the same time, the important question is: How much difference would such computation make in identifying monopoly and in estimating its extent? The latter part of this question will be discussed later.

In the absence of concrete data it is not clear that regional ratios would be consistently higher than national ratios. Many might be lower.[10] We know little about the over-all effect on concentration ratios for manufacturing industries which follows from computing them on a regional basis, since evidence is extremely meager.[11] On the other hand, concentration ratios which make allowance for the international scope of markets—that is, which are computed with imports included in total output—will invariably be smaller if the firms producing the imports are not taken into account. These firms should not be taken into account if one is interested in studying monopoly within the jurisdiction of the United States. Since this is the problem toward which the present study is directed, we may assume that the relevant concentration ratios will be lowered for industries whose products are imported as well as produced domestically.

The fact that concentration ratios might be changed is unimportant in itself. The important question is whether the changes would be large enough to affect judgments about the monopolistic character of an industry. In the case of common brick, ratios were significantly raised by computing them on a regional basis.[12] But the results for a single industry can scarcely be generalized. Neither Means nor Crowder considered the case of international markets. George J. Stigler, however, presented this table in his review article of the Thorp and Crowder

	Concentration Ratio	
	Monograph No. 27	Revised to Include Imports
Newsprint	68.1	15.2
Crude glycerine	40.2	24.8
Acetic acid	73.4	58.4
Sodium sulphate	63.0	35.2
Tin	89.6	0.4
Cigarette paper	71.6	50.4
Burlap	39.6	23.4
Rayon waste	70.9	32.6
Whiskey	40.0	25.1

monograph, showing the effect on concentration ratios if imports are included in total output.[13] The downward revision for some industries, like tin, is startling indeed. However, it is also difficult to draw any general conclusions from this relatively small sample of industries.

In summarizing this discussion of what can be learned from the

Means and Crowder studies about the existence of monopoly, we can make the following statements. First, the studies are useful only for identifying monopolistic manufacturing industries. Second, concentration of output is the only indicator of monopoly, and any conclusions drawn on this basis should be subject to revision on the basis of other evidence. Third, neither of the adopted solutions of the problem of defining industries is clearly superior; each has certain advantages and disadvantages. Concentration ratios for census products and for census industries should both be used in identifying monopoly, but the critical ratios for census products should, in general, be higher than those for census industries. And, fourth, the failure in both studies to take account of geographic limits to markets means that some ratios are overstated and others are understated. The net bias cannot be determined from available evidence.

Estimation of the Extent of Monopoly.   Since the Means and Crowder studies are limited almost exclusively to manufacturing industries, it is necessary to exercise extreme care in drawing conclusions from them about the comparative extent of monopoly in the whole economy. Grant for the moment that it is possible to identify monopoly from the results of these studies. It would still be dangerous to generalize from any indications of the extent of monopoly in manufacturing, since manufacturing accounts for a relatively small proportion of market production. In 1939, for example, less than 25 per cent of national income originated in manufacturing. This fact would in itself be unimportant if monopolistic conditions in manufacturing were characteristic of those in other sections of the economy. However, as we shall show later, monopoly is much less prevalent in other areas with equally large production.

The Means study presents little information from which a clear impression of the relative extent of monopoly in manufacturing can be gained. The concentration data are summarized in the form of charts which list industries and their concentration ratios.[14] From these charts it is possible to compile a list of industries with concentration ratios above some critical level. Such a list would be a poor indicator of the extent of monopoly.

TABLE 1

Percentage of National Income Originating in Manufacturing Industries with High Concentration of Output and in All Manufacturing Industries, by Major Industry Group: 1939

	Highly Concentrated Industries			
	121 Census Products[a]	54 Census Industries[b]	42 Census Industries[c]	All Industries
Foods	0.10	0.31	0.41	3.14
Tobacco products	0.31	0.27	0.05	0.41
Textile products	0.04	0.02	0.12	1.74
Apparel			0.01	1.40
Lumber				0.68
Furniture	0.04	0.02	0.03	0.70
Paper	0.01			0.77
Printing and publishing			0.01	1.66
Chemicals	0.13	0.39	0.03	1.66
Petroleum and coal products	0.01	0.00		0.63
Rubber products	0.20	0.24		0.38
Leather products	0.01			0.58
Stone, clay, and glass products	0.11	0.08	0.09	0.91
Iron and steel products	0.42	0.16	0.13	3.11
Nonferrous products	0.11	0.17	0.11	0.82
Electrical machinery	0.28			1.17
Machinery	0.18	0.27	0.04	2.06
Automobiles	0.85	1.64		1.64
Transportation equipment	0.06	0.10	0.18	0.55
Miscellaneous products	0.06	0.17	0.10	0.71
Total	2.92	3.84	1.31	24.73

Source: Tables A-2 through A-4.

[a] Those valued at $10,000,000 or more and with concentration ratios of 3/4 or larger in 1937.

[b] Those with concentration ratios of 2/3 or larger in 1935.

[c] Those with concentration ratios of 1/2 to 2/3 in 1935.

Table 1 shows for 1939 the percentage of national income originating in three groups of highly concentrated industries. The first group includes 121 census products of major value found in the Crowder study to have concentration ratios of 3/4 or larger in 1937. The second group includes 54 census industries found in the Means study to have concentration ratios of 2/3 or larger in 1935. The third group includes 42 additional census industries found in the Means study to have concentration ratios of 1/2 to 2/3 in 1935.[15] The 54 census industries accounted for 3.8 per cent of national income or for about 16 per cent of manufacturing production.[16] The 42 census industries accounted for only 1.3 per cent of national income or for only about 5 per cent of manufacturing production. Adding the two groups together, we find that the 96 census industries accounted for 5.1 per cent of national income or for about 21 per cent of manufacturing production. The 121 census products, on the other hand, accounted for only 2.9 per cent of national income or for about 12 per cent of manufacturing production. From these figures it is evident that absolute numbers of industries are not satisfactory indices of the extent of monopoly.

Relative numbers serve no better. In the 1935 Census there were 275 census industries; in the 1937 Census there were approximately 3,600 census products. The 54 industries represent about 19 per cent of the total number; the 42 industries, about 15 per cent; the 121 products, about 3 per cent. The 19 per cent of census industries with highest concentration ratios accounted for 16 per cent of manufacturing production, but the 15 per cent of census industries with next highest concentration ratios accounted for only 5 per cent of manufacturing production. On the other hand, the 3 per cent of census products with highest concentration ratios accounted for 12 per cent of manufacturing production.[17]

Crowder did summarize findings in frequency distributions of both the number and the value of products by concentration classes.[18] But he used gross-value instead of value-added data. The total gross value and total value added accounted for by a group of industries with high concentration ratios will probably not coincide if there is any correlation between degrees of concentration and "vertical integration." The two do not correspond for the 121 products of major value with concentration ratios of 3/4 or larger. In 1939 these products accounted for 11 per cent of value added but for about 10 per cent of gross value[19] of all manufactured products.

Both studies present evidence on the relative importance of regional, but not of international, industries. From this evidence we can at least estimate the maximum possible error in measuring the extent of monopoly which could result from failure to compute concentration ratios on a regional basis. Unfortunately, the error resulting from failure to consider the international scope of markets cannot be estimated. The census industries which Means classified as having regional markets accounted for about 16 per cent of total value added in manufacturing in 1939.[20] The census products which were similarly classified by Crowder accounted for 14 per cent of the total gross value of manufactured products in 1937.[21] Therefore, at most, 4 per cent of national income was produced in these regional census industries or products in 1939. Moreover, many of the census products classified as regional had "high" (national) concentration ratios. Those with ratios above 7/10 accounted for more than 30 per cent of the gross value of all regional products; those with ratios above 1/2 accounted for about 50 per cent.[22]

THE WILCOX STUDY

The Wilcox study differs from the Means and Crowder studies in two important respects. First, it is a survey of available evidence on monopoly and competition in the United States since World War I; it is not a primary source of information. Second, its purpose is the identification of monopoly and competition in the whole economy.

Wilcox did not rely on any single test of monopoly or competition.[23] He realized that definitive identification of either is extremely difficult but made the following suggestion:

Within those fields, however, where producers are numerous, where the degree of concentration is low, where the prices charged by different firms are not identical, where these prices are not rigidly maintained over long periods of time, where the volume of production is not drastically curtailed at the onset of depression, where productive capacity is largely utilized during each of the phases of the trade cycle, where profits are moderate, where the turnover of producing units is rapid, and where the rate of business mortality is high, there is a presumption that effective competition prevails.[24]

By a careful and flexible application of these broad criteria, Wilcox separated effectively competitive industries from effectively monopolistic ones. The monopolistic area was further subdivided into situations in which supply was predominantly accounted for by one or two firms (monopoly and duopoly); by only a few firms (oligopoly); by one or a

few dominant firms and many smaller ones (dominant-firm industries);
and by several or many firms acting in collusion (cartels, pools, and
effective trade associations). The oligopoly, dominant-firm, and cartel
situations were further subdivided according to type of behavior.
Industries which were characterized by more than one type of behavior
were correctly discussed in all appropriate sections and were not
arbitrarily assigned to any one category.

Although Wilcox performed ably the task of classifying industries, he
purposely failed to provide a concise quantitative summary of the
comparative extent of monopoly and competition.[25] It would, however,
be grossly unreasonable to demand all things of the Wilcox study. The
main problem which it attacked—namely, the identification of monopoly
and competition—was competently handled. Indeed, no other study of
comparable success exists. The Wilcox monograph is a solid foundation
upon which to build.

THE FINDINGS OF THE PRESENT STUDY

The primary objective of the present inquiry is the development of a
quantitative measure of the relative extent of monopoly. We shall not
reconstruct foundations but shall build upon existing ones.

Our list of monopolistic industries[26] was drawn mainly from the
Wilcox study. Of the monopolistic situations which he described, only
the "pure" cartels[27] and the industries whose production occurs
entirely outside the United States have not been included. Contract
construction and fluid-milk production, which are fundamentally
cartelized, are, however, included as monopolistic areas, since there is
evidence of output concentration in many local markets.

To the group of industries taken from the Wilcox monograph we have
added any manufacturing census industries with concentration ratios[28]
in 1935 of 1/2 or larger and any census products of major value with
concentration ratios in 1937 of 3/4 or larger which were not covered by
Wilcox, leaving out only those which he had characterized as effectively
competitive for other reasons.[29] It should be noted that Wilcox took
into account the regional nature of markets in deciding whether an
industry was monopolistic.[30] He did not, on the other hand, give much

attention to the international scope of markets. Therefore, our list of monopolistic industries is, if anything, an overstatement on this score.

Our measures of the relative extent of monopoly are based on estimates of the income which originated in monopolistic industries. The practical difficulties that arise in applying the concept of "income originating" to specific industries and the techniques adopted in handling them are discussed in Appendix A.

Table 2 presents the estimates of the percentages of national income produced in effectively monopolistic areas in 1937 and 1939, broken down by major industrial divisions. Also included are estimates of the percentages originating in governmental activities and governmentally supervised industries, households and nonprofit institutions, and workably competitive industries.[31] We find that in these two years (1) the effectively monopolistic industries accounted for between 20 and 21 per cent of national income; (2) the workably competitive industries, between 55 and 56 per cent; (3) the governmental and "regulated" sector, between 19 and 20 per cent; and (4) households and nonprofit enterprises, about 4 per cent.

Other measures of the relative extent of monopoly may be more relevant to the question of the "inevitability" of monopoly than one based on total national income. We really want to know the prevalence of monopoly in that sector of the economy which is—or could be—organized by private enterprise. We want to eliminate from consideration the income derived from purely governmental activities. An approximation to the income figure that we desire is nongovernmental production.[32] The concept of monopolistic industry must now be expanded to include governmentally supervised industries that would act like private monopolies in the absence of supervision. Public utilities and (possibly) radio broadcasting would fall into this category. Transportation is, however, a much more doubtful area. With the exception of facilities to some comparatively isolated communities, the effectively supervised transportation services were probably produced, in general, more under competitive than under monopolistic conditions in the 1930's. Some specialized types of transportation, like pipelines, were monopolized. For the case of pipelines there is no problem, since the industry was not effectively supervised.

TABLE 2

Percentage Distribution of National Income by Industrial Origin and by

	Effectively Monopolistic	
	1937	1939
Agriculture	0.98	0.96
Mining	0.71	0.57
Contract construction	2.74	3.11
Manufacturing	10.22	9.79
Trade	1.59	1.45
Finance	2.34	2.39
Transportation	0.18	0.18
Communication	1.25	1.39
Public utilities		
Services	0.58	0.59
Government and government enterprises		
Nonallocable		
Total	20.59	20.43

Source: Tables A-10 and A-13 through A-16; *Survey of Current Business Supplement,* July 1947, p. 26.

ª We assume that supervised communication and public utilities would have been

Monopolistic industries, including public utilities and radio broadcasting, accounted for 26 per cent of nongovernmental production in 1937 and 1939.[33] The remainder, 74 per cent, was produced under workably competitive or nonprofit conditions.

Table 3 shows the extent of monopoly in major industrial divisions in 1937 and 1939. The data indicate that monopolistic production is relatively most extensive in contract construction, communication, public utilities, manufacturing, mining, and finance. It is relatively least extensive in transportation, services, trade, and agriculture. These results will scarcely come as a surprise.

Consider, further, the areas in which monopoly is most extensive. There is no need to look into the construction trades, communication, or public utilities, for we have already arbitrarily designated these entire areas as monopolistic. The handling of these areas could undoubtedly be improved upon with additional study. In Table 4 are the relevant data for major industry groups in mining and manufacturing. More detailed information is in Appendix A. We note from Table 4

Type of Productive Organization: 1937 and 1939

Workably Competitive		Governmental or Governmentally Supervised[a]		All Types	
1937	1939	1937	1939	1937	1939
8.87	7.48			9.85	8.44
1.93	1.64			2.64	2.21
				2.74	3.11
16.00	14.94			26.22	24.73
14.62	15.27			16.21	16.72
8.45	8.94			10.79	11.33
0.24	0.27	5.73	5.81	6.15	6.26
		0.09	0.11	1.34	1.50
		2.34	2.45	2.34	2.45
10.35[b]	10.55[b]			10.93	11.14
		10.59	11.79	10.59	11.79
				0.20	0.34
60.46	59.09	18.75	20.16	100.00	100.02

effectively monopolistic in the absence of governmental supervision, while supervised transportation would have been workably competitive.

[b] Includes 4.04 per cent for 1937 and 4.11 per cent for 1939 attributable to households and nonprofit institutions.

TABLE 3

Relative Extent of Monopoly[a] in Major Industry Divisions: 1937 and 1939 (per cent)

	1937	1939
Contract construction	100.0	100.0
Communication	100.0[b]	100.0[b]
Public utilities	100.0[b]	100.0[b]
Manufacturing	39.0	39.6
Mining	26.9	25.8
Finance	21.1	21.7
Agriculture	10.0	11.4
Trade	9.8	8.7
Services	5.3	5.3
Transportation	2.9	2.9

Source: Table 2.

[a] Measured by percentage of income originating in each division accounted for by monopolistic industries.

[b] Includes effectively supervised industries. If these are excluded, the percentages become:

	1937	1939
Communication	93.3	92.7
Public utilities	0.0	0.0

TABLE 4

Relative Extent of Monoploy in and Relative Size of Major Industry Groups in Mining and Manufacturing: 1937 and 1939 (per cent)

	Relative Extent of Monopoly[a]		Relative Size of Group[b]	
	1937	1939	1937	1939
Mining				
Anthracite	100.0	100.0	7.2	7.7
Metal	64.7	61.7	23.5	21.7
Nonmetal	63.2	55.5	7.2	8.1
Soft coal			31.1	31.2
Crude petroleum			31.1	31.2
Manufacturing				
Automobiles	99.4	100.0	6.7	6.6
Petroleum and coal products	79.0	81.0	3.1	2.5
Electrical machinery	80.5	79.5	4.7	4.7
Tobacco products	76.9	78.1	1.0	1.7
Stone, clay, and glass products	72.7	73.6	3.4	3.7
Transportation equipment	68.9	72.7	1.7	2.2
Foods	49.7	50.3	12.4	12.7
Chemicals	51.9	50.0	6.0	6.7
Nonferrous products	46.3	50.0	3.6	3.3
Iron and steel products	39.6	38.9	13.4	12.6
Miscellaneous products	39.1	38.0	2.6	2.9
Lumber	21.1	26.5	2.9	2.7
Machinery	22.2	21.4	9.1	8.3
Textile products	12.9	13.2	8.3	7.0
Furniture	13.0	12.9	2.6	2.8
Rubber products	10.0	5.3	1.5	1.5
Paper	4.0	5.2	2.9	3.1
Leather products	1.6	1.7	2.4	2.3
Apparel	0.8	0.7	5.1	5.7
Printing and publishing			6.4	6.7

Source: Tables A-10, A-11, and A-12; *Survey of Current Business Supplement*, July 1947, p. 26.

[a] Measured by percentage of income originating in each group accounted for by monopolistic industries.

[b] Measured by percentage of total mining or manufacturing production accounted for by each group.

[c] The relative extent of monopoly was computed on the basis of gross-value data for 1937 and of value-added data for 1939.

that only soft coal mining and crude petroleum extraction escaped widespread monopolistic conditions in mining. Manufacturing industry groups can be separated into four categories: (1) a very high percentage of production was monopolistic in automobiles, petroleum and coal products, electrical machinery, tobacco products, transportation equipment, and stone, clay, and glass products; (2) a moderately high percentage in foods, chemicals, nonferrous products, iron and steel products, and miscellaneous products; (3) a low percentage in lumber, machinery, textile products, and furniture; and (4) a very low percentage in rubber products, paper, leather products, apparel, and printing and publishing. The comparative importance of each of these categories is shown by the proportion of manufacturing production which the industry groups account for. In 1939, 21 per cent of manufacturing production originated in the groups in the first category; 38 per cent in the groups in the second category; 21 per cent in the groups in the third category; and 19 per cent in the groups in the fourth category.[34]

In the communication sector, the telephone and telegraph systems comprised the ineffectively supervised monopolistic industries; radio broadcasting was considered monopolistic but effectively supervised. Banking and insurance carriers were classified as monopolistic in the field of finance.

The monopolistic industries in transportation, services, trade, and agriculture were (1) pipelines in transportation, (2) motion pictures in the services sector, (3) milk distribution and the retailing of new automobiles in trade, and (4) milk production in agriculture. In the transportation area, "services allied to transportation" were considered as neither effectively supervised nor monopolistic. All effectively supervised activities in transportation were taken as potentially workably competitive.

We can probably best conclude our discussion of the extent of monopoly in the late 1930's with some words of qualification. No quantitative measure of the extent of monopoly is more reliable than the data and techniques upon which it is based. If there is no consistent dissatisfaction with our list of monopolistic industries or with our techniques of measurement, the findings of this study should be useful for some purposes. Some industries have undoubtedly been erroneously omitted from our list of monopolies. On the other hand, it is also likely that some have been erroneously included. The effects of both types of error should be weighed before any final judgments are made. The same statement applies to the determination of a possible net bias in our techniques of measurement.

It cannot be too strongly stressed that the measures of extent, as defined in this study, are not measures of importance in any other sense. We cannot determine from our estimates just how different conditions would have been if competitive pricing has replaced monopolistic pricing everywhere. The findings of our study indicate only that workably competitive production was about two and a half to three times as prevalent as monopolistic production in the late 1930's. This estimate, with proper qualifications, should at least serve as a basis for more fruitful discussion of the "inevitability" of monopoly.

CHAPTER 3

Growth of Monopoly: 1899–1939

INTRODUCTION

Those who debate the question of a "decline of competition" should realize that there simply are no quantitative estimates of the growth of enterprise monopoly over the last fifty years. The absence of such data frequently makes it difficult to know what the debate is about. Each side tends to phrase its arguments in unverifiable terms. One side maintains that monopoly has grown significantly; the other counters that it has not. One side asserts that economies of scale are more important now than fifty years ago; the other says that they are not. Without quantitative definitions of "significant growth" and of "importance," there is no way of knowing who is right and what difference it makes.

Nonquantitative reasoning probably leads, in general, to an overestimation of the growth of monopoly. In the first place, the observer notices a mass of statistical information on monopoly in the 1930's as against a relative dearth of evidence on monopoly in the 1890's. In the second place, many of the signs of growth are much more spectacular than are the signs of counteracting tendencies. The rise of giant corporations is more striking than is the concomitant expansion of markets. Novel monopolistic practices quickly gain notoriety, while the spreading of competitive forces passes unadvertised. Finally, there is a tendency to romanticize the past, to look upon the end of the nineteenth century as a period of Christian morality, prosperity, and competition.

To indicate how tenuous reasoning can be on this level, we shall undertake an extremely brief and superficial survey of factors which might have strengthened or weakened the bases of monopoly in the United States over the period from 1899 to 1939. Our main evidence on the growth of monopoly, however, will be the quantitative data submitted in the concluding section of this chapter.

Before proceeding, the reader should remind himself that the matter being examined is the change in the extent of enterprise monopoly. This is not a study of the development of noncompetitiveness in general or of shifts in the distribution of "economic power" or wealth. In so far as one is concerned with discovering in what sense a private-enterprise economy might be self-destructive, the other issues are certainly important. The present study does not pretend to deal with them.

FACTORS AFFECTING THE GROWTH OF MONOPOLY

The difficult task in any analysis is to limit the factors investigated to manageable proportions and still not to omit any important ones. The amount of monopoly is, of course, dependent ultimately on everything else, and everything else is dependent on the amount of monopoly. But, in recognizing this pervasive interdependence, we have added nothing useful to our previous knowledge. For present purposes the pertinent issue is: Has everything else changed in the last fifty years in such a way as to lead to more extensive monopolistic conditions? The problem thus posed is obviously unmanageable.

We shall be concerned with observing some of the probable effects of changes in the following: (1) the extent of markets, (2) the rate of innovation, (3) uncertainty, (4) the composition of national income, (5) the effective framework of rules, and (6) economies of scale.

Changes in the Extent of Markets. The most striking development leading to expanded market areas has been the lowered cost of transportation and communication.[1] The scope of markets has increased on the supply side; the knowledge of and access to markets have expanded on the demand side.[2] The national or international area is a much more representative market today than it was in 1899. The implications for monopoly are apparent. Unless monopolistic firms have increased their output at a rate faster than the expansion of total output in the relevant market areas, their monopolistic positions have probably been impaired.

On the other side, factors like tariffs and regional barriers to trade may have operated to restrict market areas. A trade barrier will strengthen the bases of monopoly if the industry "protected" is domestically monopolistic or if demand conditions facing an "exporting" industry are incidentally so reduced that the firm of most efficient size becomes monopolistic. Otherwise the results will be cartel-like. An extensive analysis of conditions in industries affected by tariffs would be required before any sound generalizations on effects could be made.

It seems reasonably safe to conclude, however, that changes in the extent of markets have, on balance, worked against an increase in monopoly.

Changes in the Rate of Innovation. Innovation is the anathema of monopoly. Few monopolies can be stable in the face of continual changes in technology and tastes. Specific commodities cannot for long fail to have very close substitutes; technological advantages in production may dwindle away; demand conditions may frequently shift in favor of other products. The more rapidly such changes occur, the smaller the opportunity for any firm to develop a long-run monopolistic position.

There seems little reason for supposing that the rate of innovation has slowed up over the last half-century. In fact, evidence points toward an acceleration. The authors of the National Resources Committee study of technological trends reached this conclusion:

The large number of inventions made every year shows no tendency to diminish. On the contrary the trend is toward further increases. No cessation of social changes due to invention is to be expected. It is customary to speak of the present age as one of great change, as though it were a turbulent transition period between two plateaus of calm, but such a conclusion is illusory. Though the rate of change may vary in the future there is no evidence whatever of a changeless peace ahead.[3]

The data on issuance of patents support this position. More patents were issued in the ten-year period from 1931 through 1940 than in the twenty-year period from 1881 through 1900; more than twice as many were issued from 1931 through 1940 as from 1891 through 1900.[4] Even these data do not reflect adequately the large number of new products which have been introduced in the last fifty years.

The rapid rate of innovation is likely to have favored monopoly in general only if such widespread advantages of large-scale production have resulted that all other effects have been more than offset. Discussion of this possibility will be postponed until a later point.

Changes in Uncertainty. "Uncertainty" has become a catchall term for economists. It summarizes all the imponderables and incalculables that disturb the smooth operation of the economy. Unpredictable fluctuations in demand and cost conditions, in capital values, and in general price levels are important sources of uncertainty for the entrepreneur or investor. The pertinent question for this discussion is twofold. First, to what extent are monopolies favored by uncertainty? Second, has uncertainty increased or decreased over the last fifty years? Unfortunately, neither question is easily answered.

In some senses an economy characterized by unpredictable business fluctuations offers a climate favorable to monopolies. Venture investment is inhibited, especially in view of the type of progressive taxation that has existed. Moreover, investment diversification for one reason or another has probably been accomplished in large part through giant operating firms; hence, in so far as monopoly accompanies large size, it may be stimulated by uncertainty. Finally, the established concern may enjoy a differential advantage in capital markets because one of the few accepted tests of future survival is survival in the past.

But competitive firms also have advantages. If the degree of flexibility and specialization of investment in an industry is narrowly limited by cost factors, uncertainty may favor relatively small firms (investments) because of possibly greater ease of disinvestment. Disinvestment may be more costly for a single large firm than for a number of small firms with the same total investment. Furthermore, there is little evidence that flexibility and lack of specialization can be gained only by expanding the size of plants or firms or, if so, that the costs may not exceed the gains. The inducement to diversify may greatly restrict the incentive and ability to monopolize. Finally, the small management unit may possess many advantages. Adjustments to unforeseen changes can be made more rapidly, and errors in judgment are likely to be less costly. Even if these advantages are not sufficient to make for small firms, they may cause such decentralization of control that the giant firm will act as if it were a collection of relatively small, independently operated firms.

It is likewise difficult to say that conditions in general have become either more or less uncertain over the last fifty years. The recent record of forecasts of broad industrial fluctuations has been, to say the least, notably poor; but we have little reason to suspect that the record in the 1890's or early 1900's was either any better or much worse. There are some areas in which uncertainty has rather clearly lessened. The prediction of conditions facing particular firms or industries has probably improved with the development of statistical techniques and the collection of data. The increased speed and lowered cost of communication have decreased the delay in learning about events. On the other hand, there are other areas in which uncertainty has increased. This is perhaps most clearly true of the political sector. The insecurity of international politics, the unpredictability of internal economic policy, the uncertainty growing out of the intensifying rivalry of economic blocs—all these have probably increased during the last fifty years.

This brief and superficial discussion indicates the difficulties involved in making any simple generalizations about changes in uncertainty or the effects of those changes. In some respects conditions may be more uncertain now than fifty years ago; in others they may be less uncertain. Uncertainty may favor both monopolistic and competitive situations. The effects may vary with the times, depending on the "optimism"—or, better, "the gambling spirit"—of the public. We actually know very little about that broad area of problems that are thrown together under the heading of "uncertainty." We shall most likely never know as much about them as we should like to know.

Changes in the Composition of National Income. Monopoly has typically concentrated in certain areas of the economy. Contract construction, manufacturing, communication, public utilities, mining, and finance were most monopolistic in the late 1930's; agriculture, trade, and services were most competitive. The latter area accounted for about 53 per cent of national income in 1899 but for only 37 per cent in 1937.[5] Therefore, there was a decline of about 16 per cent of national income in that sector. This decline was largely matched by the increased share of government, which produced 10 per cent more of national income in 1937 than in 1899. The remainder of the decline—6 per cent of national income—represents the increased share of the area which was most monopolistic in 1937. Hence the shift in the composition of national income has apparently created a more favorable breeding ground for monopoly. If significant shifts in the location of monopoly have not occurred, the relative extent of monopoly has increased.

Changes in the Effective Framework of Rules. If any trend of thought is detectable in the history of the last half-century, it is a growing disaffection with the ideology of the free market. Antithetical systems of economic organization have been receiving increasing approval. The "welfare state," bloc rivalry, cartelization, syndicalism, "group democracy," and similar organizational schemes are replacing the free market in popularity. We need not inquire into the reasons for this development. It will suffice to point out some of the consequences with respect to enterprise monopoly.

Legal restrictions on enterprise monopoly have remained in force. Antimonopoly prosecutions and rules, although not all that might be desired, have probably become increasingly effective in recent years. Moreover, the mere existence of antitrust laws has probably deterred many monopolistic schemes that would have been carried out if legally sanctioned. There seems to be little reason to doubt that less monopoly exists than would have obtained in the absence of statutes forbidding private restraint of trade.

On the other hand, as other groups are steadily exempted from similar restrictions, the climate becomes more and more healthy for enterprise monopoly. In the first place, the exempted groups find mounting difficulty in maintaining that "all monopoly is wicked save ours." Their interests may be better served by repressing antimonopoly sentiment. Attention may be diverted in other directions, such as toward the "unfair" profits of business in general. Or all enterprise monopolies may be explained as the natural result of mass production and as therefore ineradicable under a system of private ownership. In the second place, it may be profitable for a labor union, for instance—or "convenient" for a governmental agency—to deal with a single monopolistic concern rather than with a host of small "unco-ordinated" and "nonconforming" firms. A strong union and a monopolistic firm may find it to their mutual interest to work together and share the spoils, for each may provide a partial barrier against competitors of the other. Finally, the mere existence of well-organized blocs of sellers of productive services may present a formidable obstacle to the entrance of venture capital even into industries which are otherwise reasonably competitive.

Other changes in rules have been mentioned. These include progressive taxation and trade barriers, both apparently favorable to monopoly. So far as the traditional antimonopoly exemption—the patent—is concerned, it would be difficult without extensive study to know whether its role has become relatively more important. The number of patents issued per year has apparently increased, but the total number of products has also become much larger.

In summary, we can conclude that changes in the effective framework of rules have probably favored indirectly the development of enterprise monopolies. This consequence has been only incidental to the main trend toward what might be termed "bloc cartelization." But we cannot therefore suppose that it has been insignificant.

Changes in Economies of Scale. Little that is conclusive can be drawn from the discussion up to this point. The expansion of markets and the rapid rate of innovations have apparently worked against the growth of monopoly; shifts in the composition of national income and changes in the framework of rules have, on the other hand, probably favored such growth. It would be next to impossible in this type of discussion to determine whether the two tendencies offset each other. In any event, the factors so far considered have not figured prominently in the debate over the growth of monopoly. Argument has centered mainly around the question of changes in economies of scale. Those holding the "decline of competition" thesis maintain that monopoly has increased as the result of technological imperatives. According to their view, modern production is symbolized by the assembly line, and the assembly line means that the most efficient plants and firms must become monopolistic in size. Those of the opposite persuasion argue that there is no foundation for these beliefs. They assert that the evidence shows only an increase in the absolute size of plants and firms and does not indicate that the larger ones have, in general, grown faster than the smaller ones or than the extent of markets. They say, in addition, that, even if there had been such a differential growth, a change in social economies of scale would be only one of many possible explanations.

It is extremely doubtful that any reliable method for directly measuring social economies of scale can be developed. However, such measurement may not be required to resolve the dispute. The important question is: Has there been any significant general trend toward monopolistic plant or firm size? If empirical evidence shows no such trend, the question of cause becomes rather immaterial. If a trend has been observed, the matter of cause will still be at issue. But, by knowing something definite about the magnitude of the trend, we can better determine how important the issue really is.

The data for studies of tendencies toward monopolistic plant (but not firm) size are readily available for manufacturing industries. It is surprising that more studies have not been made. One was undertaken by the Temporary National Economic Committee,[6] but it exhibits many deficiencies. An "absolute index of concentration" was formed as the reciprocal of the percentage change in the number of top establishments, which together employed half the wage earners in an industry. Thus, if the 100 largest establishments in an industry employed half the wage earners in 1914 and only the 50 largest employed half in 1937, the "absolute index" for 1937 would be 200. The index was computed for each of 195 selected census industries for the census years between 1914 and 1937, 1914 serving as the base year. A separate index was also computed for the 195 industries as a group. Table 5 records the movements of the latter index.[7] The most interesting observation is the fact that the major upward movements seem to be positively correlated with depression and wartime. Notice the slight movement between

TABLE 5

TNEC Absolute Index of Concentration
of Employment[a]

	Index		Index
1914	100	1929	109
1919	119	1933	134
1921	102	1935	129
1923	109	1937	122

[a] See text for source and meaning of the index.

1921 and 1929. Nevertheless, some increase in concentration is indicated.

The study is subject, however, to several important criticisms. In the first place, only certain industries were selected for investigation. The author gives no basis for the selection except that these were the industries "for which comparable data were available."[8] We can interpret this to mean that industries were selected which had existed throughout the entire period from 1914 to 1937. Such a basis of selection arbitrarily eliminates industries which died or were born between 1914 and 1937. Results might be substantially affected by including those industries.

In the second place, the index cannot be literally interpreted as presenting a measure of change in concentration. In so far as we are concerned with discovering to what extent the larger plants have grown at the expense of the smaller, we should find out the change in the fraction of wage earners which was employed by a fixed number of the largest plants. The TNEC index tells us only the change in the number of establishments which employed a fixed fraction of wage earners. An index of 122 for 1937, with 1914 as the base year, would be more meaningful if it showed that, in 1937, 61 per cent of all workers were employed by the same number of plants which had hired only 50 per cent of all workers in 1914. But under the TNEC construction the index means only that 50 per cent of all workers were employed by about 18 per cent fewer plants in 1937 than in 1914. An extreme example shows readily that the two do not come down to the same thing.

Suppose that there were 100,000 plants in 1914 and that the top 10,000 employed 50 per cent of the workers. Suppose, in addition, that the top 5,000 employed 45 per cent of the workers. If between 1914 and 1937 the number of plants hiring 50 per cent of the workers fell by half (from 10,000 to 5,000), the TNEC index would record an increase in concentration of 100 per cent. But this is obviously a gross over-statement. Actually, the market share of the largest 5,000 plants has increased by only a little more than 11 per cent (5/45).

In the third place, concentration of employment is not directly relevant to studies of monopoly. The important factor is concentration of output; concentration of employment relates directly to problems of monopsony, if it relates to anything.

These difficulties can be largely avoided by comparing Lorenz distributions of manufacturing establishments (plants) classified by value of products (which we shall term "output"). A Lorenz distribution shows the cumulative percentages of one variable associated with specified cumulative percentages of a related variable. In the present case each pair of values in a distribution represents a cumulative percentage of manufacturing plants (ranged from those with smallest to those with largest outputs) and the cumulative percentage of output accounted for by that percentage of plants. If all plants have the same output, the percentages in each pair will be identical. That is, the lowest 10 per cent of plants will account for 10 per cent of output; the lowest 20 per cent, for 20 per cent; and so on. A Lorenz curve in this case is a straight line connecting the 0 per cent value for both plants and output with the 100 per cent value for both. We can call this the "equality line." If output is not the same in all plants, the Lorenz curve will bulge down below the equality line, provided that the cumulative percentage of plants is plotted on the horizontal axis. That is, the lowest 10 per cent of plants will account for less than 10 per cent of output, and so on. In rather loose terms, the larger the proportional share of output accounted for by plants with higher outputs, the greater will be the bulge.[9]

The problem to be investigated is whether there has been a tendency for the output of larger plants to grow more proportionally than the output of smaller plants, that is, for larger plants to account for an increasing proportional share of output. Such a tendency would be reflected in the downward shifting of Lorenz curves.

Lorenz curves can be plotted from census data for census years from 1904 through 1939. The data are not comparable, however, because of the manner in which samples of manufacturing plants were drawn. Censuses before 1923 included all plants with a value of products of $500 or more; those since then, all plants with a value of products of $5,000 or more. This method of arbitrarily setting lower limits is not suitable for the problem at hand, since the relative range of outputs in the distributions will vary not only with shifts in concentration of output but also with shifts in productivity of capital and in the price level, as certain small plants move into or out of the sample.

One solution is to set lower value-of-products limits in two years so that they are in the same ratio as aggregate value of products. This procedure amounts to making the prior assumption that the outputs of plants of every size class have increased by the same proportion, that is, that the proportional distribution of plants by *relative* output classes has remained the same. The procedure is warranted if, in fact, the derived Lorenz curves for the two years do not materially differ; for the assumption tends to be substantiated. The procedure is obviously not warranted if the Lorenz curves differ significantly.

To derive the desired Lorenz curves, it is necessary to eliminate from existing distributions all plants with outputs below the relevant lower limits. The elimination can be accomplished for most years only through intraclass interpolation in existing distributions. The simpler inter-polation techniques do not yield plausible results, as can be seen from the discussion in Appendix B. Consequently, no attempt was made to derive the appropriate Lorenz curves for all census years from 1904 through 1939. Conditions in 1904 and 1939 can, however, be compared without resorting to intraclass interpolation. Comparison of conditions in two terminal years obviously does not provide conclusive evidence on trend, but it does contribute pertinent information.

Aggregate value of products was approximately four times as great in 1939 as in 1904.[10] Therefore, the smallest plant to be considered in 1904 should have one-fourth the value of products of the smallest plant in 1939. We can set the smallest value of products at $5,000 for 1904 and at $20,000 for 1939 and thereby avoid intraclass interpolation.[11] The resulting Lorenz curves, illustrated in Figure 1, differ significantly

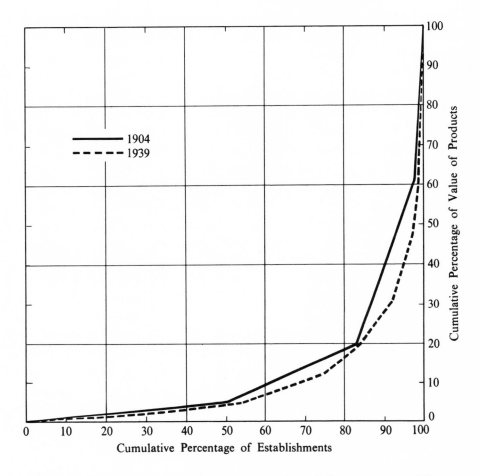

Figure 1. Lorenz Curves of the Concentration of Output among Manufacturing Establishments: 1904 and 1939. (Source: Table B–1. See text for adjustments made.)

only because of the larger number of observations for 1939 than for 1904. If both curves are smoothed out, they become almost identical. This evidence suggests that the outputs of plants of all relative sizes were greater by about the same proportion in 1939 as compared with 1904. There is no indication here that larger plants have grown at the expense of smaller ones.

At the same time, every plant within each output class tended to account for a larger proportion of manufacturing output in 1939 than in 1904, since the aggregate number of plants in the relevant output ranges declined from 142,631 to 123,637. The meaning of this change is not at all clear. In the first place, as we saw above, the evidence on manufacturing plants as a whole does not suggest that the increased proportion of manufacturing output accounted for by each plant resulted from developments of economies of large size. The death rate for plants of each relative output class was about the same.[12] It must be recognized, however, that study of changes in Lorenz distributions, industry by industry, might yield considerably different results and make economies of scale a more plausible explanation. In the second place, the increase in the proportion of manufacturing output accounted for by each plant might not be significant from the point of view of monopoly because of the expansion of relevant market areas from 1904 to 1939. The same proportion of national output represents a smaller proportion of output in relevant market areas in 1939 than in 1904.

The actual changes in concentration of output among plants can be shown by changes in the proportional distribution of output among a specified number of the largest plants. Consider the top 184,230 plants in any year, that number having been covered by the Census of 1939 and being smaller than the number covered in all but two other censuses.[13] These plants accounted for at least 99 per cent of aggregate value of products in every year considered.[14]

Changes in concentration are presented in Table 6. The top one-tenth of plants—i.e., the top 18,423 plants—accounted for about 75.5 per cent of the total value of manufactured products in 1904, about 78.5 per cent in 1919, and about 78.2 per cent in 1939. The top one-tenth, therefore, accounted for about 2.7 per cent more of output in 1939 than in 1904. The top five-tenths, on the other hand, accounted for only about 1 per cent more of output in 1939 than in 1904. An index of concentration comparing the percentage of output accounted for by the largest 92,115 establishments (five-tenths of the total considered), with 1914 as the base year, would read 100.7 for 1919 and 100.3 for 1929 and 1939. Compare these magnitudes with the TNEC index, which shows 119 for 1919, 109 for 1929, and 122 for 1937, recognizing at the same time that the two indices do not measure the same changes.

TABLE 6

Percentage of Total Value of Manufactured Products Produced by
Specified Fractions of Largest 184,230 Manufacturing Establishments

	Top 1/10	Top 2/10	Top 3/10	Top 4/10	Top 5/10
1904	75.5	85.4	90.3	94.1	96.2
1909	72.1	85.8	90.6	93.7	96.0
1914	75.8	87.1	91.4	94.6	96.8
1919	78.5	87.2	93.0	95.9	97.5
1921	75.1	85.2	91.7	94.9	96.5
1923	77.2	87.1	92.3	95.4	97.2
1925[a]	77.2	86.7	92.3	96.1	97.9
1929	77.0	88.1	94.2	96.2	97.0
1939	78.2	88.9	94.2	96.1	97.1

Source: Derived from smoothed Lorenz curves based on data in Table B-4.
[a] Only 183,877 establishments were reported in the *Census of Manufactures* for
this year.

No such index is very useful in any event, since it obscures shifts in
concentration within the entire range of half of plants or of employment,
as the case may be.

We may summarize this discussion of changes in the relative size of
manufacturing plants as follows. The proportion of total value of
manufactured products accounted for by the largest plants rose rather
steadily from 1904 through 1939. The significance of this trend, as far
as monopoly is concerned, is not clear, since market areas also expanded
in the same period. Furthermore, the evidence surveyed suggests that
the increased concentration of output did not result from the displacement of smaller plants by larger ones. Instead, the number of plants in
every comparable output class diminished by about the same proportion; that is, the diminution in number of plants was not reflected
in any substantial change in the proportional distribution of plants by
relative output class. The latter conclusions might not be supported by
a study of shifts in output distribution, industry by industry. Finally, the
limited conclusions apply only to plants and not to firms.

Thus we can say that the evidence points toward the conclusion that
there has been a growing tendency toward monopolistic plant size in
manufacturing but does not clearly support this point of view. No
definite statements can be made about cause without considerably

more detailed investigation. Nor can these limited conclusions be legitimately extended to areas other than manufacturing.

QUANTITATIVE ESTIMATES OF THE GROWTH OF MONOPOLY

Mere speculation about factors which might have affected the growth of monopoly will not provide meaningful quantitative measures of growth. We shall now direct attention to that problem.

The year 1899 may be an unfortunate choice as the initial point for a study of the growth of monopoly, since the period of most significant growth may be arbitrarily eliminated. The late 1890's and early 1900's have typically been characterized as the "trust era," a decade within which the movement toward industrial combination reached its peak. However, practicable and conceptual difficulties inhibit the study of conditions before 1899.

On the level of feasibility we may merely note the lack of detailed information about monopoly in the period preceding the 1890's. For that matter, data for the nineties are by no means comprehensive; no large-scale systematic investigations were made of this period. However, widespread concern over the "trust problem" did stimulate empirical study by the government and certain students of monopoly. The findings, though incomplete and unsystematic, provide some basis for estimating the extent of monopoly. We have relied on such sources as the reports of the Industrial Commission, census materials, and studies by Moody, Van Hise, Dewing, and Laidler.[15] No similar materials exist for the years preceding the 1890's.

On the conceptual level we may point out that the problem of identifying monopoly becomes more difficult, the farther back into the nineteenth century we move, because of the regional nature of the economy. Obviously, no single year, decade, or quarter of a century can be selected as marking the sudden emergence of "the" national market. Economists are more likely to reach general agreement on the nineties as a convenient starting point, however, than on the sixties, seventies, or eighties. From this point of view, incidentally, the usual conclusion that the trust movement implied a drastic increase in the degree and extent of monopoly is not beyond dispute.

Even if these factors are ignored, there still remain cogent arguments in favor of studying the period between 1899 and 1939. For many other reasons the beginning of the twentieth century is a significant turning point in economic history. Moreover, the decisive split of opinion among economists pertains to the interpretation of monopolistic developments in this century, not in the last. Finally, in testing the hypothesis that monopoly is automatically generated in a private-enterprise system, knowledge of the growth of monopoly over a recent forty years is as important as knowledge of that over the preceding years.

As we stated above, no single well-organized and comprehensive source of information on monopoly in the later 1890's exists. Moreover, most of the available data concern concentration of output. A list of industries in which the four largest firms controlled at least half the total output at some time between 1895 and 1904 has been compiled from various sources, which took some account of the regional nature of markets. Table B-6 in Appendix B contains these industries. Commercial banking, public utilities, and railroad transportation are the only important ones in the list which did not have national concentration ratios of 1/2 or larger. A survey of the list shows that in all but a small number of the industries the largest firm alone produced over half the total national output. We have no way of determining exactly how accurate these estimates of output concentration are. They were for the most part based on much less reliable data than those used for studies of the 1930's. However, there appears to be a fairly wide margin for error before judgments about the monopolistic nature of these industries would be changed. We have therefore taken these industries as monopolistic in 1899.

The criterion of monopoly chosen for the 1890's seems to be more restrictive than the criteria used in Chapter 2 for the 1930's. In the first place, many industries with concentration ratios below 1/2 were considered monopolistic in the 1930's on other grounds. In the second place, a concentration ratio of 1/2 in the 1890's suggests a lower elasticity of demand for the largest firms than the same ratio in the 1930's. For the 1890's, as compared with the 1930's, gaps in substitution among products in the same and in different industries were more pronounced,[16] and market areas were more restricted.

These considerations are offset by the possibility that concentration ratios for the 1890's were overestimated relative to those for the 1930's. There is little question that they were less accurately measured; and, in view of powerful antimonopoly sentiments, grounds exist for believing that the bias was toward overstatement.

It is impossible to determine which set of factors outweighs the other and, consequently, what sets of criteria would be comparable for both periods. We can, however, indicate the range of results that follows from appropriate variation in the criteria of monopoly for the 1930's.

Table 7 shows an estimate of the percentage of national income

TABLE 7

Percentage Distribution of National Income by Industrial Origin and by Type of Productive Organization: 1899

	Effectively Monopolistic	Workably Competitive[a]	Govern- mental	All Types
Agriculture		18.9		18.9
Mining	1.1	1.6		2.7
Contract construction		4.2		4.2
Manufacturing	5.6	11.9		17.5
Trade		16.6		16.6
Finance	1.2	4.3		5.5
Transportation and communication	9.1	0.8		9.9
Public utilities	0.4			0.4
Services		11.3		11.3
Government and government enterprises			6.5	6.5
Miscellaneous		6.5		6.5
Total	17.4	76.1	6.5	100.0

Source: Tables B-5, B-8, and B-10 and text, pp. 145–46.
[a] Includes some household and nonprofit activities.

originating in effectively monopolistic and workably competitive industries in 1899. Monopolistic industries accounted for 17.4 per cent, and workably competitive industries[17] for 76.1 per cent. The remainder, 6.5 per cent, represents government's share. Monopolistic industries thus accounted for about 19 per cent of nongovernmental production, while workably competitive industries represented about 81 per cent.

These figures should not be compared directly with those in Table 2, since the two sets of estimates are based on different criteria of monopoly and on different national income series. The estimates for 1937 and 1939 were based on the new Department of Commerce national income series; those for 1899, on Dr. Robert Martin's national income series. Since the latter extends through 1937, our original estimates for that year can be adjusted to be comparable, on this score, with those for 1899.[18] Table 8 presents the data for effectively monopolistic industries

TABLE 8

Percentage of National Income Produced by Effectively Monopolistic Industries, by Major Industry Division: 1899 and 1937

| | 1899[a] | 1937[b] | |
		Estimate I[c]	Estimate II[d]
Agriculture		1.0	
Mining	1.1	0.7	0.7
Contract construction		2.6	
Manufacturing	5.6	9.2	6.7
Trade		1.7	
Finance	1.2	2.0	2.0
Transportation and communication	9.1	1.6[e]	1.6[e]
Public utilities	0.4	[e]	[e]
Services		0.5	
Total	17.4	19.3[e]	11.0[e]

[a] From Table 7.

[b] Based on Dr. Robert Martin's income data (see Tables B-12 and B-13 and text, pp. 145–46).

[c] Based on the criteria of monopoly developed in Chapter 2.

[d] Based on criteria of monopoly similar to those for 1899 (see text, pp. 48–49).

[e] Including effectively supervised but otherwise monopolistic industries, the percentages are as follows: transportation and communication, 1.7; public utilities, 1.8; total, 21.2 (Estimate I) and 12.9 (Estimate II).

in both 1899 and 1937 as computed on the basis of the Martin income series. The following analysis is based on these data.

Two estimates are presented for 1937. Estimate I includes all the industries classified as monopolistic on the basis of the criteria developed in Chapter 2. Estimate II includes only the industries classified as monopolistic on the basis of criteria similar to those developed for 1899 in this chapter, that is, only those mining and manufacturing census industries with concentration ratios of 1/2 or larger.[19] In addition, industries in finance, transportation, communication, and public utilities that were classified as monopolistic in Chapter 2 are retained as monopolistic. All industries previously classified as monopolistic in agriculture, contract construction, trade, and services have been eliminated because data for 1899 on monopoly in those areas, however monopoly might be defined, are essentially nonexistent. Estimate I is in a limited sense an "upper" estimate for 1937; Estimate II, a "lower" estimate.

If the upper estimate for 1937 is used, the fraction of national income originating in privately organized monopolistic industries rose from 17.4 per cent in 1899 to 19.3 per cent in 1937, an increase of 1.9 percentage points; the fraction originating in privately organized workably competitive industries fell from 76.1 to 55.5 per cent, a decrease of 20.6 percentage points; and the fraction originating in government and governmentally supervised industries rose from 6.5 to 25.2 per cent, an increase of 18.7 percentage points.[20] On the same basis the fraction of nongovernmental production originating in all monopolistic industries, both privately organized and governmentally supervised,[21] rose from 19 per cent in 1899 to 25 per cent in 1937, an increase of 6 percentage points; the fraction of nongovernmental production originating in all workably competitive industries correspondingly fell from 81 to 75 per cent, a decrease of 6 percentage points. Therefore, it would appear on the basis of Estimate I for 1937 that the extent of monopoly had increased only slightly relative to the whole economy but substantially relative to the extent of competition.

On the other hand, opposite conclusions are reached if the lower estimate for 1937 is used. Using Estimate II, we find that the fraction of national income originating in privately organized monopolistic industries fell from 17.4 per cent in 1899 to 11.0 per cent in 1937, a decrease of 6.4 percentage points; the fraction originating in privately organized workably competitive industries fell from 76.1 to 63.8 per cent, a decrease of 12.3 percentage points. The fraction of nongovernmental production originating in all monopolistic industries fell from 19 per cent in 1899 to 15 per cent in 1937, a decrease of 4 percentage points; the fraction originating in all workably competitive industries correspondingly rose from 81 to 85 per cent, an increase of 4 percentage points. Hence, on the basis of Estimate II for 1937, it would seem that the extent of monopoly had declined significantly, relative both to the whole economy and to the extent of competition.

If we use averages of the two sets of estimates for 1937, we find that the fraction of income originating in privately organized monopolistic industries fell from 17.4 per cent in 1899 to 15.2 per cent in 1937, a decrease of 2.2 percentage points; the fraction originating in privately organized workably competitive industries fell from 76.1 to 59.6 per cent, a decrease of 16.5 percentage points. The fraction of non-governmental production originating in all monopolistic industries rose from 19 per cent in 1899 to 20 per cent in 1937. This indicates a slight decline in the extent of monopoly relative to the economy but a very slight increase relative to the extent of competition.

Changes between 1899 and 1937 are analyzed in more detail in Tables 9 and 10. Changes in the relative extent of monopoly in broad industrial divisions are shown in Table 9 under both sets of definitions

TABLE 9

Relative Extent of Monopoly in and Relative Size of Major Industry Divisions: 1899 and 1937 (per cent)

| | Relative Extent of Monopoly[a] | | | Relative Size of Division[b] | |
| | | 1937 | | | |
	1899	Estimate I[c]	Estimate II[d]	1899	1937
Public utilities	100.0	100.0[e]	100.0[e]	0.4	1.9
Transportation and communication	91.9	20.0[e]	20.0[e]	9.9	8.5
Mining	40.2	27.0	27.0	2.7	2.5
Manufacturing	32.0	38.3	28.0	17.5	24.0
Finance	21.7	30.4	30.4	5.5	6.6
Services		5.3		11.3	10.3
Agriculture		10.3		18.9	9.7
Trade		14.0		16.6	12.1
Contract construction		100.0		4.2	2.6

Source: Tables 3, 7, 8, B-5, and B-13.

[a] Measured by percentage of income originating in each division accounted for by monopolistic industries.

[b] Percentage of national income originating in the division.

[c] Based on the criteria of monopoly developed in Chapter 2.

[d] Based on criteria of monopoly similar to those for 1899 (see text, pp. 48–49).

[e] Includes effectively supervised industries. If these are excluded, the percentages become as follows: public utilities, 0.0; transportation and communication, 18.8.

TABLE 10

Relative Extent of Monopoly in and Relative Size of Major Industry Groups in Mining and Manufacturing: 1899 and 1937 (per cent)

| | Relative Extent of Monopoly[a] | | | Relative Size of Group[b] | |
| | | 1937 | | | |
	1899	Estimate I[c]	Estimate II[d]	1899	1937
Mining					
Anthracite	100.0	100.0	100.0	15.0	7.2
Nonmetal	69.9	63.2	63.2	10.0	7.2
Metal	56.6	64.7	64.7	32.1	23.5
Soft coal and petroleum				42.9	62.1
Manufacturing					
Rubber products	100.0	10.0	67.5	1.5	2.6
Iron and steel products	78.8	39.6	36.5	9.3	14.1
Paper	71.0	4.0	4.0	2.0	3.3
Transportation equipment[e]	57.3	93.2	93.2	3.9	8.2
Tobacco products	49.9	76.9	76.9	3.1	1.0
Petroleum and coal products	46.8	79.0		0.8	2.2
Nonferrous products	45.7	46.3	40.0	4.8	3.5
Machinery[f]	41.4	42.0	18.0	10.5	14.3
Foods[g]	39.1	49.7	24.5	12.8	10.7
Leather products	26.2	1.6	4.8	4.2	2.3
Chemicals	24.3	51.9	33.5	3.6	6.3
Textile products[h]	20.2	8.9	7.1	16.0	11.8
Stone, clay, and glass products	13.3	72.7	25.0	4.7	3.5
Miscellaneous products	2.7	39.1	39.1	3.8	4.4
Printing and publishing	0.9			5.9	6.8
Forest products[i]	0.5	17.2	16.7	13.0	5.0

Source: Tables 8, A-10, A-12, B-7, B-8, and B-10.

[a] Measured by percentage of income originating in the group accounted for by monopolistic industries.

[b] Measured by percentage of total mining or manufacturing production accounted for by the group.

[c] Based on the criteria of monopoly developed in Chapter 2.

[d] Based on the criteria of monopoly similar to those for 1899 (see text, pp. 48–49).

[e] Includes automobiles.   [f] Includes electrical machinery.   [g] Includes beverages.

[h] Includes apparel.   [i] Includes furniture

of monopoly used for 1937. We note that, no matter which of these definitions is used, the fraction of income originating in monopolistic industries increased in finance; remained the same in public utilities, if governmental supervision is ignored; and declined in mining and in transportation and communication. The decline in transportation and communication is most pronounced and reflects the invention of the automobile and airplane rather than governmental interference.[22]

Under Estimate I for 1937, the fraction of income originating in monopolistic industries increased in manufacturing, services, agriculture, trade, and contract construction. Under Estimate II, on the other hand, the fraction of income originating in monopolistic industries declined in manufacturing and remained the same in agriculture, services, trade, and contract construction.

We need analyze further only the discrepancy in findings for manufacturing. The discrepancy for agriculture, services, trade, and contract construction reflects basically the extreme insufficiency of data on productive conditions in those areas in 1899. No matter how monopoly is defined, an increase in the extent of it in those areas between 1899 and 1937 is almost certain to show up in any study because of this paucity of data. An increase does not show up under Estimate II for 1937 because the expedient adopted was to disregard monopoly in those areas.[23]

Since more detailed data are available for mining and manufacturing than for other areas, a more thorough analysis of changes is more meaningful as well as more practicable. Table 10 contains information on the relative extent of monopoly in major industry groups and on the relative sizes of those groups.

We note from Table 9 that the fraction of national income originating in monopolistic mining industries declined substantially between 1899 and 1937. The data in Table 10 indicate that the decline was due almost entirely to shifts in the sizes of major industry groups rather than to a decrease in the extent of monopoly within groups. If the relative extents of monopoly within groups as of 1899 had remained constant, the actual shifts in the relative sizes of the groups would have caused the fraction of mining income originating in monopolistic industry to decline by 14.7 instead of the observed 13.2 percentage points. On the other hand, if relative sizes of groups as of 1899 had remained constant, the actual changes in the relative extents of monopoly would have caused the fraction of mining income originating in monopolistic industries to increase by 1.9 percentage points. Therefore, the changes in relative extents of monopoly within groups essentially restricted the over-all decline in the extent of monopoly in mining.

The situation in manufacturing is much more ambiguous. Under Estimate I for 1937,[24] an increase by about 6 percentage points is indicated for the fraction of manufacturing income originating in monopolistic industries, as can be seen from Table 9. Under Estimate II for 1937,[25] on the other hand, a decrease by about 4 percentage points is indicated.

Considering the indicated decrease first, we note that it reflects primarily changes in the relative extents of monopoly within major industry groups. If relative sizes of groups as of 1899 had remained constant, actual shifts in the relative extents of monopoly within groups (under the criteria of monopoly used) would have caused the fraction of manufacturing income originating in monopolistic industries to decline by 9 percentage points instead of by the observed 4 percentage points. If relative extents of monopoly within groups as of 1899 had remained constant, actual changes in the relative sizes of groups would have caused the fraction to increase by 7.2 percentage points instead of to decrease by the observed 4 percentage points.

If we suppose that the criteria of monopoly used in Estimate I for 1937 are more appropriate than those used in Estimate II, it still is not clear that the resulting increase in extent of monopoly is characteristic of manufacturing industries as a whole. In the first place, the entire increase of 6.3 percentage points can be more than accounted for by the rise of the automobile industry. About 6.6 per cent of manufacturing income originated in this industry in 1937, as compared with a completely insignificant proportion in 1899.[26] In the second place, the relative extent of monopoly decreased in four groups, remained the same in three, and increased in nine. Using standardized averages again, we note that, if only the relative extent of monopoly within groups had changed between 1899 and 1937, while relative sizes of groups remained the same, the fraction of manufacturing income originating in monopolistic industries would have increased by only 2.2 instead of the observed 6.3 percentage points.

The data in Table 11 suggest that monopoly was irregularly unstable

TABLE 11

Rankings of Manufacturing Major Industry Groups by Relative Extent of Monopoly: 1899 and 1937

| | | 1937 | |
	1899	Estimate I	Estimate II
Rubber products	1	12	3
Iron and steel products	2	9	6
Paper products	3	14	13
Transportation equipment	4	1	1
Tobacco products	5	3	2
Petroleum and coal products	6	2	15.5
Nonferrous products	7	7	4
Machinery	8	8	10
Foods	9	6	9
Leather products	10	15	12
Chemicals	11	5	7
Textile products	12	13	11
Stone, clay, and glass products	13	4	8
Miscellaneous products	14	10	5
Printing and publishing	15	16	15.5
Forest products	16	11	14

Source: Table 10.

within manufacturing industry groups, no matter which of the two sets of criteria of monopoly is used for 1937. The major industry groups are listed with their rankings in 1899 and 1937 on the basis of relative extent of monopoly. There is no significant correlation between the set of rankings for 1899 and either of the two sets for 1937.[27]

The findings of our study of changes in the extent of monopoly are obviously inconclusive. Although it is unfortunate that more definite conclusions cannot be drawn, the ambiguity is in itself significant. In any event, the quantitative data can perhaps provide a useful basis for future discussion. The magnitude of change is at least somewhat narrowed and put into more definite terms than is ordinarily the case.

CHAPTER 4

Growth of Monopoly: 1939–1958

In extending the quantitative analysis of monopoly to recent years, the first problem encountered is the absence of any comprehensive classification of industries similar to that of Clair Wilcox for the 1930's. Fortunately, there have been periodic calculations of concentration ratios for the manufacturing sector, so that the task of identifying monopolistic industries in that area is facilitated, but for other sectors it is necessary to use a variety of sources. The disparity in data availability dictates flexible standards of classification that vary by industry. The data available and the classification standards used are described in detail in Appendix C. This appendix also includes detailed descriptions of the individual industrial classifications mentioned in this chapter. The classifications themselves are those utilized in considering the earlier period: workably competitive, effectively monopolistic, and government or governmentally supervised.

Table 12 indicates the share of national income originating in the three competitive classes of industries. The effectively monopolistic industries declined in importance between 1939 and 1954 and 1958, but this decline reflects some rather controversial classifications. The most significant of these occur in the contract construction, agriculture, communications, services, and trades industrial divisions. In some instances rivalry has changed considerably, and many of the non-competitive factors have declined in importance or disappeared since the late 1930's. Consequently, many of the industry classifications for 1954 and 1958 differ from Nutter's classifications for 1939.

The government and government-supervised sector probably is the least controversial of the three competitive classifications derived. This sector includes all government activities listed in the national income accounts and those industries in which the government regulates

TABLE 12

Percentage Distribution of National Income by Industrial Origin and by

	Effectively Monopolistic		
	1939	1954	1958
Manufacturing	9.79	11.54	10.68
Trade	1.45	1.69	1.79
Government and government enterprises			
Services	0.59		
Financial and real estate	2.39	2.79	2.97
Contract construction	3.11		
Agriculture	0.96		
Transportation	0.18		
Mining	0.57	0.29	0.23
Public Utilities			
Communication	1.39	1.62	0.21
Nonallocable			
Total	20.43	17.93	15.88

Sums and detail may not agree because of rounding.
Source: Tables 2, C-8, C-9, C-16, C-19, and C-20.
ᵃ We assume that supervised agriculture, communication, and public utilities would

the price or entry so as to preclude the exercise of power by the private sector authorities. Unless otherwise stated, the existence of government regulation has been accepted as effective supervision. In 1954 this sector accounted for 19.37 per cent of national income, not much less than the 20.16 per cent of 1939, while 21.52 per cent of national income was provided in 1958. Only three major reclassifications have affected the government sector since 1939. In 1954 and 1958 the fluid milk-producing industry was considered as government-regulated, because the industry's marketing structure had altered sufficiently since 1939 to warrant a change from the previous classification as effectively monopolistic. The second reclassification occurred in the communication division, where the radio broadcasting industry was reclassified from government-supervised to effectively monopolistic in 1954 and 1958. Finally, in 1958 telegraph and telephone service was considered as government-supervised rather than effectively monopolistic as in earlier years.

The workably competitive sector provided the largest share of national

Type of Productive Organization: 1939, 1954, and 1958

Workably Competitive			Governmental or Governmentally Supervised[a]			All Types		
1939	1954	1958	1939	1954	1958	1939	1954	1958
14.94	18.63	17.58				24.73	30.17	28.26
15.27	15.09	14.83				16.72	16.78	16.64
			11.79	11.88	12.69	11.79	11.88	12.69
10.55[b]	10.01[b]	11.41[b]				11.14	10.01	11.41
8.94	6.92	7.25				11.33	9.71	10.22
	5.32	5.41				3.11	5.32	5.41
7.48	4.86	4.28		0.75	0.71	8.44	5.61	4.99
0.27			5.81	4.79	4.47	6.26	4.79	4.47
1.64	1.33	1.24		0.01	0.00	2.21	1.63	1.48
			2.45	1.94	2.01	2.45	1.94	2.01
			0.11		1.64	1.50	1.62	1.85
						0.34	0.54	0.57
59.09	62.16	62.02	20.16	19.37	21.52	100.00	100.00	100.50

have been effectively monopolistic in the absence of governmental supervision, while supervised transportation and mining would have been workably competitive.

[b] Includes 4.11 per cent for 1939, 3.76 per cent for 1954, and 4.42 per cent for 1958 attributable to households and nonprofit institutions.

income. It includes industries with the traditional competitive characteristics as well as industries in which the competitive characteristics outweigh the noncompetitive ones. The more controversial industrial classifications are included in the competitive and monopolistic sectors. The share of national income originating in the competitive sector increased from 59.09 per cent in 1939 to 62.16 per cent in 1954, but declined slightly to 62.02 per cent in 1958. This 1939–1958 over-all increase reflects (1) a sizable increase in the workably competitive manufacturing industries, and (2) the reclassification of the construction division from effectively monopolistic in 1939 to workably competitive in 1954 and 1958. If the same construction classification were used for all years, the share of national income originating in the workably competitive sector would show a 2.48 percentage point decline from 1939 through 1958.

The share of national income originating in the effectively monopolistic industries declined substantially between 1939 and 1958. This sector includes those industries in which (1) price and output decisions are effectively determined by the top four companies, or (2) the non-competitive characteristics outweigh the competitive characteristics. In 1939, 20.43 per cent of national income originated in effectively monopolistic industries; this share dropped to 17.93 per cent in 1954 and to 15.88 per cent in 1958. The pattern of national income originating in the effectively monopolistic sector contrasts with the pattern for the competitive sector. These contrasting patterns reflect problems that occur in classifying industries for which few or no relevant data are available.

The manufacturing division originated the single largest portion of national income from 1939 through 1958. Its share of national income contributions rose from 24.73 per cent in 1939 to 30.17 per cent in 1954, but declined slightly to 28.26 per cent in 1958. In 1958, 37.8 per cent of the national income originating in the manufacturing division was derived from effectively monopolistic industries, as contrasted to 39.6 per cent in 1939. No part of the manufacturing division is considered as effectively government-supervised in any of the census years studied. During this period the greater part of the national income originating in manufacturing was provided by workably competitive industries. The several criteria used in classifying manufacturing industries include: (1) concentration ratios showing the share of output provided by the four largest companies in an industry or product line, (2) legal evidence of cartel behavior, and (3) national trends of basically local market industries. The manufacturing division is subjected to more detailed analysis in the following chapter.

The second largest originator of national income was the trade division, which includes both wholesale and retail trade units. No major classification changes occurred after 1939. The trade division's share of national income originations remained constant during this period: 16.72 per cent in 1939, 16.78 per cent in 1954, and 16.64 per cent in 1958. Trade industries are characterized by local and regional markets; this fact has two effects on the classification procedure: (1) national structural indicators cannot be used in classifying industries, and (2) classifications must be based on industry-wide trends in anti-competitive behavior. Of the two trade industries classified as effectively monopolistic, fluid milk distribution was characterized by the dominance of a few large distributors, while automobile distribution reflected the continued exercise of control by automobile manufacturers over some important aspects of the industry. Some of these same factors are present in other industries, such as bread baking and food retailing, that still display the dominant characteristic of workably competitive industries. In the absence of any method for measuring these particular noncompetitive local markets, the industries must be classified as a whole and thus as workably competitive.

The third largest originator of national income was the government division, whose relative contributions to national income showed a slight upward trend from 11.79 per cent in 1939 to 12.69 per cent in 1958. This growth has helped to balance the declining share of national income provided by some government-supervised industries and accounts for about two-thirds of the increased national income originating in the combined government and government-supervised sector. The government division provides just under 60 per cent of all national income originating in the government and government-supervised sector.

The services division is the fourth largest of the industrial divisions, as measured by contributions to national income. This division's share of national income has hovered around the 11 per cent mark since 1939, and its industries were classified as workably competitive during the 1950's. The movie industry was classified as effectively monopolistic in 1939, but different conditions required a changed classification for 1954 and 1958. In classifying this division's industries, some of the same problems presented by the trade industries are encountered. The traditionally local markets and close personal buyer-seller relationships are important factors in limiting the size of service industry markets. These conditions support a noncompetitive classification only if demand is somewhat inelastic and these close relationships are not derived from a voluntary basis. A noncompetitive classification of service industries must be based on specific evidence of widespread noncompetitive behavior by or between producers and/or consumers.

The finance and real estate industry division was the fifth largest originator of national income; its relative contributions declined from 11.33 per cent in 1939 to 9.71 per cent in 1954 but rose slightly to 10.22

per cent in 1958. Concurrently, the division seems to have become relatively more monopolistic. These changes reflect the significance of large financial institutions, such as banks and insurance companies, which are growing more rapidly than the traditionally more important real estate industries. Some of the most complex competitive relationships enter into the classification of these industries: it is necessary to evaluate interindustry competition, varying degrees of government regulation, a widespread reluctance to engage in price competition, and overlapping market areas that further complicate intraindustry competitive relationships. Reflecting these complex conditions, previous studies have provided differing evaluations of competitive situations in the several banking and insurance industries. Consequently, these classifications must be considered among the more controversial in this report.

Each remaining industrial division originated a much smaller share of national income than those already mentioned. The contract construction division presents some of the most difficult and controversial classification and data problems. Consequently, personal judgment and the evaluation of nonquantitative information more directly affect this classification than any of the others. Almost no useful concentration data and no comprehensive study of competitive conditions are available for this industry division. Information is needed concerning the relative importance of local versus regional or national markets, the degree of competition between different types of contractors and subcontractors, the importance of specialization in these industries, and the effect of unions and contractor's associations in promulgating price and service practices or rules that limit competition. The industry's 1939 monopolistic classification was changed to workably competitive in the 1950's. This change reflects very limited information and rests on the negative foundation that the conditions of 1939 were not generally extant during the 1950's.

The agriculture division, which provided 8.44 per cent of national income in 1939, originated 4.99 per cent in 1958. This decline was the largest of all the major industry divisions. The classification of this division was approached in a rather different manner from that used for the other industrial divisions. The basic assumption was that agriculture is competitive and that farmer co-operatives serve to improve the competitive balance between the farmers and their customers. However, fluid milk was believed to be an exception to this rule, and the industry was included in the regulated sector during the 1950's. The industry was considered effectively cartelized in 1939, but subsequent government controls were increased through more comprehensive milk market orders. No other agricultural industries reflect conditions justifying a noncompetitive classification.

The entire transportation division, which produced 6.26 per cent of national income in 1939 but only 4.47 per cent in 1958, was classified as government-regulated in the 1950's. The division's decline in national income originations was second only to that of the agriculture division. The transportation division involves much more interindustry competition than the banking industries; it generally is assumed that the transportation industries are organized in a basically competitive fashion. Government regulation allegedly stifles price, entry, and other competitive behavior in the transportation industries. Although not all parts of the transportation industries are effectively regulated, industry-wide classification is dictated by the absence of means to apportion national income data by local markets and individual industries. Post-1939 changes include the reclassification of the pipeline industry from monopolistic to regulated. Highway freight transportation is classified as government-supervised in the 1950's, because government regulations are important factors in a businessman's decision to own, hire, or rent the truck transportation that his company needs. Government regulation may have a similar indirect effect in other industries, but it is a particularly important factor in highway transportation.

The mining division's contribution to national income diminished from 2.21 per cent in 1939 to 1.48 per cent in 1958. Some mining classifications have been altered, but these changes have not significantly affected the three competitive sectors. Appendix C includes a detailed description of the several standards applied in evaluating extreme vertical integration, high concentration of mine ownership, imports, and other factors peculiar to the individual mining industries.

The share of national income originating in the utility division declined from 2.45 per cent in 1939 to 2.01 per cent in 1958. In each census year the entire division was classified as government-supervised; this reflects the nature of utility businesses and regulation. The classifications are based on the assumption that utilities are effectively regulated; as indicated in Appendix C, this assumption may not be completely valid in every instance.

The communications division originated 1.85 per cent of national income in 1958, up slightly from 1.50 per cent in 1939. There were two major changes in the competitive classification of communications industries after 1939: (1) the telephone and telegraph industry was classified as government-supervised in 1958 rather than monopolistic as in the earlier years, and (2) radio and television was classified as monopolistic in the 1950's rather than effectively regulated as in 1939. Both changes require an evaluation of (*a*) the effectiveness of government regulation, and (*b*) the relation between a large national company and many small local concerns. These altered classifications provided much of the 1954–1958 increase in the share of national income originating in government and government-supervised industries.

Table 13 indicates the extent of effective monopoly in each of the major industrial divisions for 1939, 1954, and 1958. These figures show, for each division, the relative share of the national income contribution that is provided by the effectively monopolistic industries. Here, we must consider the basic conditions in government-supervised industries. The values for effective monopoly in Table 13 include government-supervised industries if they are basically monopolistically structured (such as utilities) but not if they are fundamentally competitive (such as transportation). This procedure provides a better picture of the extent to which monopolistic forces "really" affect the domestic economy. The data indicate a decline in the relative importance of effective monopoly.

For the broad industrial divisions, the data reflect the structural or competitive adjustments that are experienced as industries mature or decline and as the government's role in economic affairs is redefined. These statistical shifts indicate no general trend toward either an increase or a decline in the effective monopolization of American industry between 1939 and 1958. Five of the divisions indicate less

TABLE 13

Relative Extent of Monopoly[a] in Major Industry
Divisions: 1939, 1954, and 1958 (per cent)

	1939	1954	1958
Contract construction	100.0[b]	0.0[b]	0.0[b]
Communication	100.0[c]	100.0[c]	100.0[c]
Public utilities	100.0[c]	100.0[c]	100.0[c]
Manufacturing	39.6	38.2	37.8
Mining	25.8[b]	18.0[b]	15.9[b]
Finance	21.7	28.7	29.1
Agriculture	11.4[c]	13.4[c]	14.2[c]
Trade	8.7	10.1	10.8
Services	5.3	0.0	0.0
Transportation	2.9	0.0	0.0

Source: Tables 3 and 12, and Appendices A through C.

[a] Measured by percentage of income originating in each division
accounted for by monopolistic industries.

[b] These estimates are particularly sensitive to personal judgments
on the proper classification of industries. See the relevant appendices
for explanation of our judgments.

[c] Includes effectively supervised industries. If these are excluded,
the percentages become:

	1939	1954	1958
Communication	92.7	100.0	11.4
Public utilities	0.0	0.0	0.0
Agriculture	0.0	0.0	0.0

effectively monopolistic components in 1958 than in 1939, three divisions
reflect increases, and two have experienced no change. However, the
qualified nature of some shifts, plus the rather slight changes in some
divisions, would cast doubts on any general trends that might be
deduced for the economy as a whole. The changes in industrial
structure, the adjustments in competitive relations, and the shifts in
government economic activity which are summarized by industrial
division in Table 13, are described in Appendix C.

CHAPTER 5

Concentration in Manufacturing: 1939–1958

INTRODUCTION

Since output concentration, relevantly defined, is closely related to monopoly, trends in the one shed light on trends in the other. In this chapter, we examine what happened to concentration among both establishments and companies in the manufacturing sector between 1939 and 1958. The manufacturing industries are studied in more detail than other industrial divisions, because more data are available for manufacturing activity. Post-1939 trends in the structure of domestic manufacturing are identified by examining alternative concepts and measures of concentration. Establishment and company concentration measures are presented below; they describe the manufacturing division as a whole, as well as industry groups and industries. The establishment is almost always synonymous with a single plant and is the most common producing unit, but a large number of companies operate two or more establishments. Establishment comparisons indicate the concentration of output, or other measure, by the basic production facilities. Establishment size distributions are believed to provide estimates of the most competitive scales of production as well as of the resources required to enter an industry. Company data describe concentrations by an industry's separate financial organizations; this measure is more closely related to the public's concern with concentration of output by a few economic interests.

Separate data describe both the establishment and the company bases; similarly, no public data permit the analysis of both absolute and relative concentration. The establishment data identify only relative concentrations, that is, the relative shares of industrial output provided by relative portions of the manufacturing industry. The company data permit the comparison of absolute concentrations, that is, the shares of output provided by a given number of largest companies. Each measure has its vociferous advocates, but both measures must be considered in a balanced study.

It is difficult to select the size criteria most useful in classifying establishments: sales, capital invested, value added by manufacture, etc. The classification used in this study is the census series grouping establishments by number of employees. An establishment classification on this basis is both useful and defensible for intraindustry comparisons, because industry establishments with the most employees generally have been the largest also in terms of output, net asset size, and other relevant size characteristics. However, a classification based on number of employees is not ideal for interindustry comparisons. The employee-output relationship varies widely between the labor-intensive and capital-intensive industries, and even within an industry these vital relationships will differ from establishment to establishment.

Formerly, a value-of-products classification was available for use in classifying manufacturing establishments by size, but its compilation was discontinued after the 1939 Census. This classification groups establishments according to the factory value of their annual production; thus the size of the industry's establishments and its market output are measured in comparable terms. The value-of-product classification does not indicate an establishment's relative economic size and importance, since the value of a product includes the contributions of suppliers as well as the reporting establishment's own value added by manufacture. The value-of-product (or a value-of-shipments) classification sometimes reflects large amounts of raw materials supplied by closely allied establishments in the same industry. The duplication generally is not significant within individual industries and raises no problems in most industry comparisons. However, the repetition is significant in the aggregate for all manufacturing industries and for some major industry groups, such as steelworks and rolling mills, motor vehicles and parts, and aircraft. Also, value-of-shipments comparisons are affected by the large difference in the ratio of raw-materials costs to labor and other manufacturing costs.

Value added by manufacture would provide a better criterion for comparing the relative economic characteristics of establishments, companies, and industries. A value-added distribution avoids the duplication of materials costs by subtracting these costs from the value of shipments. This procedure provides a truer picture of each producing unit's contribution to total output. Unfortunately, data are not available on a value-added classification; hence another means of grouping establishments must be considered.

Asset size was used as a basis of a classification in some earlier studies but would be unsatisfactory for this one. Assets are a good measure of size when size is considered as a result of past competitive conditions. However, intertemporal price changes would preclude asset valuation on a common basis. Also, the use of assets data generates a controversy as to which assets should be included in such comparisons.[1] Most important for this study of concentration is the lack of asset data in a form which reveals the intraindustry distribution of the particular assets.

LORENZ DISTRIBUTIONS

As in Chapter 3, Lorenz curves[2] may be used to illustrate the degree of inequality in establishment size. Figure 2 presents the curves and Table 14 the data for 1939, 1947, 1954, and 1958. In this instance manufacturing establishments are grouped by size according to their number of employees, and manufacturing output is measured by value added by manufacture. Linear interpolations of the distributions are sufficient since rather large differences exist between approximately similar points for the four years. Because the top 5 percentile is difficult to plot clearly, computed values are included in Table 15. Two separate estimates are given in order to provide a comparison for two contrasting interpolating procedures.

One set of computations in Table 15 consists of linear interpolation for the largest 5, 4, 2, 1, and $\frac{1}{2}$ per cent of all manufacturing establishments. This method assumes that relative concentration of establishments is distributed uniformly within each class. This assumption has no a priori basis in fact, but it avoids the even more arbitrary selection of the changing and more complex functions that probably exist within each class.

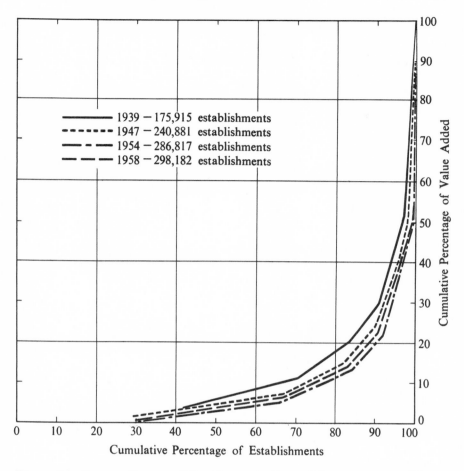

1939 — 175,915 establishments
1947 — 240,881 establishments
1954 — 286,817 establishments
1958 — 298,182 establishments

Figure 2. Lorenz Curves of the Concentration of Output among Manufacturing Establishments: 1939, 1947, 1954, and 1958. (Source: Table 14.)

The second set of computations utilizes the sum-of-the-digits method for estimating the intraclass distribution. This procedure tacitly assumes that intraclass distributions are arranged unevenly, with a proportionately large number of firms concentrated in the lower extremities of each class and a few large firms providing the greater portion of value added by manufacture within any given class.

The linear method indicates an uneven trend toward greater relative concentration of manufacturing output through 1954, followed by a mild decline in 1958. With two slight exceptions this pattern is duplicated by the sum-of-the-digits method. This procedure indicates a very

TABLE 14
Size Distributions of Manufacturing Establishments, 1939–1958

Size Class (number of employees)	Establishments		Value Added	
	Number	Per Cent	Thousand Dollars	Per Cent
1939				
1 to 6	75,930	43.163	887,511	3.633
6 to 21	49,015	27.863	1,824,457	7.469
21 to 51	23,646	13.442	2,314,867	9.477
51 to 101	11,908	6.769	2,494,711	10.213
101 to 251	9,458	5.376	4,273,985	17.497
251 to 501	3,653	2.077	3,601,323	14.743
501 to 1,001	1,495	0.850	3,118,114	12.765
1,001 to 2,501	634	0.360	3,130,284	12.815
2,501 and over	176	0.100	2,781,816	11.388
Total	175,915	100.000	24,427,068	100.000
1947				
1 to 5	70,384	29.219	905,693	1.217
5 to 10	46,622	19.355	1,446,978	1.944
10 to 20	40,645	16.873	2,601,176	3.495
20 to 50	40,016	16.612	6,050,163	8.129
50 to 100	18,672	7.752	6,593,104	8.859
100 to 250	14,323	5.946	11,793,823	15.846
250 to 500	5,555	2.306	10,450,830	14.042
500 to 1,000	2,729	1.133	10,128,788	13.609
1,000 to 2,500	1,431	0.594	11,619,386	15.612
2,500 and over	504	0.209	12,835,884	17.247
Total	240,881	99.999	74,425,825	100.000
1954				
1 to 5	106,960	37.292	1,554,297	1.329
5 to 10	47,402	16.527	2,008,156	1.718
10 to 20	41,982	14.637	3,644,743	3.117
20 to 50	42,798	14.922	8,351,209	7.143
50 to 100	21,091	7.353	9,661,529	8.264
100 to 250	15,647	5.455	17,143,425	14.663
250 to 500	6,092	2.124	15,834,820	13.544
500 to 1,000	2,837	0.989	15,454,350	13.219
1,000 to 2,500	1,473	0.514	18,927,036	16.189
2,500 and over	535	0.187	24,332,963	20.813
Total	286,817	100.000	116,912,526	99.999
1958				
1 to 5	105,641	35.428	1,831,999	1.297
5 to 10	50,660	16.990	2,543,890	1.801
10 to 20	46,820	15.702	4,837,994	3.425
20 to 50	46,307	15.530	11,089,100	7.850
50 to 100	21,764	7.299	12,023,698	8.511
100 to 250	16,132	5.410	21,162,398	14.980
250 to 500	6,240	2.093	19,291,058	13.655
500 to 1,000	2,759	0.925	18,103,226	12.815
1,000 to 2,500	1,363	0.457	21,448,943	15.183
2,500 and over	498	0.167	28,937,990	20.484
Total	298,182	100.001	141,270,297	100.001

Sums and detail may not agree because of rounding.
Source: U.S. Bureau of the Census, *Census of Manufactures: 1939, 1948, 1954*, and *1958*, Government Printing Office, Washington.

TABLE 15

Interpolated Percentages of Total Value Added by Manufacture Accounted for by the Specified Portions of the Largest Manufacturing Establishments: Census and Survey Years, 1939–1958

	Top ½ Per Cent	Top 1 Per Cent	Top 2 Per Cent	Top 4 Per Cent	Top 5 Per Cent
	Uniform-Ratio Interpolation[a]				
1939	24.8	32.3	41.9	53.7	57.0
1947	24.7	35.2	46.8	59.0	62.5
1950	29.2	39.8	51.4	63.5	64.5
1951	28.8	39.8	51.4	63.1	65.4
1952	29.6	40.7	52.2	63.7	67.1
1954	30.7	41.0	52.2	64.3	67.0
1955	32.2	42.8	53.8	65.6	68.1
1958	31.5	40.9	51.4	63.1	64.9
	Sum-of-Digits Interpolation[b]				
1939	25.4	35.2	45.1	55.5	60.7
1947	28.8	37.2	47.2	60.4	64.3
1950	33.2	42.2	52.4	63.5	64.8
1951	32.9	41.6	51.8	64.9	65.6
1952	33.7	42.4	52.4	65.2	68.5
1954	34.5	43.1	53.9	64.8	69.4
1955	36.2	45.2	55.1	65.6	70.1
1958	34.6	44.0	53.7	64.1	68.7

Source: Tables 14 and 16.

[a] Value added within a size class of establishments is taken to be uniformly distributed. For example, for the class represented by 1–5 employees, a proportional share of the value added would be assigned to each establishment.

[b] Value added within a size class of establishments is taken to be distributed by the sum-of-digits ratio: $sum = (n/2)(n + 1)$. This procedure apportions greater shares to the largest member of each class.

slight rise in the importance of the largest 1 per cent of manufacturing establishments from 1954 through 1958. The other exception involves the top ½ per cent of manufacturers between 1939 and 1947, when a very slight decline was indicated by the linear procedure; for the same percentile, a slight 1954–1958 rise was shown by both procedures. On balance, these slight deviations would not in themselves refute any conclusions derived by the otherwise consistent results.

SURVEYS OF MANUFACTURES DATA: 1950, 1951, 1952, AND 1955

Within specific tolerances, four additional comparisons are possible by using data from the annual *Survey of Manufactures*. Although the surveys are not compiled in precisely the same manner as the censuses, specific tolerance limits are provided for particular statistics, including the concentration series. Because the six smallest size classes are combined into only one class in each survey, data are available for only half as many size classifications as are listed in each census report. This reduction in the number of size classes effectively prevents the construction of meaningful Lorenz distributions for all but the largest manufacturing establishments.

These Lorenz distributions have been prepared by using the two interpolating procedures already described: the linear and the sum-of-the-digits methods. These distributions can be accepted only within the tolerance limits provided for the survey data. Table 16 gives the number of establishments and the value added by manufacture for each establishment size class listed in the annual surveys. Table 15 presents, in chronological order, the Lorenz distributions for the largest 5, 4, 2, 1, and $\frac{1}{2}$ per cent establishments listed in each manufacturing survey, as well as census, from 1939 through 1958.

The survey samples covered 45,000 plants in each year, but sampling rates varied by employee-number classification, with the largest classes receiving complete coverage. The standard errors of estimate were provided by the Bureau of the Census and vary between 0 and 3 per cent. The percentage standard errors of estimate:

... indicate the differences that can be expected between the estimates and comparable complete canvass totals, because of sampling fluctuations. The estimates will differ from the complete totals by less than:
  (i) the percentage shown: approximately 2 times out of 3;
  (ii) twice the percentage shown: approximately 19 times out of 20; and
(iii) three times the percentage shown: almost always.[3]

The survey data can be interpreted only in light of the standard errors of estimate, and valid conclusions would seem to require applied tolerances of three times the standard errors of estimate. Application of these tolerances provides overlapping ranges of possible annual values. Consequently, the Lorenz distributions obtained from the survey data do not reveal so clear a trend as those derived from the census data. Although the survey data seem to support the trend of

TABLE 16

Size Distributions of Manufacturing Establishments Estimated from Sample Surveys: 1950, 1951, 1952, and 1955

Size Class (number of employees)	Establishments		Value Added	
	Number	Per Cent	Million Dollars	Per Cent
1950				
1 to 250	249,678(2)[a]	95.9	32,167(2)	35.8
250 to 500	5,962(2)	2.3	12,437(2)	13.9
500 to 1,000	2,794(1)	1.1	12,344(1)	13.7
1,000 to 2,500	1,433(0)	0.6	14,626(0)	16.3
2,500 and over	516(0)	0.2	18,186(0)	20.3
Total	260,383(2)	100.0	89,750(1)	100.0
1951				
1 to 250	250,520(2)	95.6	35,542(2)	34.8
250 to 500	6,364(2)	2.4	14,438(2)	14.1
500 to 1,000	2,922(1)	1.1	13,798(1)	13.5
1,000 to 2,500	1,574(0)	0.6	16,990(0)	16.6
2,500 and over	564(0)	0.2	21,317(0)	20.9
Total	261,944(2)	100.0	102,086(1)	100.0
1952				
1 to 100	239,443(3)	89.7	22,030(2)	20.3
100 to 250	15,953(3)	6.0	15,448(3)	14.2
250 to 500	6,305(2)	2.4	14,711(2)	13.6
500 to 1,000	3,036(1)	1.1	14,870(1)	13.7
1,000 to 2,500	1,574(0)	0.6	17,771(0)	16.4
2,500 and over	587(0)	0.2	23,648(0)	21.8
Total	266,898(2)	100.0	108,477(1)	100.0
1955				
1 to 100	255,684(1)	90.3	26,894(1)	20.4
100 to 250	16,032(2)	5.7	18,324(2)	13.9
250 to 500	6,363(1)	2.2	17,478(1)	13.3
500 to 1,000	2,862(1)	1.0	16,856(1)	12.8
1,000 to 2,500	1,519(0)	0.5	21,286(0)	16.2
2,500 and over	587(0)	0.2	30,760(0)	23.4
Total	283,047(1)	100.0	131,598(1)	100.0

Sums and detail may not agree because of rounding.

[a] Figures in parentheses represent percentage standard errors of estimate.

Source: U.S. Bureau of the Census, *Surveys of Manufactures: 1950, 1951, 1952,* and *1955,* Government Printing Office, Washington.

the census data, the standard errors of estimate raise the possibility of a change. Conceivably, concentration declined slightly throughout the period or did not follow any consistent pattern. However, it seems most likely that concentration increased from 1939 through the early 1950's and then declined.

The results of the survey data vary with the interpolating procedure, but, on balance, neither method yields more consistent results than the other. Both procedures provide some indication of declines from year-earlier levels, but these inconsistent periods differ with the method used, and generally we would not expect a trend to consist of a constant, undeviating progression from one year to another. For these few deviations, the average variations (from the minimum values consistent with a trend toward increased concentration) are greater for the sum-of-the-digits method. However, in neither case are the differences large enough to refute the existence of a trend toward greater concentration during the 1939–1958 period. These deviations fall within the tolerances set by the standard errors of estimate, and they are not inconsistent with the general trend.

TWO-DIGIT SIC MAJOR INDUSTRY GROUPS

Trends in inequality of plant size by major industry groups are shown in Table 17, where each complete Lorenz distribution for a group is summarized by its Gini coefficient. The latter, a commonly used index of inequality, measures the area between the equality line (the 45-degree line) and the actual Lorenz curve as a fraction of the total area under the equality line, and hence tends to be directly proportional to the degree of inequality shown by the Lorenz curve.[4] We note an irregular but generally upward trend in inequality of plant size for the industry groups that can be compared: a rise in inequality is shown for 12 out of 13 groups between 1939 and 1947 and for 17 out of 20 between 1947 and 1954, but for only 4 out of 20 between 1954 and 1958. A rise is evident for 12 out of 13 groups between 1939 and 1958, but for only 13 out of 20 between 1947 and 1958. For manufacturing as a whole, the Gini coefficient shows an upward trend, as we should expect from the earlier examination of complete Lorenz distributions.

TABLE 17

Gini Coefficients[a] for Lorenz Distributions of Manufacturing Establishments, by Major Industry Group: 1939, 1947, 1954, and 1958

	1939	1947	1954	1958
Food and kindred products	0.7397	0.7812	0.7907	0.7830
Tobacco manufactures	0.8930	0.9100	0.8968	0.6916
Textile mill products	0.6482	0.7355	0.7126	0.7098
Apparel and related products	0.5434	0.5989	0.6190	0.6052
Lumber and timber basic products	0.6837	n.a.	n.a.	n.a.
Furniture and finished lumber products	0.6464	n.a.	n.a.	n.a.
Paper and allied products	0.6325	0.6644	0.7169	0.7362
Printing and publishing	0.7476	0.8095	0.8119	0.8074
Chemicals and allied products	0.7846	0.8175	0.8574	0.8451
Petroleum and coal products	0.7724	0.7969	0.8187	0.8343
Rubber products	0.7984	0.8578	0.8610	0.8417
Leather and leather products	0.6694	0.6663	0.7228	0.7005
Stone, clay, and glass products	0.7490	0.8371	0.8274	0.7847
Iron and steel products	0.7827	n.a.	n.a.	n.a.
Nonferrous metals	0.8128	n.a.	n.a.	n.a.
Electrical machinery	0.8271	0.8327	0.8451	0.8388
Machinery except electrical	0.7946	0.8389	0.8511	0.8465
Automobiles	0.8509	n.a.	n.a.	n.a.
Transportation equipment except automobiles	0.8557	n.a.	n.a.	n.a.
Miscellaneous manufactures	0.7403	n.a.	n.a.	n.a.
Lumber and wood products	n.a.	0.7284	0.7591	0.7640
Furniture and fixtures	n.a.	0.7409	0.7585	0.7480
Primary metal industries	n.a.	0.8179	0.8487	0.8601
Fabricated metal products	n.a.	0.7869	0.7924	0.7786
Transportation equipment	n.a.	0.8839	0.9094	0.8988
Instruments and related products	n.a.	0.8505	0.8813	0.8754
Miscellaneous manufactures	n.a.	0.7777	0.8316	0.7619
All industries	0.7808	0.8206	0.8480	0.8311

n.a.: not applicable because of changes in industrial classification.

Source: Gini coefficients were calculated from census data by electronic computer on the basis of a program prepared by Miss Juanita Johnson of the National Bureau of Economic Research, Inc.

[a] The Gini coefficient measures the area between the equality line (the 45-degree line) and the actual Lorenz curve as a fraction of the total area under the equality line.

TRUNCATED DISTRIBUTIONS OF LARGEST 175,915 ESTABLISHMENTS

In the Lorenz distributions discussed previously, the apparent increase in concentration may reflect cyclical conditions rather than a trend toward increased concentration. Lorenz distributions are affected by numerous small establishments that are opened during times of prosperity, contribute less than their proportional share of value added by manufacture, and are the first and most serious casualties during the trough phase of a business cycle. The observed increase in inequality of plant size could mean either that larger plants grew more percentage-wise than smaller ones or that the absolute number of plants increased relatively more over the smaller size classes than over the larger ones. The total number of plants rose from 175,915 in 1939 to 240,881 in

TABLE 18

Lorenz Distributions for the Largest 175,915 Manufacturing
Establishments: 1939, 1947, 1954, and 1958

Cumulative Percentage of Establishments	Percentage of Value Added[a]			
	1939	1947[b]	1954[b]	1958[b]
10	0.8	0.6	0.6	0.6
20	1.7	1.4	1.3	1.3
30	2.5	2.1	2.3	2.6
40	3.4	3.7	3.6	3.9
50	5.5	5.2	5.2	6.0
60	8.2	8.2	8.2	9.0
70	10.8	11.9	11.1	12.0
80	17.4	17.7	17.0	18.1
90	28.9	30.6	29.0	30.3
100	100.0	100.0	100.0	100.0

Source: Table 14 as adjusted (see note 5 for this chapter).
[a] Based on linear interpolation of original data.
[b] Value added for largest 175,915 establishments, accounting for following portion of total value added by manufacture: 1947, 98.9 per cent; 1954, 98.5 per cent; 1958, 98.1 per cent.

1947, 286,817 in 1954, and 298,182 in 1958. If we analyze the Lorenz distributions for a fixed number (175,915) of the largest plants for all years, we can test which of the two explanations for increased inequality is more likely.

The Lorenz distributions for the fixed number of plants[5] are listed, by interpolated decile classes, in Table 18. In 1947, 1954, and 1958 the largest 175,915 establishments constituted 73.0, 61.3, and 59.0 per cent, respectively, of the total manufacturing establishments covered. The exclusion of the smaller establishments in the 1947, 1954, and 1958 distributions would naturally serve to increase the equality indicated by the Lorenz distributions. Any comparison of these restricted distributions with the more inclusive distribution would automatically indicate less relative concentration than actually exists within groups composed of comparable establishment-size classes. The internal distribution of value added by manufacture did not vary significantly within the largest 175,915 establishments. For example, the largest 50 per cent of these establishments provided 94.5 per cent of value added by these largest manufacturing establishments in 1939, while the share was 94.8 per cent in 1947, 94.8 per cent in 1954, and 94.0 per cent in 1958. The shares of value added by individual decile classes of manufacturing companies also remained relatively constant during this period, showing very slight upward drift in concentration for relatively larger plants and a downward drift for relatively smaller ones.

When allowance is made for statistical and interpolative errors, the distributions would seem to display no significant change over the period under review. Hence the increase in inequality observed in the complete Lorenz distributions appears to be attributable to the fact that the number of establishments rose more percentagewise in lower size classes than in upper ones. Such a development does not imply that larger plants were displacing smaller ones, or that economies of scale at the plant level were becoming more favorable to monopolistic conditions.

This conclusion is reinforced by considering changes in the average contributions to value added by manufacture, which do not vary significantly within the largest 175,915 establishments. One would expect the largest firms to displace the smallest, while gaining larger market shares, if the relative changes in average contribution to value added had increased with establishment size. However, these changes failed to occur. Table 19 indicates that the smallest establishments experienced average contributions to value added which were, at their most favorable rates, smaller and rose much less than those for the middle-sized and largest manufacturing establishments. However, from 1954 to 1958 a different pattern seemed to exist with relatively smaller and more equal increases in average value added per establishment size class. This changed pattern was accompanied by a decline in the number of smallest (1–5 employees) establishments, and it would appear that in 1958 the number of these establishments was more nearly in line with the demand for goods and services obtainable from small manufacturing establishments.

TABLE 19

Average Value Added by Manufacture, by Establishment Class: 1939,

Establishment Size Class	Average Value Added by Manufacture ($1,000)			
	1939	1947	1954	1948
1 to 6	11.7			
1 to 5		12.9	14.5	17.3
5 to 10		35.6	42.4	50.2
10 to 20		64.0	86.8	103.3
6 to 21	37.2			
5 to 20 combined		(49.8)	(63.2)	(75.7)
21 to 51	97.9			
20 to 50		151.2	195.1	239.5
51 to 101	209.5			
50 to 100		353.1	458.1	552.5
101 to 251	451.9			
100 to 250		823.4	1,095.6	1,311.8
251 to 501	985.9			
250 to 500		1,881.3	2,599.2	3,091.5
501 to 1,001	2,085.7			
500 to 1,000		3,711.5	5,447.4	6,566.3
1,001 to 2,501	4,937.3			
1,000 to 2,500		8,119.7	12,849.3	15,736.6
2,501 and over	15,805.7			
2,500 and over		25,468.0	45,482.2	58,108.4
Overall average	138.9	309.0	407.6	473.8

Source: Table 14.

These two findings focus on the apparent inconsistency in levels and trends of concentration for the manufacturing sector as a whole and for the largest domestic establishments in particular. The truncated Lorenz distributions show no marked changes in relative concentration among the largest establishments from 1939 through 1958. However, the Lorenz distributions for all manufacturing establishments indicate increased concentration from 1939 through 1954 and a subsequent decline in 1958. The increased relative concentration from 1939 through 1958 reflects two factors:

1. The large and rather equal increases in average contributions to value added by manufacture have prevented any large shifts in the relative positions of establishment size groups comprising the largest 175,915 establishments.

2. The smallest establishments seem to have increased far faster than

1947, 1954, and 1958

Establishment Size Class	Percentage Changes from:					
	1939 to 1947	1939 to 1954	1947 to 1954	1939 to 1958	1947 to 1958	1954 to 1958
1 to 6	{10.3}					
1 to 5		23.9	12.4	47.9	34.1	19.3
5 to 10			19.1		41.0	18.4
10 to 20			35.6		61.4	19.0
6 to 21	{33.9}					
5 to 20 combined		69.9	26.9	103.5	52.0	19.8
21 to 51	{54.4}					
20 to 50		99.3	29.0	144.6	58.4	22.8
51 to 101	{68.5}					
50 to 100		118.7	29.7	163.7	56.5	20.6
101 to 251	{82.2}					
100 to 250		142.4	33.1	190.3	59.3	19.7
251 to 501						
250 to 500	90.8	163.6	38.2	213.6	64.3	18.9
501 to 1,001						
500 to 1,000	77.9	161.2	46.8	214.8	76.9	20.5
1,001 to 2,501						
1,000 to 2,500	64.5	160.2	58.2	218.7	93.8	22.5
2,501 and over						
2,500 and over	61.1	187.8	78.6	267.6	128.2	27.8
Overall average	122.5	193.4	31.9	241.1	53.3	16.2

the limited markets that they can enter. This is indicated by their generally small and slowly rising average contributions to value added by manufacture. The number of these smallest establishments has risen in each census since 1933, when there were 139,325 as compared to a 1929 high of 206,663. The importance of this factor is strengthened by the 1954–1958 decline in the number of smallest establishments simultaneously with a decrease in relative concentration for manufacturing establishments as a whole.

EXTENT OF HIGH ABSOLUTE CONCENTRATION

Because Lorenz distributions can provide paradoxical results, the absolute concentration of domestic manufacturing also must be examined. The extent of highly concentrated manufacturing industries in 1939, 1954, and 1958 is shown in Table 20 for major industry groups.

TABLE 20

Relative Extent of High Concentration in Manufacturing: 1939, 1954, and 1958 (per cent)

	Relative Extent of High Concentration[a]			Relative Size of Group[b]		
	1939	1954	1958	1939	1954	1958
Food and kindred products	24.0	18.7	17.2	12.7	8.7	9.0
Tobacco products	76.7	83.3	100.0	1.7	0.7	0.8
Textile mill products	9.8	6.5	6.0	7.0	4.2	3.8
Apparel and related products	0.5	1.4	3.4	5.7	4.2	4.2
Forest products	8.4	1.6	2.0	5.6	4.7	4.4
Furniture and fixtures	n.a.	2.2	4.0	2.8	3.0	1.7
Lumber and wood products	n.a.	0.5	0.5	2.8	1.7	2.7
Paper and allied products	2.6	5.4	9.6	3.1	3.7	3.8
Printing and publishing	0.0	0.0	1.2	6.8	5.1	5.5
Chemicals and allied products	28.2	51.5	49.5	6.7	6.9	7.6
Petroleum and coal products	0.2	15.4	1.1	2.4	4.1	3.5
Rubber products	64.2	51.1	56.4	1.6	1.5	1.7
Leather and leather products	1.9	2.1	1.9	2.4	1.5	1.3
Stone, clay, and glass products	19.8	50.7	40.1	3.7	3.5	3.6
Iron and steel, nonferrous, and *miscellaneous products*	27.7	38.4	38.9	18.8	20.4	20.9
Iron and steel products	22.2	n.a.	n.a.	12.6	n.a.	n.a.
Nonferrous metals	39.0	n.a.	n.a.	3.3	n.a.	n.a.
Primary metal industries	n.a.	67.9	65.4	n.a.	8.4	8.8
Fabricated metal products	n.a.	13.8	13.8	n.a.	7.4	7.4
Instruments and related products	n.a.	53.7	45.7	n.a.	2.1	2.3
Miscellaneous manufacturing	38.2	7.9	11.0	2.9	2.4	2.5
Electrical machinery	1.1	51.3	35.5	4.8	6.9	7.6
Machinery except electrical	19.3	21.6	24.1	8.3	10.7	10.2
Transportation equipment	89.6	59.0	83.2	8.8	13.3	11.8
Automobiles	99.8	n.a.	n.a.	6.6	7.0	5.1
Transportation equipment except automobiles	61.2	n.a.	n.a.	2.2	6.3	6.8
All industries	27.2	31.6	30.6	100.0	100.0	100.0

Sums and detail may not agree because of rounding.

n.a.: not applicable because of changes in industrial classification.

Source: Tables 4, A-10, C-8, and underlying data.

[a] Measured by percentage of income originating in each group accounted for by industries with high concentration. The latter are those with concentration ratios for the four leading firms of 50 per cent or greater, plus any products with concentration ratios of 75 per cent or more not included among such industries.

[b] Percentage of income originating in manufacturing accounted for by group.

In this instance, "high concentration" is indicated by a four-company concentration ratio of 50 per cent or more for an industry or of 75 per cent or greater for those additional products not found in the highly concentrated industries. The heavily concentrated industries and products rose from 27.2 per cent of all national income originating in the·manufacturing division in 1939 to 31.6 per cent in 1954, falling thereafter to 30.6 per cent in 1958. This upward but irregular trend in the relative extent of high concentration contrasts with the earlier finding on changes in the relative extent of monopoly (see Table 13). During this period, national income originating in manufacturing rose from $17.9 billion in 1939 to $91.1 billion in 1954 and $103.8 billion in 1958.

The increased importance of concentrated manufacturing industries reflects (1) the growth of 1939's heavily concentrated industries and products, and (2) the increased concentration of industries and products that had not been considered heavily concentrated in 1939. However, there does not appear to be any unambiguous relationship between changes in the relative extent of high concentration, on the one hand, and either growth in relative size or changing major industry group importance, on the other.

In 11 of 16 major manufacturing industry groupings that are comparable over the 1939–1958 period, the highly concentrated sectors increased in importance as originators of their major group's national income contributions. In five major industry groups a lower share of each group's originations of national income was attributable to its highly concentrated industries. Of course, the changes were neither constant nor consistent in direction during this period. Of the 11 major industry groups showing rises in the relative extent of high concentration, about half increased and about half decreased in relative size. A similar split was reflected by the five major groups whose highly concentrated sectors declined relative to the other sectors.

SUMMARY

The manufacturing division experienced increasing relative concentration from 1939 through 1954 with a slight decline from 1954 through

1958. This generally rising trend reflected an increased number of smallest-size manufacturing establishments and not the displacement of small establishments by larger ones; i.e., rather than the very largest establishments increasing in size, the smallest manufacturing establishments apparently grew in numbers far faster than the demand for their goods and services between 1939 and 1958.

The absolute concentration of manufacturing industries also reflects an increasing trend during this period. However, this rise in concentration was not reflected in a relatively greater extent of monopoly (Tables 13 and 20). Structural and behavioral changes apparently limited the relative growth of monopoly. During these 20 years, an increasing share of manufacturing output was provided by industries considered workably competitive.

CHAPTER 6

Growth of Monopoly: 1899–1958

Having studied trends in productive structure separately for the periods 1899–1939 and 1939–1958, we turn now to examine the entire span from 1899 to 1958. There are two ways to do this: first, by combining the findings for the two briefer periods; and, second, by directly comparing conditions in the initial and terminal years. The first possibility need not detain us, since we have already noted that there are no clearly discernible trends in either direction over the lesser periods in the extent of monopoly and hence none over the two periods combined.

For a direct comparison of conditions in 1899 and 1958, we may proceed as in Chapter 3 by taking account of the fact that the criteria for classifying an industry as monopolistic are much more restrictive for 1899 than for 1958. In addition, we face the problem that the Martin national income series, on which the calculations for 1899 are based, does not extend to 1958. There is no way to resolve this problem, but we can indicate from data given earlier how much difference is made in estimates for 1937 when the Department of Commerce series is used instead of Martin's.

Using the classificatory criteria applied to 1899, we derive for 1958 the revised percentage distribution of national income among types of productive organization as given in Table 21. Comparing the results with those obtained earlier under broader criteria for monopoly (see Tables 12 and 22), we see that the percentage of national income attributable to effectively monopolistic industries falls from 15.9 to 11.5, or by 4.4 percentage points, whereas that attributable to workably competitive industries rises by the same amount from 62.0 to 66.4. If we may judge from the data for 1937, use of a Martin-type national income series rather than the Department of Commerce series would have reduced

Growth of Monopoly: 1899–1958

TABLE 21

Percentage Distribution of National Income in 1958 by Industrial Origin and by Type of Productive Organization, Based on Criteria Similar to Those Used for 1899

	Effectively Monopolistic	Workably Competitive	Governmental or Governmentally Supervised[a]	All Types
Agriculture		4.3	0.7	5.0
Mining	0.2	1.2	0.0	1.5
Contract construction		5.4		5.4
Manufacturing	8.1	20.2		28.3
Trade		16.6		16.6
Finance	3.0	7.3		10.2
Transportation and communication	0.2		6.1	6.3
Public utilities			2.0	2.0
Services		11.4[b]		11.4
Government and government enterprises			12.7	12.7
Nonallocable				0.6
Total	11.5	66.4	21.5	100.0

Sums and detail may not agree because of rounding.

Source: Table 12 as adjusted on the basis of the more restrictive criteria used to define monopoly in 1899 (see pp. 48–49).

[a] We assume that supervised communication, public utilities, and agriculture would have been effectively monopolistic in the absence of supervision, while supervised transportation and mining would have been workably competitive. For this case, the percentages of national income are to be reclassified as follows:

Effectively Monopolistic		Workably Competitive	
Communication	1.6	Transportation	4.5
Public utilities	2.0	Mining	0.0
Agriculture	0.7		

[b] Includes 4.4 per cent attributable to households and nonprofit institutions.

the percentage attributable to effective monopoly by a slight additional amount (see Table 23).

If the upper figure for 1958 (Estimate I) is used, the fraction of national income originating in privately organized monopolistic industries is shown as falling from 17.4 per cent in 1899 to 15.9 per cent in 1958, or by 1.5 percentage points; the fraction originating in privately organized competitive industries, as falling from 76.1 to 62.0 per cent, or by 14.1 percentage points; and the fraction originating in government and governmentally supervised industries, as rising from 6.5 to 21.5 per

TABLE 22

Percentage of National Income Produced by Effectively Monopolistic Industries, by Major Industry Division: 1899 and 1958

		1958	
	1899	Estimate I[a]	Estimate II[b]
Agriculture		c	c
Mining	1.1	0.2	0.2
Contract construction			
Manufacturing	5.6	10.7	8.1
Trade		1.8	
Finance	1.2	3.0	3.0
Transportation and communication	9.1	0.2c	0.2c
Public utilities	0.4	c	c
Total	17.4	15.9c	11.5c

Source: Tables 8, 12, and 21.

[a] Based on the criteria of monopoly developed in Chapters 2 and 4.

[b] Based on criteria of monopoly similar to those for 1899 (see text, pp. 48–49).

[c] Including effectively supervised but otherwise monopolistic industries, the percentages are as follows: agriculture, 0.7; transportation and communication, 1.8; public utilities, 2.0; and total, 20.2 (Estimate I) and 15.8 (Estimate II). See note a of Table 21.

cent, or by 15.0 percentage points. On the same basis the fraction of nongovernmental production originating in all monopolistic industries, both privately organized and governmentally supervised, rose from 19 per cent in 1899 to 23 per cent in 1958, or by 4 percentage points; the fraction originating in all workably competitive industries fell correspondingly from 80 to 77 per cent. Hence, use of Estimate I for 1958 implies that the extent of monopoly declined somewhat relative to the whole economy but rose significantly relative to the extent of competition.

If the lower figure for 1958 (Estimate II) is used, the extent of monopoly is indicated as declining significantly relative to the economy as a whole and as remaining about the same relative to the extent of competition. The fraction of national income originating in privately organized monopolistic industries is shown as falling from 17.4 per cent in 1899 to 11.5 per cent in 1958, or by 5.9 percentage points; the

TABLE 23

Percentage of National Income Produced by Effectively Monopolistic Industries in 1937, Based on Criteria Similar to Those Used for 1899, by Major Industry Division and National Income Series

	Martin Income Series[a]	Department of Commerce Income Series[b]
Agriculture		
Mining	0.7	0.7
Contract construction		
Manufacturing	6.7	7.1
Trade		
Finance	2.0	2.3
Transportation and communication	1.6[c]	1.4[c]
Public utilities	[c]	[c]
Services		
Total	11.0[c]	11.5[c]

[a] From Table 8, Estimate II.

[b] From Table 2 as adjusted on the basis of the more restrictive criteria used to define monopoly in 8919 (see pp. 48–49).

[c] Including effectively supervised but otherwise monopolistic industries, the percentages are as follows:

	Martin	Commerce
Transportation and communication	1.7	1.5
Public utilities	1.8	2.3
Total	12.9	13.9

fraction originating in privately organized competitive industries, as falling from 76.1 to 66.4 per cent, or by 9.7 percentage points. The fraction of nongovernmental production originating in all monopolistic industries, both privately organized and governmentally supervised, is shown as 19 per cent in 1899 and 18 per cent in 1958, while the corresponding fractions originating in all competitive industries are shown as 81 and 82 per cent.

We see from Table 24 that, according to both Estimates I and II, the extent of monopoly broadly defined (i.e., including governmentally supervised monopolies) declined for transportation and communication and for mining, increased for finance, and remained the same for public utilities. According to Estimate I, it increased as well for agriculture and trade, but in these cases there simply was not enough information to measure the extent of monopoly in 1899. Manufacturing shows a rise in the extent of monopoly under Estimate I but a fall under Estimate II.

The changes for mining and manufacturing are analyzed in more detail in Table 25. Within mining the extent of monopoly shows a decline for nonmetals and an increase for metals, just as in the period 1899–1937 (see Table 10). In a more controversial case, anthracite mining—whose relative importance has diminished sharply—has been judged as shifting to the competitive category in recent years. We note that for mining as a whole the observed decline by 24.3 percentage points in the fraction of mining income originating in monopolistic industries (see Table 24) is attributable to changes in both the relative extents of monopoly within groups and the relative sizes of groups, but primarily to the latter. If the relative extents of monopoly within

TABLE 24

Relative Extent of Monopoly in and Relative Size of Major Industry Divisions: 1899 and 1958

	Relative Extent of Monopoly[a]			Relative Size of Division[b]	
		1958			
	1899	Estimate I[c]	Estimate II[d]	1899	1958
Public utilities	100.0	100.0[e]	100.0[e]	0.4	2.0
Transportation and communication	91.9	29.3[e]	29.3[e]	9.9	6.3
Mining	40.2	15.9	15.9	2.7	1.5
Manufacturing	32.0	37.8	28.8	17.5	28.3
Finance	21.7	29.1	29.1	5.5	10.2
Services				11.3	11.4
Agriculture		14.2[e]		18.9	5.0
Trade		10.8		16.6	16.6
Contract construction				4.2	5.4

Source: Tables 9, 13, B-5, and B-13.

[a] Measured by percentage of income originating in each division accounted for by monopolistic industries.

[b] Percentage of national income (Martin series for 1899 and Commerce series for 1958) originating in the division.

[c] Based on the criteria of monopoly developed in Chapters 2 and 4.

[d] Based on criteria of monopoly similar to those for 1899 (see text, pp. 48–49).

[e] Includes effectively supervised industries. If these are excluded, the percentages become as follows: public utilities, 0.0; transportation and communication, 3.3; and agriculture, 0.0.

TABLE 25

Relative Extent of Monopoly in and Relative Size of Major Industry Groups in Mining and Manufacturing: 1899 and 1958

	Relative Extent of Monopoly[a]			Relative Size of Group[b]	
		1958			
	1899	Estimate I[c]	Estimate II[d]	1899	1958
Mining					
Anthracite	100.0			15.0	2.7
Nonmetal	69.9	23.5	23.5	10.0	13.8
Metal	56.6	90.7	90.7	32.1	13.9
Soft coal and petroleum				42.9	69.6
Manufacturing					
Rubber products	100.0	50.1	56.4	1.5	1.7
Paper products	71.0	9.3	9.3	2.0	3.8
Transportation equipment[e]	57.3	63.4	63.4	3.9	11.8
Iron and steel, nonferrous, and misc. products	54.0	38.5	38.5	17.9	20.9
Tobacco products	49.9	100.0	100.0	3.1	0.8
Petroleum and coal products	46.8	85.2	1.1	0.8	3.5
Machinery[f]	41.4	35.8	30.9	10.5	18.0
Foods[g]	39.1	35.0	19.4	12.8	9.0
Leather products	26.2	1.9	1.9	4.2	1.3
Chemicals	24.3	49.2	49.3	3.6	7.6
Textile products[h]	20.2	4.5	4.5	16.0	8.0
Stone, clay, and glass products	13.3	43.5	44.5	4.7	3.6
Printing and publishing	0.9	33.1	1.2	5.9	5.5
Forest products[i]	0.5	1.8	1.8	13.0	4.4

Source: Tables 10, A-10, A-12, B-7, B-8, B-10, C-8, and C-19.

[a] Measured by percentage of income originating in the group accounted for by monopolistic industries.

[b] Percentage of income originating in mining or manufacturing accounted for by the group.

[c] Based on the criteria of monopoly developed in Chapters 2 and 4.

[d] Based on criteria of monopoly similar to those for 1899 (see text, pp. 48–49).

[e] Includes automobiles.   [f] Includes electrical machinery.   [g] Includes beverages.

[h] Includes apparel.   [i] Includes furniture.

groups had remained the same as in 1899 while the relative sizes of groups changed as they did, the observed decline would have been 20.0 percentage points; if the relative sizes of groups had remained the same while the relative extents of monopoly changed as they did, the observed decline would have been only 8.7 percentage points.

For manufacturing, the extent of monopoly is shown as increasing for six industry groups and decreasing for eight, in Estimate and evenly split if Estimate II is used for 1958. If the relative sizes of industry

TABLE 26

Rankings of Manufacturing Major Industry Groups by
Relative Extent of Monopoly: 1899 and 1958

		1958	
	1899	Estimate I	Estimate II
Rubber products	1	4	3
Paper products	2	11	9
Transportation equipment	3	3	2
Iron and steel, nonferrous, and misc. products	4	7	6
Tobacco products	5	1	1
Petroleum and coal products	6	12	14
Machinery	7	8	7
Foods	8	9	8
Leather products	9	13	11
Chemicals	10	5	4
Textile products	11	12	10
Stone, clay, and glass products	12	6	5
Printing and publishing	13	10	13
Forest products	14	14	12

Source: Table 25.

groups within manufacturing had not changed between 1899 and 1958,
a decline in the extent of monopoly in manufacturing would have been
observed under either Estimate I or Estimate II for 1958, by 5.2 percentage points in the former case and 7.8 in the latter. On the other
hand, if the relative extents of monopoly within groups had remained
the same as in 1899 while the relative sizes of groups changed as they
did, the extent of monopoly in manufacturing would have shown an
increase by 7.8 percentage points, or 2.0 percentage points more than
under Estimate I (see Table 24). In this sense, then, a decline in the
extent of monopoly seems to have been generally characteristic
of industry groups within manufacturing. Comparison of rankings of
groups by extent of monopoly (Table 26) suggests that the pattern of
monopoly changed significantly over the period 1899–1958 regardless
of which estimate is used for 1958.[1]

CHAPTER 7

Summary and Qualifications

This study provides quantitative estimates of the extent and growth of enterprise monopoly in the United States for the period 1899–1958. Conditions are compared for intervening as well as terminal years, so that some evidence is provided on the stability of trends.

Data on output concentration were the primary source of information on monopoly around the turn of the century. All industries for which evidence was found to indicate high concentration ratios for the four leading firms were taken as monopolistic. Several other industries in finance, transportation, and communication were also regarded as monopolistic. All other industries in the private sector of the economy were considered workably competitive. The remaining economic activities were those undertaken by the government. The extent of monopoly, competition, or governmental activities was measured by the fraction of national income originating in each area, Dr. Robert Martin's income data being used as the basis for all calculations.

For 1899, we find that 17.4 per cent of national income originated in monopolistic industries, 76.1 per cent in workably competitive industries, and 6.5 per cent in government. Therefore, workably competitive industries accounted for about 81 per cent of nongovernmental production; monopolistic industries, for about 19 per cent.

If similar criteria of monopoly are used for 1958, we find that 11.5 per cent of national income originated in monopolistic industries, 66.4 per cent in workably competitive industries, and 21.5 per cent in government and governmentally supervised industries. This breakdown differs somewhat from that for 1899 in that several industries have been removed from the private sector and added to government on the grounds that they were effectively supervised. It may be useful to assign these industries to the competitive or monopolistic sector on the basis of judgments as to how they would behave in the absence of effective supervision. If supervised public utilities, communications, and agriculture are accordingly assigned to the monopolistic sector and supervised mining and transportation to the competitive sector, all competitive industries accounted for about 82 per cent of nongovernmental production and all monopolistic industries accounted for about 18 per cent. According to these estimates, the fraction of national income originating in privately organized monopolistic industries declined by 5.9 percentage points between 1899 and 1958; and the fraction of nongovernmental production originating in all monopolistic industries, both privately organized and governmentally supervised, declined by about 1 percentage point. Therefore, it would appear that the extent of monopoly decreased significantly relative to the economy as a whole while remaining about the same relative to the competitive sector.

Since the structural and behavioral characteristics of industries have been studied much more extensively for recent years than for the period around the turn of the century, broader criteria of monopoly (described in Appendix C) may be applied to recent years. On the basis of these broader criteria, we find that in 1958 15.9 per cent of national income originated in monopolistic industries, 62.0 per cent in competitive industries, and 21.5 per cent in government and governmentally supervised industries. All monopolistic industries, both privately organized and governmentally supervised, accounted for about 23 per cent of nongovernmental production; all competitive industries, for about 77 per cent. By these estimates, the fraction of national income originating in privately organized monopolistic industries decreased by 1.5 percentage points between 1899 and 1958, while the fraction of nongovernmental production originating in all monopolistic industries increased by 4 percentage points. The extent of monopoly is shown as decreasing slightly relative to the whole economy while increasing significantly relative to the competitive sector.

The change in the extent of monopoly between 1899 and 1958 may also be estimated by linking the findings for two subperiods, 1899–1937 and 1939–1958. In the former case, two estimates were made for 1937 similar in nature to those used for comparing 1899 and 1958. If the two estimates are averaged, the extent of monopoly is shown as declining slightly (by 2.2 percentage points) relative to the whole economy and remaining about the same relative to the competitive sector. Comparison of 1939 with 1954 and 1958 can be based on uniformly detailed information and unchanging criteria of monopoly. For those years a slight and persisting decline is shown in the extent of monopoly relative to both the whole economy and the competitive sector. Combining the findings for the two periods, we would seem to be justified in saying that there is no evidence of a significant increase in the extent of monopoly relative to either the economy or the competitive sector between 1899 and 1958.

For both early and late years the relevant data are more detailed for manufacturing than for other sectors. According to our estimates based on comparable criteria of monopoly, monopolistic industries accounted for 32 per cent of manufacturing income in 1899, 28 per cent in 1937, and 29 per cent in 1958. Under broader criteria of monopoly, the fractions rise to 39 per cent for 1937, 40 per cent for 1939, and 38 per cent for 1954 and 1958. Hence there seems to have been a remarkable stability in the extent of monopoly within manufacturing as a whole. This over-all stability was accompanied by significant changes in the extent of monopoly within industry groups, so that the location and intensity of monopolistic elements shifted considerably over the years. Moreover, if the relative size of industry groups had remained constant, an over-all decline in the extent of monopoly would have been registered.

Study of size distributions of manufacturing plants (establishments) reveals a trend toward increasing inequality, particularly between 1939 and 1958, but this trend has resulted from the fact that the observed increase in the number of plants has been concentrated in the lower size classes, not from a displacement of smaller plants by larger ones. Concentration of output among a fixed number of plants displays little change over the period examined. There seems, therefore, to be no evidence of a secular increase in economies of scale at the plant level throughout manufacturing as a whole.

These conclusions are all subject to serious qualification because of probable inaccuracies in measurement and the arbitrary nature of definitions of monopoly. The problem of definition aside, the measurement of income originating in monopolistic industries is subject to error of unknown magnitude and direction. The estimates will, for instance, vary with the national income series used. The set of estimates for 1899 and the comparable set for 1937 were based on the National Industrial Conference Board series compiled by Robert Martin, while a second set for 1937 and those for all later years were based on the Department of Commerce series. If the Department of Commerce series is used, the fraction of national income originating in monopolistic industries in 1937 turns out to be 21 per cent, or 2 percentage points more than the estimate based on the Martin series. However, the estimate of the extent of monopoly relative to the competitive sector is the same in both cases. No matter which series is used, estimates of change in the extent of monopoly over time are subject to an undeterminable error because of the greater inaccuracy of income data for the earlier than for the later years.

Other biases are probably introduced by the methods used for apportioning income by origin among subdivisions of the industrial groups for which data are published. Wherever possible, income originating was apportioned by value added, a procedure not likely to introduce bias. In some cases, however, it was necessary to apportion on the basis of gross value of output. To obtain some evidence on the possible bias introduced by the latter procedure, income was apportioned to a group of randomly selected monopolistic industries in manufacturing by both value added and gross value of output. The apportioned income was larger in the latter case than in the former, and hence there may be some overstatement in our estimates of income originating in monopolistic industries.

The conclusions are subject to further qualification because of deficiencies in the data on monopoly, however defined. For any particular year, more data are available for some industrial divisions than for others; for any span of time, more data are available for the later years. The first factor tends to cause an understatement of the extent of monopoly at any particular time; the second, an overstatement of the extent of monopoly in later years relative to earlier ones. For the last three decades, more or less comprehensive information is available for manufacturing and mining; information for other sectors is scattered and meager. For the 1890's this difference in information is even more pronounced, and, in addition, the information on output concentration in manufacturing is much less comprehensive than for the last three decades.

Estimates of the extent of monopoly for particular years may not be representative for immediately adjacent years. For instance, the position of a particular year in the "business cycle" might be an important factor affecting the proportion of national income originating in monopolistic industries. Some evidence on possible effects of this kind is provided by independent estimates for 1937 and 1939. On the basis of Department of Commerce income data, the fraction of national income originating in the same monopolistic industries was 20.6 per cent in 1937 and 20.4 per cent in 1939, a difference of only 0.2 percentage point.

The question of accuracy of measurement aside, estimates of extent of monopoly will vary with different definitions of monopoly. If output concentration is used as the basic criterion of monopoly, results will depend on the critical degree of concentration chosen and on the definitions of industries used. The evidence for manufacturing indicates that varying the critical degree of concentration over a rather wide range, holding definitions of industries constant, produces widely different effects, depending on the year. Manufacturing census industries with concentration ratios of 2/3 or larger accounted for 3.8 per cent of national income in 1939; those with concentration ratios of 1/2 to 2/3 represented only an additional 1.3 per cent. On the other hand, for 1958 the former fraction was 3.4 per cent, while the latter rose to 4.7 per cent.

The introduction of factors other than output concentration causes a pronounced change in estimates of extent of monopoly. The possible magnitude of changes may be indicated by our two estimates for 1937. Using a fairly rigid test of monopoly on the basis of output concentration, we found that the fraction of national income originated in monopolistic industries was 11.0 per cent. When much broader criteria were substituted, we obtained a fraction of 19.3 per cent. This substantial difference in results raises the question of which sets of criteria are comparable for both the 1890's and the 1930's and 1950's. There is no completely satisfactory answer to this question. It is unfortunately not even clear that the same tests of output concentration are equally applicable to both periods in view of the changes in so many other dimensions of competition.

There is a multitude of other possible changes that could result from altering definitions of monopoly and judgments on the classification of industries. In addition, this study is severely limited in the following respects: first, it considers only enterprise and not labor monopoly; second, it deals only with monopoly within the jurisdiction of the United States; and, third, it does not examine the role of "pure" cartels.

The measures presented here must therefore be interpreted with extreme caution. They obviously cannot provide information relevant to all important "monopoly questions." Above all, they do not tell us the importance to the economy of the observed extent and growth of monopoly. They do provide some concrete information on the amount of production originating in monopolistic industries that should be useful for resolving the disagreement among economists about the desirability of policies designed to maintain competition. Whoever uses the measures must bear the responsibility for applying them wisely. As Humpty-Dumpty put it, "The question is, which is to be master— that's all."

Basic Data on Extent of Monopoly: 1937 and 1939

This appendix presents the basic data[1] and explains the procedures used to estimate the extent of monopoly in 1937 and 1939. It is divided into four sections, dealing, in turn, with (1) manufacturing, (2) mining, (3) agriculture and trade, and (4) all other industrial divisions.

The basic national income data are those of the Department of Commerce. The proportional distribution of national income by major industrial division is given in Table 2. The figures are further subdivided as required in the appropriate sections of the appendix.

All computations involving division have been carried to six decimal places and rounded to four.

MANUFACTURING

Source of Data and Industrial Classification. The primary source of data on manufacturing is the *Census of Manufactures.*[2] The particular census from which data were derived is noted in each of the tables which follow in this section. The industrial classification adopted for the present study is the one used in the 1939 Census. In all tables in which data are classified by industry or major industry group, titles are given in abbreviated form. The number which was assigned to each industry in the 1939 industrial classification is also presented for the convenience of those who wish to look up more complete descriptions of industries.[3] In general, the complete titles of census products are given whenever products appear in the tables.

The 1939 industrial classification was chosen because the new Department of Commerce series on national income by industrial origin was computed on the basis of the major industry groups as defined in the 1939 Census. That fact is important because of the methods we used for apportioning income among industries. Using that classification raises two problems, since the National Resources Committee and the Temporary National Economic Committee investigations were made on the basis of the 1935 and 1937 censuses, respectively. In the first place, the Bureau of the Census presents complete data under the 1939 classification only for 1937 and 1939, and study is therefore limited to those two years. The concentration ratios calculated by the NRC for 1935 and by the TNEC for 1937 were assumed to be valid for 1937 and 1939. In the second place, definitions of products and industries changed in some cases between the 1935, 1937, and 1939 censuses. These changes were traced in each case, and compensating adjustments were made. As one result, a meticulous observer may note that Table A-2 covers only 119 products instead of the 121 listed by Wilcox. The discrepancy is, however, merely illusory, being caused by changes in definitions of products.

Adjustments in Census Data. The adjustments which were made did not affect the fact that the 1939 major industry groups were the basis for our study, since they did not change the area of activities included within any group. The only reason for the adjustments was to make sure that all the commodities which were found to be produced under highly concentrated conditions in 1935 and 1937 were included in our estimates for 1937 and 1939. Whenever an industry was split up, the new industries were very seldom distributed among different major industry groups; they were almost always kept together in the same group.

When the scope of a census industry was changed between 1935 and 1939, value data for 1937 are usually available under both definitions. Consequently, the value figure for 1939 was adjusted by multiplying it by the ratio of the two sets of 1937 data. For example, a larger number of commodities is included in the "cereals" industry in the 1935 than in the 1939 Census, so that the 1937 value added for the industry as defined in 1935 is 1.0595 times the 1937 value added for the industry as defined in 1939. It is then assumed that the 1939 value added for "cereals" as defined in 1935— if known—would also be 1.0595 times as large as that for "cereals" as defined in 1939. The latter figure is accordingly multiplied by 1.0595. All adjustments of this nature are presented in Table A-8.

Value data for some census products are not available for 1939. In all such instances the value figures for 1939 were considered as bearing the same ratio as in 1937 to the figure for the next most inclusive product group for which both 1937 and 1939 data are published. For instance, the value of "machine-finished book paper" is published for both 1937 and 1939, whereas the value of "machine-finished book paper containing ground wood" is available only for 1937, when the latter value was 0.1585 of the former. The 1939 figure for "ground-wood book paper" was therefore estimated by multiplying the value of "book paper" by 0.1585. All estimates of this nature are noted in the footnotes to Table A-2.

Apportionment of Income by Origin. The Department of Commerce data on national income by industrial origin are broken down for manufacturing industries only to the level of the major industry group. It was necessary for the purposes of this study to apportion income by origin among census industries within a major industry group and among census products within a census industry. The income originating in a major industry group was prorated among member-industries on the basis of relative value added. That is, an industry was allocated the same proportion of income by origin as it had of value added. Since value added is a net production datum closely related to income by origin, no systematic bias should be introduced by this procedure.[4]

It is not possible to follow the same procedure in allocating income by origin among census products, however, since value-added data are not available for them. Consequently, the apportionment was made on the basis of gross-value data. This procedure might produce a systematic downward bias if the establishments manufacturing census products with high concentration ratios possessed, in general, a higher degree of "vertical integration" than other establishments in the same industry. For, if this were true, the proportion of total value of products in an industry accounted for by products with high concentration ratios would consistently understate the proportion of net production (value added). We can test for the existence of such a bias by computing for census industries with high concentration ratios the value added on the basis of gross-value data and by comparing the computed with the actual value added. Table A-1 presents such a comparison for the year 1937 for eleven census industries selected at random from among the fifty-four with concentration ratios of 2/3 or larger in 1935.[5] From that table it is seen that the bias is by no means consistent in direction. As a matter of fact, for these eleven industries the net result is an overstatement of value added by almost 10 per cent. It therefore seems that the procedure for allocating income by origin among products within an industry is likely, if anything, to lead to an overestimation.

Another complicating factor is that the value added for an industry and the value of separate products are calculated in the census on different bases. The value added in an industry is determined by summing the value added by all establishments which are classified in that industry. Since an establishment is classified according to its product or products of chief value, value added as determined on an establishment basis will seldom correspond exactly to the net production of all commodities which are classified in an industry. The value of separate products in an industry, on the other hand, is computed on a commodity basis. That is, the total value of a product is summed without regard to the industrial classification of the establishments in which it is manufactured. The total value of products in an industry ordinarily is computed on both bases.[6]

The problem which emerges is apparent. We can easily find the proportion of total value of products in an industry accounted for by products with high concentration ratios, since the required data are available on a commodity basis. However, it would not be appropriate to multiply value added by this proportion, since value added has been calculated on an establishment basis and hence may be smaller or larger than value added on a commodity basis and in either case should be adjusted. For example, the total value of products of the industry "colors and pigments" in 1937 was $119 million and $84 million on a commodity and an establishment basis, respectively. Value added was derived from the latter figure and therefore understates value added on a commodity basis. The major issue is to decide by how much this value added should be adjusted upward. The simplest assumption is that the two sets of value-added data are in the same ratio as the comparable sets of value-of-products data. On this assumption, value added should be multiplied by the ratio 119/84.

The example which was chosen required an upward adjustment in value added. The same argument would hold, of course, for cases requiring a downward adjustment. It can be easily shown that the adjustment, whether up or down, is properly made if we simply substitute total value of products on an establishment basis for that on a commodity basis in computing the proportion of total value of products in an industry which is accounted for by products with high concentration ratios. Suppose we let

VP represent total value of products in an industry;
vp represent the value of a product with high concentration which is in that industry;
VA represent value added for the industry;
va represent value added for the product;
(c) represent computation on a commodity basis; and
(e) represent computation on an establishment basis.

Then

$$va(c) = \frac{vp(c)}{VP(c)} \cdot VA(c).$$

But

$$VA(c) = \frac{VP(c)}{VP(e)} \cdot VA(e).$$

Therefore

$$va(c) = \frac{vp(c)}{VP(c)} \cdot \frac{VP(c)}{VP(e)} \cdot VA(e)$$

$$= \frac{vp(c)}{VP(e)} \cdot VA(e).$$

We have consequently used total value of products on an establishment basis in all such computations in Tables A-2 and A-9, with the exception of those for the "tobacco and snuff" industry in 1937. There was no need to adjust value added in this industry because all commodities were produced by establishments in either the "tobacco and snuff" or the "cigarettes" industry and the entire value added for the latter was included in computing income by origin for products with high concentration ratios. The 1939 value of separate products in the "tobacco and snuff" industry is available on an establishment basis, and hence total value of products on this basis was used for that year. But the 1937 data are given only on a commodity basis. Since no adjustment in value added is required, calculations for 1937 were therefore made by using total value of products also on a commodity basis.

MINING

Source of Data and Industrial Classification. Data on mineral industries are prepared by the Bureau of the Census and by the Bureau of Mines.[7] The latter gathers data on a commodity basis and presents only the value of minerals as they leave the mining establishments. The former provides a decennial census of mining industries, presenting data on an establishment basis. Value added can be derived from the census data but not from the Bureau of Mines data. Unfortunately, census data are not available for 1937.

The 1939 industrial classification is used in this study, for reasons given on page 95.

Apportionment of Income by Origin. Allocation of income by origin among industries was made on the basis of relative value added in 1939 and gross value of products in 1937. Value added was computed by subtracting purchases of supplies, fuel, and electrical energy from total value of products.

AGRICULTURE AND TRADE

Wilcox classified the agricultural industries of bananas and fluid-milk production as monopolized. He also considered the distribution of fluid milk and new automobiles to be monopolistic. The banana industry is not studied because production occurs outside the United States.

TABLE A-1

Actual and Apportioned Value Added in 1937 for Eleven Randomly 1935 (thousand dollars)

	Value of Products	
	Industry (1)	Major Industry Group (2)
Aluminum products, n.e.c.	129,052	2,779,961
Typewriters	45,006[b]	3,902,967
Photographic equipment	115,888	1,077,573
Fire extinguishers	8,889	1,077,573
Chocolate and cocoa products	102,346	11,294,890
Cigarettes	968,927	1,272,688
Linseed products	90,357	3,718,406
Explosives	67,343	3,718,406
Writing ink	3,476	3,718,406
Gypsum products	42,617	1,428,411
Firearms	21,555	3,818,789
Total		

Source: U.S. Bureau of the Census, *Sixteenth Census of the United States: 1940: Manufactures: 1939*, Vol. II, Government Printing Office, Washington, 1942; and Gardiner C. Means, *The Structure of the American Economy*, Part I, Government Printing Office, Washington, 1939, pp. 239–63.

Data for the production and distribution of fluid milk are presented in Table A-14. They are derived mainly from the publication, *Price Spreads between Farmers and Consumers for Food Products, 1913–44*.[8] The procedure for estimating the proportion of national income originating in production and distribution was as follows. Total consumption of fluid milk was estimated as the product of average per capita consumption for the period 1935–1939 (84.4 quarts)[9] times total population (128,825,000 and 130,880,000 in 1937 and 1939, respectively).[10] The value of production on farms was taken as total consumption times the price of milk on the farm. The value added in distribution was estimated as total consumption times the retail margin per quart. These figures were reduced to proportions of national income by dividing by total national income.

The proportion of national income originating in the retailing of new automobiles was estimated in a similar manner. The Automobile Manufacturer's Association published in 1940 an estimate of the average retail margin of automobile dealers in 1935-1936 expressed as a proportion of net sales.[11] This figure was 0.179 and represented the ratio:

$$\frac{\text{Retail sales} - \text{wholesale sales}}{\text{Retail sales}}.$$

Selected Census Industries with Concentration Ratios of 2/3 or Larger in

Ratio of (1) to (2) (3)	Value Added	
	Apportioned[a] (4)	Actual (5)
0.0464	39,244	49,018
0.0115	26,813	31,614[b]
0.1075	68,227	79,235
0.0082	5,204	5,307
0.0091	30,674	28,215
0.7613	247,467	197,405
0.0243	43,161	15,875
0.0181	32,148	39,746
0.0009	1,599	1,976
0.0298	26,529	25,935
0.0056	18,978	17,222
	540,044	491,548

[a] Ratio in col. 3 times value added for the major industry group.
[b] From U.S. Bureau of the Census, *Biennial Census of Manufactures: 1937*, Part I, Government Printing Office, Washington, 1939, p. 1089.

Since we have reliable data only for the wholesale sales of new automobiles, to find the total retail margin the denominator of the ratio must be replaced by wholesale sales. That is, we want the ratio of retail margin to wholesale sales. It is apparent that this ratio is 0.179/0.821, or 0.218. The total retail margin ("value added" in retailing) is then wholesale sales multiplied by 0.218.

ALL OTHER INDUSTRIAL DIVISIONS

The other industries which Wilcox classified as monopolistic and the proportions of national income assignable to them are given in Table A-16. All data were taken from the new Department of Commerce income series.

"Services allied to transportation," accounting for 0.24 per cent of national income in 1937 and 0.27 per cent in 1939, was considered a competitive area.

The estimates of national income originating in households and nonprofit enterprises were also taken from the new Department of Commerce income series.[12]

TABLE A-2

Basic Data for Manufactured Products, Each Valued at $10,000,000 or More, with Concentration Ratios of 3/4 or Larger in 1937,[a] by Major Industry Group and Industry: 1937 and 1939

	Industry Number[b]	Ratio of Value for Concentrated Products to Total Value[c]		Ratio of Value Added for Concentrated Products to Total Value Added[d]		Proportion of National Income Originating in Concentrated Products[e]	
		1937	1939	1937	1939	1937	1939
Foods	1			0.0255	0.0304	0.0008	0.0010
Meat packing	111	0.0125	0.0120[f]				
Canned vegetables, etc.	133	0.1013	0.1293				
Beet sugar	163	0.9270	0.9331				
Cane sugar	162	0.0532	0.0519				
Corn products	194	0.4547	0.4596				
Tobacco products	2			0.7386	0.7537	0.0019	0.0031
Cigarettes	211	1.0000	1.0000				
Tobacco and snuff	231	0.9331[g]	0.8869[h]				
Textile products	3			0.0253	0.0252	0.0005	0.0004
Cotton broad goods	311	0.0552	0.0552[i]				
Woolens and worsteds[j]	341	0.0309	0.0314[k]				
Linoleum	374	0.2901	0.3089				
Furniture	6			0.0516	0.0532	0.0004	0.0004
Mattresses, etc.	611	0.3957	0.4192				
Upholstered furniture	612	0.1025	0.0931[l]				
Matches	693	0.5931	0.4890				
Paper	7			0.0105	0.0115	0.0001	0.0001
Paper mills	720	0.0232	0.0249[m]				
Chemicals	9			0.0931	0.0802	0.0015	0.0013
Paints, etc.	911	0.0312	0.0244				
Colors and pigments	912	0.7523	0.5679				
Rayon products	951	0.2289	0.2140				
Coal-tar products	981	0.7927	0.6915				
Plastic materials	982	0.2504	0.2419				
Compressed gases	985	0.8019	0.7612				
Chemicals, n.e.c.	999	0.0586	0.0419				
Ammunition	988	1.0000	1.0000				
Petroleum and coal products	10			0.0118	0.0123	0.0001	0.0001
Petroleum refining	1011	0.0152	0.0158				
Rubber products	11			0.5325	0.5250	0.0021	0.0020
Tires and inner tubes	1111	0.8083	0.8305				
Rubber boots and shoes	1121	0.7422	0.7211				
Leather products	12			0.0239	0.0189	0.0001	0.0001
Footwear	1240	0.0397	0.0319				
Stone, clay, and glass products	13			0.1525	0.1251	0.0013	0.0011
Flat glass	1310	0.7401	0.6528				
Glass containers	1321	0.2468	0.2072				
Tableware, etc.	1329	0.2443	0.2578				
Gypsum products	1372	0.2727	0.2761				
Wallboard	1374	0.9596	0.8528				
Asbestos products	1392–93	0.1806	0.0757				

(continued)

TABLE A-2 (*concluded*)

	Industry Number[b]	Ratio of Value for Concentrated Products to Total Value[c]		Ratio of Value Added for Concentrated Products to Total Value Added[d]		Proportion of National Income Originating in Concentrated Products[e]	
		1937	1939	1937	1939	1937	1939
Iron and steel products	14			0.1439	0.1358	0.0051	0.0042
Steel works	1412	0.2455	0.2297				
Tin cans, etc.	1430	0.5551	0.5374				
Files	1453	0.9050	0.9475				
Hardware, n.e.c.	1459	0.5113	0.4482				
Stoves, etc.	1465	0.0608	0.0609				
Steam fittings	1466	0.1985	0.1793				
Nonferrous products	15			0.1190	0.1397	0.0011	0.0011
Alloying, etc.	1520	0.1793	0.1756				
Aluminum ware	1592	1.0000	1.0000				
Aluminum products, n.e.c.	1593	0.8729	0.9247				
Sheet-metal work	1594	0.1026	0.1256				
Electrical machinery	16			0.2795	0.2432	0.0034	0.0028
Carbon products	1612	0.5952	0.7213				
Measuring instruments	1613	0.5258	0.4215				
Generating apparatus, etc.[n]	1619	0.3274	0.3098				
Electrical appliances	1620	0.1833	0.1111				
Insulated wire	1630	0.3477	0.2367				
Automotive electrical equipment	1640	0.3258	0.3580				
Radios and tubes, etc.	1661	0.0618	0.0094				
Communication equipment	1662	0.5093	0.4939				
Batteries	1691	0.2795	0.3095				
Machinery	17			0.0908	0.0862	0.0022	0.0018
Steam engines, etc.	1711	0.5735	0.2856				
Tractors[j]	1721	0.3859	0.3673				
Agriculture machinery	1729	0.1432[o]	0.1865[o]				
Office machinery	1771	0.4305	0.4472				
Refrigerators, etc.	1784	0.3432	0.3993				
Automobiles	18			0.5134	0.5211	0.0090	0.0085
Motor vehicles and parts	1810	0.5153	0.5223				
Transportation equipment	19			0.0593	0.1033	0.0003	0.0006
Aircraft and parts	1921	0.2577	0.2658				
Miscellaneous	20			0.0799	0.0875	0.0006	0.0006
Photographic equipment	2012	0.6403	0.6621				

Source: W. L. Thorp and W. F. Crowder, *The Structure of Industry*, Temporary National Economic Committee Monograph No. 27, Government Printing Office, Washington, 1941, pp. 420-81; U.S. Bureau of the Census, *Census of Manufactures: 1939*, Vol. II, Government Printing Office, Washington, 1940, and *Survey of Current Business Supplement*, July 1947, p. 26.

[a] Each industry includes the following products with concentration ratios of 3/4 or larger:
  - 111 Canned meats other than vacuum-cooked; wool, in meat-packing establishments.
  - 133 Canned soups.
  - 163 Granulated beet sugar.
  - 162 Refined sugar, soft or brown.
  - 194 Mixtures of corn and other syrups; corn sugar; corn starch.
  - 231 Smoking tobacco; scrap chewing tobacco; plug chewing tobacco; snuff.
  - 311 Tobacco and cheese cloth; chambrays and cheviots; turkish and terry woven towels and toweling and huck towels and toweling.

(*continued*)

NOTES TO TABLE A-2 (*continued*)

341 Men's-wear suitings and pantings; other worsted (except all wool).
374 Inlaid lineoleum.
611 Innerspring mattresses.
612 Metal upholstered davenports, sofas, day beds, studio couches, etc.
693 Matches, strike-anywhere.
720 Ground-wood printing paper; machine-finished book paper containing ground wood; machine-glazed kraft wrapping paper.
911 White lead in oil, pure.
912 Litharge (lead oxide); zinc oxide (Chinese white, zinc white); lithopone; other oxides.
951 Rayon yarns, 100 denier; rayon yarns, 300 denier.
981 Coal-tar crudes.
982 Coal-tar resins derived from phenol and/or cresol.
985 Hydrocarbon-acetylene; oxygen.
999 Ferro-alloys, electric furnace.
1011 Partially refined oils, sold for re-running.
1111 Passenger-car pneumatic tires and casings; truck and bus pneumatic tires and casings; passenger-car, truck, and bus inner tubes.
1121 Canvas rubber-soled shoes; arctics and gaiters; other shoes, rubbers, and footholds.
1240 Men's work shoes, wood or metal fastened.
1310 Window glass; other flat glass.
1321 Milk bottles; narrow-neck packers' ware; beer bottles.
1329 Machine-made tumblers, goblets, and barware; other lighting glassware, including electric light bulbs and oil lamps.
1372 Base-coat plaster.
1374 Fiberboard made of wood or other vegetable pulp, laminated lumber with paper liners; insulation.
1392–3 Asbestos roofing shingles.
1412 Semifinished rolled products: blooms, billets, and slabs; rolled blooms and billets for forging; sheet and tin plate bars. Finished hot-rolled products and forgings: pierced billets rounds, and blanks, for seamless pipes and tubes; rails; heavy structural shapes; universal plates; sheets, No. 13 and thinner, black for tinning; stainless-steel plates and sheets; strips and flats (hot-rolled) for cold-rolling; skelp; axles, rolled and forged; car and locomotive wheels, rolled and forged.
1430 Venthole-top cans; sanitary cans, including sweetened condensed milk cans; beer cans.
1453 Metalworking files and rasps.
1459 Motor-vehicle hardware, including lock units.
1465 Kerosene cooking stoves and ranges.
1466 Thermostats.
1520 Copper plates and sheets; nickel-alloy plates and sheets; brass and bronze tubing (seamless) and pipe.
1593 Ingots; other aluminum products.
1594 Culverts, flumes, irrigation pipe, etc.
1612 Electrodes and miscellaneous specialties for electrical uses, including packing rings for steam seal.
1613 Watt-hour meters, a-c.
1619 Generators, except railway and vehicle power generators (not including generators, other drives); distribution transformers, $1\frac{1}{2}$–500 kv-a; power transformers, 501 kv-a and over; motors, $\frac{1}{20}$ hp and over but under 1 hp: split phase, capacitor type; motors, 1 hp and over, d-c; power switchboards and parts.
1620 Household ranges, $2\frac{1}{2}$ kw and over.
1630 Paper insulated; ignition-cable or wire assemblies for internal-combustion engines.
1640 Generators for battery charging; spark plugs.
1661 Receiving sets, extending beyond standard broadcast band, socket-power operated, over $45 but not over $65.
1662 Telephone and telegraph apparatus.
1691 Storage, other than automotive or radio; dry, other than 6 in., $1\frac{1}{2}$ volt.
1711 Steam turbines other than marine.
1721 Wheel type except "all-purpose," 30 belt hp and over; wheel type, "all-purpose," under 30 belt hp, steel tires; wheel type, "all-purpose," under 30 belt hp, rubber tires.

(*continued*)

NOTES TO TABLE A-2 (*concluded*)

1729　Trailer-drawn cultivators; combines (harvester-thresher).
1771　Listing-adding machines; typewriters-standard; cash registers; card punching, sorting, and tabulating machines; fare registers and fare boxes, ticket-counting machines, and coin counters.
1784　Domestic refrigerators, electric 6 cu ft or more but under 10; refrigerating systems, complete without cabinets; refrigerator cabinets, domestic.
1810　Passenger cars; commercial cars, trucks, and buses; passenger-car chassis.
1921　Aircraft engines and engine parts.
2012　Cameras, motion picture and other; films except X-ray; sensitized photographic paper.

[b] As listed in *Census of Manufactures: 1939: Industry Classifications.*

[c] The value of each concentrated product is taken on a commodity basis, while the total value of products in an industry is taken on an establishment basis.

[d] For each industry, value added for concentrated products calculated as total value added times ratio of value added for concentrated products to total value added.

[e] Proportion of national income originating in major industry group times ratio of value added for concentrated products to total value added.

[f] Value for canned meats other than vacuum-cooked not available and therefore estimated as 0.2364 of value of all canned meats, the ratio for 1937.

[g] Total value of products in the industry is taken on a commodity basis (see text).

[h] The value of concentrated products in this industry is given only on an establishment basis.

[i] Taken to be the same as for 1937 since data were not available for concentrated products.

[j] The following concentrated products are improperly identified in the list presented in Clair Wilcox, *Competition and Monopoly in American Industry*, Temporary National Economic Committee Monograph No. 21, Government Printing Office, Washington, 1940, pp. 117–18: men's-wear suitings and pantings, other worsted (except all wool)—identified as "woolen woven goods, other"; and tractors, wheel type, "all purpose," under 30 belt hp, rubber tires—identified as "belt horsepower 30 and over."

[k] Value for men's-wear suitings and pantings, other worsted not available, and therefore estimated as 0.1180 of value of all men's-wear suitings and pantings, that ratio obtaining in 1937.

[l] Value for metal upholstered davenports, etc., not available, and therefore estimated as 0.7610 of value of all metal living-room and library furniture, the ratio for 1937.

[m] Value for machine-finished book paper containing ground wood not available, and therefore estimated as 0.1585 of value of all machine-finished book paper, the ratio for 1937.

[n] Generators, except railway and vehicle power generators, omitted by mistake from the list in Wilcox, *op. cit.*, pp. 117–18.

[o] Data for highly concentrated products taken from U.S. Bureau of the Census, *Statistical Abstract of the United States: 1940*, Government Printing Office, Washington, 1940, p. 854.

Basic Data for Manufacturing Industries with Concentration Ratios of 2/3 or Larger in 1935,[a] by Major Industry Group: 1937 and 1939

	Industry Number[b]	Ratio of Value Added for Concentrated Industries to Total Value Added		Proportion of National Income Originating in Concentrated Industries[e]	
		1937	1939	1937	1939
Foods[d]	1	0.0967	0.0999	0.0032	0.0031
Tobacco products	2	0.6073	0.6474	0.0016	0.0027
Textile products[d]	3	0.0114	0.0128	0.0002	0.0002
Furniture	6	0.0318	0.0357	0.0002	0.0002
Chemicals[d]	9	0.2383	0.2336	0.0038	0.0039
Petroleum and coal products	10	0.0034	0.0025	0.0000	0.0000
Rubber products	11	0.6670	0.6416	0.0027	0.0024
Stone, clay, and glass products	13	0.0852	0.0833	0.0007	0.0008
Iron and steel products	14	0.0426	0.0510	0.0015	0.0016
Nonferrous products[d]	15	0.1972	0.2055	0.0019	0.0017
Machinery[d]	17	0.1470	0.1290	0.0035	0.0027
Automobiles	18	0.9963	0.9977	0.0175	0.0164
Transportation equipment	19	0.3501	0.1829	0.0016	0.0010
Miscellaneous[d]	20	0.2272	0.2370	0.0016	0.0017
Total				0.0400	0.0384

Source: Means, *Structure of American Economy*, Part I, pp. 239–63; *Census of Manufactures: 1939*, Vol. II; and *Survey of Current Business Supplement*, July 1947 p. 26.

[a] Each major industry group includes the following industries with concentration ratios of 2/3 or larger:

1   Cereals, 143; Cane sugar, 162; Beet sugar, 163; Chocolate and cocoa products, 172; Chewing gum, 173; Cooking fats, etc., 192; Oleomargarine, 193; Corn products, 194.
2   Cigarettes, 211.
3   Linoleum, 374.
6   Excelsior, 691; Cork products, 692; Matches, 693.
9   Linseed products, 922; Essential oils, 924; Drug grinding, 931; Soap and glycerin, 941; Rayon, 951; Explosives, 983; Compressed gases, 985; Bone black, etc., 986; Ammunition, 988; Bluing, 995; Writing ink, 997.
10 Fuel briquettes, 1091.
11 Tires and inner tubes, 1111; Boots and shoes, 1121.
13 China firing, etc., 1365; Gypsum products, 1372; Abrasives, 1391; Natural graphite, 1394.
14 Tin cans, etc., 1430; Files, 1453; Firearms, 1497; Safes and vaults, 1498.
15 Primary smelting, etc., 1511, 1517; Aluminum ware, 1592; Aluminum products, n.e.c., 1593; Gold and silver leaf, 1595; Tinfoils, etc., 1590.
17 Tractors, 1721; Agricultural machinery, 1729; Typewriters, 1771; Sewing machines, 1783.
18 Motor vehicles and parts, 1810.
19 Locomotives, 1911; Railway cars and equipment, 1921.
20 Photographic equipment, 2012; Surgical equipment, 2022; Billiard tables, 2049; Pens and mechanical pencils, 2051; Soda fountains, etc., 2091; Fire extinguishers, 2096; Nonrubber combs, 2099.

[b] As listed in *Census of Manufactures: 1939: Industry Classifications*.

[e] Proportion of national income originating in major industry group times ratio of value added for concentrated industries to total value added.

[d] For industries defined according to the 1937 *Census of Manufactures*. See Table A-8.

Basic Data for Manufacturing Industries with Concentration Ratios of 1/2 to 2/3 in 1935,[a] by Major Industry Group: 1937 and 1939

	Industry Number[b]	Ratio of Value Added for Concentrated Industries to Total Value Added		Proportion of National Income Originating in Concentrated Industries[c]	
		1937	1939	1937	1939
Foods	1	0.1359	0.1317	0.0044	0.0041
Tobacco products	2	0.1408	0.1199	0.0004	0.0005
Textile products	3	0.0633	0.0667	0.0014	0.0012
Apparel	4	0.0051	0.0048	0.0001	0.0001
Furniture	6	0.0503	0.0460	0.0003	0.0003
Paper[d]	7	0.0175	0.0144	0.0001	0.0001
Chemicals	9	0.0217	0.0182	0.0003	0.0003
Stone, clay, and glass products	13	0.1214	0.0946	0.0011	0.0009
Iron and steel products	14	0.0485	0.0425	0.0017	0.0013
Nonferrous products[e]	15	0.1150	0.1394	0.0011	0.0011
Machinery	17	0.0174	0.0176	0.0004	0.0004
Transportation equipment[d]	19	0.2066	0.3263	0.0009	0.0018
Miscellaneous products	20	0.1620	0.1450	0.0011	0.0010
Total				0.0133	0.0131

Source: See Table A-3.

[a] Each major industry group includes the following industries with concentration ratios of 1/2 to 2/3:

1 Meat packing, 111; Custom slaughtering, 112; Liquors, distilled, 185; Baking powder, 191.
2 Tobacco and snuff, 231.
3 Carpets and rugs, wool, 371; Carpet yarn, wool, 372; Carpets and rugs, other, 373; Felt goods, etc., 390; Artificial leather, oilcloth, 395–396.
4 Suspenders, etc., 484.
6 Wood preserving, 694.
7 Two parts of die-cut paper, 791: cards, cut and designed; and cardboard, converted. See Table A-9.
9 Hardwood distillation, 961; Wood naval stores, 962; Salt, 984; Fireworks, 993; Candles, 994.
13 Mirrors, etc., 1330; Mineral ware, 1373; Wallboard, 1374; Asbestos products, 1392; Sand-lime brick, 1396.
14 Blast-furnace products, 1411; Steam-fitting products, 1454; Springs, steel, 1494.
15 Zinc smelting and refining, 1513; Secondary smelting and refining, gold, etc., 1531; Watchcases, 1542; Silverware, etc., 1561; Engraving on metal, 1571; Collapsible tubes, 1594.
17 Scales and balances, 1776; Laundry equipment, 1781.
19 Part of Aircraft and parts, 1921 (see Table A-9); Motorcycles and bicycles, 1944.
20 Optical products, 2013; Ophthalmic goods, 2014; Dental equipment, 2023; Pianos, 2031; Organs, 2032; Artists' materials, 2054; Tobacco pipes, 2088; Wool pulling, 2094; Needles, pins, etc., 2095.

[b] As listed in *Census of Manufactures: 1939: Industry Classifications.*

[c] Proportion of national income originating in major industry group times ratio of value added for concentrated industries to total value added.

[d] For one industry, only part was highly concentrated. See Table A-9.

[e] For one industry defined according to the 1937 *Census of Manufactures.* See Table A-8.

TABLE A-5

Basic Data for Manufacturing Industries Classified by Wilcox as Monopolistic[a] but Not among Those with Concentration Ratios of 1/2 or Larger, by Major Industry Group: 1937 and 1939

	Industry Number[b]	Ratio of Value Added for Monopolistic Industries to Total Value Added		Proportion of National Income Originating in Monopolistic Industries[c]	
		1937	1939	1937	1939
Foods	1	0.2506	0.2558	0.0082	0.0080
Textile products	3	0.0245	0.0240	0.0005	0.0004
Lumber	5	0.2298	0.2645	0.0016	0.0018
Paper	7	0.0175	0.0196	0.0001	0.0002
Chemicals	9	0.1906	0.1883	0.0030	0.0031
Petroleum and coal products	10	0.7960	0.8018	0.0064	0.0051
Stone, clay, and glass products	13	0.4791	0.5013	0.0042	0.0046
Iron and steel products	14	0.0321	0.0392	0.0011	0.0012
Nonferrous products	15	0.0596	0.0553	0.0006	0.0005
Electrical machinery	16	0.7818	0.7790	0.0096	0.0091
Machinery	17	0.0043	0.0049	0.0001	0.0001
Total				0.0354	0.0341

Source: Wilcox, *Competition and Monopoly in American Industry*, pp. 65–298; *Census of Manufactures: 1939*, Vol. II; and *Survey of Current Business Supplement*, July 1947, p. 26.

[a] Each major industry group includes the following monopolistic industries:

1 Ice cream, 124; Special dairy products, 125; Bread and bakery products, 151; Biscuits and crackers, 152.

2 Tire fabrics, a part of cotton broad goods, 311 (see Table A-9); Cotton thread, 314.

5 Planning mills, 531.

7 Newsprint, a part of paper mills, 720 (see Table A-9).

9 Drugs and medicine, 931, excluding drug grinding (see Table A-8); Cosmetics, 932; Coal-tar products, 981.

10 Petroleum refining, 1011; Paving blocks, etc., 1051.

13 Flat glass, 1310; Glass containers, 1321; Technical, scientific, and industrial glass, a part of tableware, etc., 1329 (see Table A-9); Cement, 1340; Brick, etc., 1351; Vitreous fixtures, 1361; Concrete products, 1371; Building stone, a part of cutstone, etc., 1380 (see Table A-9).

14 Ingots, a part of steel works, 1412 (see Table A-9); Cast-iron pipe, 1424; Enameled plumbing ware, 1461.

15 Other nonferrous smelting and refining, 1519 (see Table A-8); Aluminum ware, 1592.

16 Wiring devices, 1611; Carbon products, 1612; Measuring instruments, 1613; Electrical motors, except fractional horsepower, a part of generating apparatus, etc., 1619 (see Table A-9); Insulating wire, 1630; Automative electrical equipment, 1640; Electric lamps, 1650; Communication equipment, 1662; Batteries, 1691; X-ray apparatus, etc., 1692; Electrical products, n.e.c., 1699.

17 Shoe machinery, a part of special industrial machinery, 1759.

[b] As listed in *Census of Manufactures: 1939: Industry Classifications*.

[c] Proportion of national income originating in major industry group times ratio of value added for monopolistic industries to total value added.

TABLE A-6

Basic Data for Manufactured Products, Each Valued at $10,000,000 or More, with Concentration Ratios of 3/4 or Larger Not Included among Industries in Tables A-3, A-4, and A-5,[a] by Major Industry Group: 1937 and 1939

	Industry Number[b]	Ratio of Value Added for Concentrated Products to Total Value Added		Proportion of National Income Originating in Concentrated Products[c]	
		1937	1939	1937	1939
Foods	1	0.0072	0.0084	0.0002	0.0003
Textile products	3	0.0194	0.0182	0.0004	0.0003
Furniture	6	0.0416	0.0442	0.0003	0.0003
Paper	7	0.0105	0.0115	0.0001	0.0001
Chemicals	9	0.0367	0.0300	0.0006	0.0005
Leather products	12	0.0239	0.0189	0.0001	0.0001
Stone, clay, and glass products	13	0.0194	0.0199	0.0002	0.0002
Iron and steel products	14	0.1374	0.1280	0.0048	0.0040
Nonferrous products	15	0.0446	0.0451	0.0004	0.0004
Electrical machinery	16	0.0189	0.0110	0.0002	0.0001
Machinery	17	0.0478	0.0463	0.0011	0.0010
Transportation equipment	19	0.0593	0.1033	0.0003	0.0006
Total				0.0087	0.0079

Source: Table A-2.

[a] Each industry group includes products with concentration ratios of 3/4 or larger in the following industries (for the products in each industry, see Table A-2):

1 Canned vegetables, etc., 133.
3 Cotton broad goods, 311; Woolens and worsteds, 341–342.
6 Mattresses, etc., 611; Upholstered furniture, 612.
7 Paper mills, 720.
9 Paints, etc., 911; Colors and pigments, 912; Plastic materials, 982; Chemicals, n.e.c., 999.
12 Footwear, 1240.
13 Tableware, etc., 1329.
14 Steel works, 1412; Stoves, etc., 1465; Steam fittings, 1466; Hardware, n.e.c., 1459.
15 Alloying, etc., 1520; Sheet-metal work, 1597.
16 Electrical appliances, 1620; Radios and tubes, etc., 1661.
17 Steam engines, etc., 1711; Office machinery, excluding standard typewriters (see Table A-3), 1771; Refrigeration, etc., 1784.
19 Aircraft and parts, 1921.

[b] As listed in *Census of Manufactures: 1939: Industry Classifications.*

[c] Proportion of national income originating in major industry group times ratio of value added for concentrated products to total value added.

TABLE A-7

Basic Data for Products and Industries Classified by Wilcox as Competitive but Included in Tables A-3 through A-6, by Major Industry Group: 1937 and 1939

	Industry Number[a]	Ratio of Value Added by Competitive Industries to Total Value Added		Proportion of National Income Originating in Competitive Industries[b]	
		1937	1939	1937	1939
Textile products		0.0050	0.0049	0.0001	0.0001
Woolens and worsteds[c]	341				
	342				
Furniture		0.0310	0.0349	0.0002	0.0002
Mattresses, etc.[c]	611				
Paper		0.0105	0.0115	0.0001	0.0001
Paper mills[c]	720				
Chemicals		0.0033	0.0025	0.0001	0.0000
Paints, etc.[c]	911				
Rubber products		0.5668	0.5697	0.0023	0.0022
Tires and inner tubes	1111				
Leather products		0.0239	0.0189	0.0001	0.0001
Footwear[c]	1240				
Electrical machinery		0.0069	0.0012	0.0001	0.0000
Radios and tubes, etc.[c]	1661				
Machinery		0.0371	0.0388	0.0009	0.0008
Laundry equipment	1781				
Refrigerators, etc.[c]	1784				
Total				0.0039	0.0035

Source: Wilcox, *Competition and Monopoly in American Industry*, pp. 19–62; and Tables A-3 through A-6.

[a] As listed in *Census of Manufactures: 1939: Industry Classifications*.

[b] Proportion of national income originating in major industry group times ratio of value added by competitive industries to total value added.

[c] Only certain products in the noted industry are covered. See Table A-2 for these products.

TABLE A-8

Computation of Value Added in 1939 by Certain Manufacturing Industries as Defined in the 1937 *Census of Manufactures*

	Industry Number[a] (1)	Value Added in 1937 (thousand dollars) for Industry as Defined in		Adjustment Factor[b] (4)	Value Added in 1939 (thousand dollars) for Industry as Defined in	
		1937 (2)	1939 (3)		1939 (5)	1937[c] (6)
Cereals	143	69,589	65,680	1.0595	70,349	74,535
Linoleum	374	20,358	36,276	0.5612	41,506	23,293
Drug grinding	931	3,173	250,270	0.0127	249,713	3,171
Copper and lead smelting and refining[d]	{1511 {1512	89,587	159,671	0.5611	137,002	76,872
Zinc smelting and refining[d]	1513	40,202	159,671	0.2518	137,002	34,497
Other nonferrous smelting and refining[d]	1519	29,882	159,671	0.1871	137,002	25,633
Typewriters	1771	31,614	147,278	0.2147	121,027	25,984
Billiard tables	2049	3,709	27,519	0.1348	38,064	5,131
Combs and hairpins, other than metal and rubber[e]	2099	{391 {408	{28,861 {26,103	{0.0135 {0.0156	{30,248 {28,527	{408 {445

Source: *Biennial Census of Manufactures: 1937* and *Census of Manufactures: 1939*, Vol. II.

[a] As listed in *Census of Manufactures: 1939: Industry Classifications.*

[b] Col. 2 divided by col. 3.

[c] Col. 4 times col. 5.

[d] Although a distinction is made between these different nonferrous smelting industries in the Industry Classification of the 1939 *Census of Manufactures*, value-added data are given only for the single all-inclusive industry "primary smelting and refining." Furthermore, in the 1937 Census, data were presented only for "copper and lead" and "zinc." To find the 1937 figure for the "other nonferrous" category, the summed value added by "copper and lead" and "zinc" was subtracted from the total value added by "primary smelting and refining."

[e] This industry ceased to exist as a separate category after the 1935 Census. Consequently, it was necessary to compute the value added in 1939 by the industry as defined in 1935. This was done in two steps, the top row of figures being used to compute the value added in 1937 by the industry as defined in 1935.

TABLE A-9

Computation of Value Added in 1937 and 1939 by the Parts of Certain

| | | Value of Products (thousand dollars) | | | |
| | Industry Number[a] | Part of Industry | | Entire Industry | |
		1937	1939	1937	1939
Tire fabrics	311	46,930	37,786	1,031,724	869,354
Newsprint	720	37,087	39,765	957,940	933,016
Cards, cut and designed	791	20,528	14,558	34,044	33,264
Cardboard, converted	791	7,270	9,644	34,044	33,264
Technical, scientific, and industrial glass (pressed and blown)	1329	10,383	9,953	97,640	97,317
Building stone	1380	28,157	34,911	79,006	75,812
Ingots	1412	21,132	13,982	3,146,263	2,720,020
Electrical motors, except fractional horsepower	1619	505,962	415,426	577,685	470,462
Shoe machinery	1759	10,903	10,603	58,716	55,785
Glass-making machinery	1759	4,729	4,459	58,716	55,785
Railway air brakes[b]	1769				
Aircraft and parts	1921	108,262	205,674	149,700	279,497

Source: *Census of Manufactures: 1939*, Vol. II.

[a] Numbers refer to entire industry. As listed in *Census of Manufactures: 1939: Industry Classifications*.

Manufacturing Industries Included in Table A-4

Ratio of Value of Products in Part of Industry to Value of Products in Entire Industry		Value Added (thousand dollars)			
		Entire Industry		Part of Industry	
1937	1939	1937	1939	1937	1939
0.0455	0.0435	463,933	438,331	21,109	19,067
0.0387	0.0426	390,491	400,755	15,112	17,072
0.6030	0.4376	18,524	17,194	11,170	7,524
0.2135	0.2899	18,524	17,194	3,955	4,985
0.1063	0.1023	70,521	70,284	7,496	7,190
0.3564	0.4605	57,657	50,525	18,411	23,262
0.0067	0.0051	1,376,314	1,147,548	9,221	5,852
0.8758	0.9883	367,244	283,136	321,632	279,823
0.1857	0.1901	37,751	35,949	7,010	6,834
0.0805	0.0799	37,751	35,949	3,039	2,872
0.7232	0.7359	93,144	183,247	67,362	134,851

[b] "Railway air brakes" was classified by Wilcox as monopolistic and should have been included in Table A-4. However, no separate data were available for it.

TABLE A-10

Proportion of National Income Originating in All Manufacturing Industries Classified as Effectively Monopolistic, by Major Industry Group and Source Table: 1937 and 1939

	Table A-3[a]		Table A-4[b]	
	1937	1939	1937	1939
Foods	0.0032	0.0031	0.0044	0.0041
Tobacco products	0.0016	0.0027	0.0004	0.0005
Textile products	0.0002	0.0002	0.0014	0.0012
Apparel			0.0001	0.0001
Lumber				
Furniture	0.0002	0.0002	0.0003	0.0003
Paper			0.0001	0.0001
Printing and publishing				
Chemicals	0.0038	0.0039	0.0003	0.0003
Petroleum and coal products	0.0000	0.0000		
Rubber products	0.0027	0.0024		
Leather products				
Stone, clay, and glass products	0.0007	0.0008	0.0011	0.0009
Iron and steel products	0.0015	0.0016	0.0017	0.0013
Nonferrous products	0.0019	0.0017	0.0011	0.0011
Electrical machinery				
Machinery	0.0035	0.0027	0.0004	0.0004
Automobiles	0.0175	0.0164		
Transportation equipment	0.0016	0.0010	0.0009	0.0018
Miscellaneous	0.0016	0.0017	0.0011	0.0010
Total	0.0400	0.0384	0.0133	0.0131

[a] Census industries with concentration ratios of 2/3 or larger in 1935.

[b] Census industries with concentration ratios of 1/2 to 2/3 in 1935.

[c] Industries, in addition to those with concentration ratios of 1/2 or larger in 1935, which Wilcox classified as monopolistic.

[d] Census products, each valued at $10,000,000 or more, with concentration ratios of 3/4 or larger in 1937 which were not included in Tables A-3 through A-5. All data from

Table A-5[e]		Table A-6[d]		Table A-7[e]		Total[f]	
1937	1939	1937	1939	1937	1939	1937	1939
0.0082	0.0080	0.0004	0.0006			0.0162	0.0158
						0.0020	0.0032
0.0005	0.0004	0.0008	0.0006	−0.0001	−0.0001	0.0028	0.0023
						0.0001	0.0001
0.0016	0.0018					0.0016	0.0018
		0.0006	0.0006	−0.0002	−0.0002	0.0009	0.0009
0.0001	0.0002	0.0002	0.0002	−0.0001	−0.0001	0.0003	0.0004
0.0030	0.0031	0.0012	0.0010	−0.0001	−0.0000	0.0082	0.0083
0.0064	0.0051					0.0064	0.0051
				−0.0023	−0.0022	0.0004	0.0002
		0.0002	0.0002	−0.0001	−0.0001	0.0001	0.0001
0.0042	0.0046	0.0004	0.0004			0.0064	0.0067
0.0011	0.0012	0.0096	0.0080			0.0139	0.0121
0.0006	0.0005	0.0008	0.0008			0.0044	0.0041
0.0096	0.0091	0.0004	0.0002	−0.0001	−0.0000	0.0099	0.0093
0.0001	0.0001	0.0022	0.0020	−0.0009	−0.0008	0.0053	0.0044
						0.0175	0.0164
		0.0006	0.0012			0.0031	0.0040
						0.0027	0.0027
0.0354	0.0341	0.0174	0.0158	−0.0039	−0.0035	0.1022	0.0979

Table A-2 have been doubled, since the data in that table are based on a sample of about half of all census products.

[e] Industries or products which Wilcox classified as competitive but which were included in Tables A-3 and A-4.

[f] Summed data from Tables A-3 through A-6 less data from Table A-7.

TABLE A-11

Computation of Value Added in Mining for Major Industry Groups and

	Total Value of Products[a] (1)
Metal mining	515,009
Bauxite	2,527
Copper ore	141,635
Iron ore	150,872
Molybdenum ore	15,411
Anthracite mining	189,648
Nonmetallic mining[c]	314,164
Native asphalt and bitumens	2,968
Natural sodium compounds[d]	3,067
Gypsum	4,569
Potash	13,964
Stone	117,034
Sulfur	31,812

Source: *Sixteenth Census of the United States: 1940*; *Mineral Industries: 1939*, Vol. I; Wilcox, *Competition and Monopoly in American Industry*, pp. 63–298.

[a] From producing operations.

[b] Col. 1 minus col. 5.

for Industries Classified by Wilcox as Monopolistic: 1939 (thousand dollars)

| Purchases | | | | |
Supplies (2)	Fuel (3)	Electrical Energy (4)	Total (5)	Value Added[b] (6)
67,898	10,212	18,527	96,637	418,372
269	187	60	516	2,011
23,562	4,168	4,899	32,629	109,006
10,621	2,267	4,083	16,971	133,901
1,713	39	358	2,110	13,301
25,412	3,887	6,389	35,688	153,960
37,890	14,845	12,028	64,763	249,401
317	68	28	413	2,555
429	251	198	878	2,189
624	37	146	807	3,762
1,607	1,174		2,781	11,183
16,961	4,756	5,534	27,251	89,783
1,690	1,128	15	2,833	28,979

[c] Total for stone, sand and gravel, clay and shale, and all other nonmetallic minerals. No data are separately available for magnesium, a commodity which Wilcox classified as monopolistic.

[d] This category includes more products than borates, an industry which was classified by Wilcox as monopolized.

TABLE A-12

Basic Data for Mining Industries Classified by Wilcox as Monopolistic: 1937

| | Value of Products (thousand dollars) | | | Proportion of National Income Originating |
	Monopolistic Industries (1)	All Industries (2)	Ratio of (1) to (2) (3)	in Monopolistic Industries[a] (4)
Metal mining	414,884	641,577	0.6466	0.0040
Bauxite	2,445			
Copper ore	184,996			
Iron ore	207,352			
Molybdenum ore	20,091			
Anthracite mining	197,599	197,599	1.0000	0.0019
Nonmetallic mining	247,095	390,876	0.6322	0.0012
Asphalt	3,019			
Borates	7,233			
Gypsum	4,783			
Magnesium chloride and sulfate	1,579			
Potash	9,613			
Stone	171,619			
Sulfur	49,249			
Total				0.0071

Source: Harold Barger and S. H. Schurr, *The Mining Industries, 1899–1939*, National Bureau of Economic Research, New York, 1944, pp. 305–9; *Survey of Current Business Supplement*, July 1947, Table 13, p. 26.

[a] Proportion of national income originating in mining industry times ratio in col. 3.

TABLE A-13

Basic Data for Mining Industries Classified by Wilcox as Monopolistic: 1939

	Value Added (thousand dollars)			Proportion of National Income Originating in Monopolistic Industries[a]
	Monopolistic Industries (1)	All Industries (2)	Ratio of (1) to (2) (3)	(4)
Metal mining	258,219	418,372	0.6172	0.0030
Bauxite	2,011			
Copper ore	109,006			
Iron ore	133,901			
Molybdenum ore	13,301			
Anthracite mining	153,960	153,960	1.0000	0.0017
Nonmetallic mining	138,451	249,401	0.5551	0.0010
Native asphalt and bitumens	2,555			
Natural sodium compounds	2,189			
Gypsum	3,762			
Potash	11,183			
Stone	89,783			
Sulfur	28,979			
Total				0.0057

Source: *Survey of Current Business Supplement*, July 1947, Table 13, p. 26; and Table A-11.

[a] Proportion of national income originating in mining industry times ratio in col. 3.

TABLE A-14

Basic Data for Production and Distribution of Fluid Milk: 1937 and 1939

	Fluid Milk Produced[a] (thousand quarts) (1)	Farm Price (dollars per thousand quarts) (2)
1937	10,872,830	66
1939	11,046,272	63

Source: Bureau of Agricultural Economics, *Price Spreads between Farmers and Consumers for Food Products: 1913–44*, Government Printing Office, Washington, 1945, pp. 100 and 109; *Survey of Current Business Supplement*, July 1947, Table 13, p. 26.

[a] See text for method of estimation.

TABLE A-15

Basic Data for Retailing of New Automobiles: 1937 and 1939

	Wholesale Sales (thousand dollars) (1)	Ratio of Retail Margin to Wholesale Sales[a] (2)	Value Added in Retailing[b] (thousand dollars) (3)	Proportion of National Income Originating in Retailing[c] (4)
1937	2,847,270	0.218	620,705	0.0084
1939	2,318,857	0.218	505,511	0.0070

Source: U.S. Bureau of the Census, *Statistical Abstract of the United States: 1946*, Government Printing Office, Washington, 1946, p. 488; Automobile Manufacturers' Association, *Automobile Facts and Figures: 1940*, Detroit, 1940, p. 32.

[a] See text for method of estimation.

[b] Col. 1 times col. 2.

[c] Col. 3 divided by total national income.

Retail Margin (dollars per thousand quarts) (3)	Value Added (thousand dollars)		Proportion of National Income Originating in	
	Production[b] (4)	Distribution[c] (5)	Production[d] (6)	Distribution[e] (7)
51	717,607	554,514	0.0098	0.0075
51	695,915	563,360	0.0096	0.0075

[b] Col. 1 times col. 2.
[c] Col. 1 times col. 3.
[d] Col. 4 divided by total national income.
[e] Col. 5 divided by total national income.

TABLE A-16

Proportion of National Income Originating in Industries Other Than Manufacturing, Mining, Agriculture, and Trade Classified by Wilcox as Monopolistic: 1937 and 1939

	1937	1939
Contract construction	0.0274	0.0311
Banking	0.0121	0.0121
Insurance carriers	0.0113	0.0118
Pipeline transportation	0.0018	0.0018
Telephone and telegraph	0.0125	0.0139
Motion pictures	0.0058	0.0059

Source: *Survey of Current Business Supplement,* July 1947, Table 13, p. 26; Wilcox, *Competition and Monopoly in American Industry*, pp. 63–298.

Basic Data on Growth of Monopoly: 1899–1939

This appendix presents the basic data[1] and explains the procedures used to estimate the growth of monopoly between 1899 and 1939. It is divided into two main sections. The first covers the data concerning concentration of output among manufacturing establishments. The second deals with the estimation of enterprise monopoly in 1899 and comparison of conditions in 1899 and 1937.

CONCENTRATION OF OUTPUT AMONG MANUFACTURING ESTABLISHMENTS

Most of the censuses of manufactures since 1904 have given data on establishments (plants) classified by value-of-products size classes. The data for different years do not provide comparable coverage of industries or of establishments by size.

The difference in the coverage of industries has resulted from changes in the scope of the census. The following industries were included in some but not all censuses before 1939: (1) coffee and spices, roasting and grinding; (2) flax and hemp, dressed; (3) gas, illuminating and heating; (4) grindstones; (5) motion pictures, not including projection in theaters; (6) peanuts, walnuts, and other nuts, processed or shelled; and (7) railroad repair shops.[2] In summaries which are contained in the 1939 Census, aggregate data for earlier years have been adjusted to exclude these industries; but data for each size class of manufacturing establishments have not been so adjusted. We have removed all establishments and the corresponding value of products in the seven industries mentioned from the frequency distributions of establishments. Our adjusted totals of establishments and value of products (Table B-1) do not correspond exactly with the adjusted census totals.[3] The discrepancy can be largely explained by the nature of published

TABLE B-1

Adjustments in Data for Manufacturing Establishments Classified by Value of Products to Provide Comparability in Coverage of Industries: Census Years, 1904–1939

Value of Products Class (thousand dollars)	Establishments			Value of Products (thousand dollars)		
	Unadjusted Number[a]	Adjustment[b]	Adjusted Number	Unadjusted Value[a]	Adjustment[b]	Adjusted Value
1904						
0.5 to 5	71,147	316	70,831	176,128	881	175,247
5 to 20	72,791	645	72,146	751,048	7,335	743,713
20 to 100	48,096	861	47,235	2,129,258	41,883	2,087,375
100 to 1,000	22,246	783	21,463	6,109,013	247,792	5,861,221
1,000 and over	1,900	109	1,791	5,628,456	240,497	5,387,959
Total	216,180	2,714	213,466	14,793,903	538,388	14,255,515
1909						
0.5 to 5	93,349	585	92,764	222,464	1,442	221,002
5 to 20	86,988	871	86,117	904,646	10,150	894,496
20 to 100	57,270	1,029	56,241	2,544,427	48,513	2,495,914
100 to 1,000	27,824	1,031	26,793	7,946,935	336,117	7,610,818
1,000 and over	3,060	151	2,909	9,053,580	333,098	8,720,482
Total	268,491	3,667	264,824	20,672,052	729,320	19,942,732
1914						
0.5 to 5	95,408	547	94,861	228,654	1,339	227,315
5 to 20	86,587	893	85,694	893,459	10,259	883,200
20 to 100	56,557	1,205	55,352	2,540,949	58,249	2,482,700
100 to 1,000	30,147	1,218	28,929	8,759,391	398,259	8,361,132
1,000 and over	3,819	205	3,614	11,794,061	470,775	11,323,286
Total	272,518	4,068	268,450	24,216,514	938,881	23,277,633
1919						
0.5 to 5	60,215	240	59,975	151,631	653	150,978
5 to 20	79,699	679	79,020	866,086	8,213	857,873
20 to 100	75,627	1,316	74,311	3,487,756	66,948	3,420,808
100 to 500	39,447	1,181	38,266	8,929,364	290,331	8,639,033
500 to 1,000	9,197	371	8,826	6,457,485	267,335	6,190,150
1,000 and over	10,413	509	9,904	42,301,104	1,392,129	40,908,975
Total	274,598	4,296	270,302	62,193,426	2,025,609	60,167,817
1921						
0.5 to 5	53,999	122	53,877	136,926	320	136,606
5 to 20	71,075	287	70,788	782,977	3,550	779,427
20 to 100	72,251	780	71,471	3,330,350	39,795	2,290,555
100 to 500	38,027	564	37,463	8,405,759	127,266	8,278,493
500 to 1,000	7,581	154	7,427	5,296,721	107,780	5,188,941
1,000 and over	7,333	215	7,118	25,837,476	798,223	25,039,253
Total	250,266	2,122	248,144	43,790,209	1,076,934	42,713,275
1923						
5 to 20	61,981	583	61,398	697,997	7,005	690,992
20 to 100	72,370	1,350	71,020	3,426,434	70,308	3,356,126
100 to 500	42,075	1,269	40,806	9,496,593	306,598	9,189,995
500 to 1,000	9,556	415	9,141	6,752,818	294,855	6,457,963
1,000 and over	10,327	596	9,731	40,182,157	1,695,936	38,486,211
Total	196,309	4,213	192,096	60,555,998	2,374,702	58,181,297

(*continued*)

TABLE B-1 *(concluded)*

Value of Products Class (thousand dollars)	Establishments			Value of Products (thousand dollars)		
	Unadjusted Number[a]	Adjustment[b]	Adjusted Number	Unadjusted Value[a]	Adjustment[b]	Adjusted Value
			1925			
5 to 20	55,876	491	55,385	628,373	5,947	622,426
20 to 100	68,951	1,123	67,828	3,272,197	59,249	3,212,958
100 to 500	42,209	1,085	41,124	9,576,090	260,971	9,315,119
500 to 1,000	9,771	365	9,406	6,870,112	268,935	6,601,177
1,000 and over	10,583	449	10,134	42,366,941	1,309,381	41,057,560
Total	187,390	3,513	183,877	62,713,713	1,904,483	60,809,230
			1929			
5 to 20	68,878		68,878	765,273		765,273
20 to 50	45,924		45,924	1,473,339		1,473,339
50 to 100	27,945		27,945	2,042,580		2,042,580
100 to 250	27,892		27,892	4,436,724		4,436,724
250 to 500	14,831		14,831	5,236,144		5,236,144
500 to 1,000	9,986		9,986	7,025,455		7,025,455
1,000 to 2,500	7,057		7,057	10,791,462		10,791,462
2,500 to 5,000	2,369		2,369	8,231,219		8,231,219
5,000 and over	1,781		1,781	27,991,845		27,991,845
Total	206,663		206,663	67,994,041		67,994,041
			1937			
5 to 20	50,548		50,548	576,966		576,966
20 to 50	37,611		37,611	1,214,034		1,214,034
50 to 100	23,611		23,611	1,683,661		1,683,661
100 to 250	23,422		23,422	3,729,973		3,729,973
250 to 500	12,763		12,763	4,511,524		4,511,524
500 to 1,000	8,908		8,908	6,279,012		6,279,012
1,000 to 2,500	6,098		6,098	9,396,818		9,396,818
2,500 to 5,000	2,132		2,132	7,337,152		7,337,152
5,000 and over	1,651		1,651	25,983,732		25,983,732
Total	166,794		166,794	60,712,872		60,712,872
			1939			
5 to 20	60,593		60,593	680,777		680,777
20 to 50	42,083		42,083	1,353,676		1,353,676
50 to 100	25,490		25,490	1,811,463		1,811,463
100 to 250	24,718		24,718	3,920,974		3,920,974
250 to 500	13,066		13,066	4,626,937		4,626,937
500 to 1,000	8,706		8,706	6,110,939		6,110,939
1,000 to 2,500	6,088		6,088	9,298,230		9,298,230
2,500 to 5,000	2,013		2,013	6,918,927		6,918,927
5,000 and over	1,473		1,473	22,121,102		22,121,102
Total	184,230		184,230	56,843,025		56,843,025

[a] 1904 and 1909: U.S. Bureau of the Census, *Statistical Abstract of the United States: 1923*, Government Printing Office, Washington, 1923, p. 291; 1914–1925: *Statistical Abstract of the United States: 1932*, p. 731; 1937: *Statistical Abstract of the United States: 1940*, p. 803; 1929 and 1939: U.S. Bureau of the Census, *Census of Manufactures: 1939*, Vol. I, p. 182.
[b] *Census of Manufactures* for the appropriate year.

census data. No information is published for a group of fewer than four establishments, so that the operations of individual firms may not be revealed. Consequently, whenever three or fewer establishments were encountered in a size class in one of the eliminated industries, we were forced to estimate the corresponding value of products, which had been included in the data for an adjoining class. In such instances the estimated value for each establishment was taken as the midpoint of the class interval unless such a value was clearly contradicted by other evidence in the distribution. In the latter case the same type of estimate was made for the adjoining class, and the residual was assigned to the class in question. Adjustments to provide comparable coverage of industries are given in Table B-1.

The problem of providing comparable coverage of establishments by size is discussed on p. 41. We shall confine our remarks at this point to an explanation of the procedures used for making the adjustments there noted.

The two types of adjustment which were desired required intraclass interpolations. Three methods of linear interpolation were tried, with the restrictions that the aggregate number of establishments and the aggregate value of products within a given range of value of products should be the same in the postulated as in the known distribution. Since the interclass distributions are shaped like a backward J, the linear approximations should, in addition, be negatively inclined if they were to be consistent with the interclass information. Unfortunately, none of the methods tried yielded results which were uniformly consistent with both the interclass and the intraclass information.

It was first assumed that the density distribution of establishments is a linear function of output ("output" is used throughout the ensuing discussion as a synonym for value of products). Under this assumption, negative frequencies occurred in the upper ranges of the classes to which the method was applied. A second attempt was based on the supposition that establishments are uniformly distributed within any two parts of a given class interval. But applying this method to the $5,000–$20,000 class in 1921 and 1923 with the objective of eliminating a fixed number of establishments led to the absurd result that the derived point of division for the class interval fell below the actual lower limit. Both these results suggest that the mean output in a class is too far below the midpoint of the class interval to make the assumed distributions lead to plausible results.

Finally, we assumed that the density of establishments is a linear function of the logarithms of output. Under such an assumption the midpoint of the class interval is lowered, since it now becomes the geometric mean of the class limits. On the other hand, the sign of the slope of the derived curve will be determined by the relation between the geometric mean of total output in the class and the (redefined) midpoint of the class interval. Application

TABLE B-2

Adjusted[a] Lorenz Distributions of Manufacturing Establishments Classified
by Value of Products: Census Years, 1904–1939 (cumulative per cent)

Value of Products Class (thousand dollars)	Establishments	Value of Products	Establishments	Value of Products	Establishments	Value of Products
	1904		1909		1914	
0.5 to 5	33.2	1.2	35.1	1.1	35.3	1.0
5 to 20	67.0	6.4	67.6	5.6	67.2	4.8
20 to 50	89.1	21.0	88.8	18.1	87.8	15.5
100 to 1,000	99.2	62.1	98.9	56.3	98.6	51.4
1,000 and over	100.0	100.0	100.0	100.0	100.0	100.0
	1919		1921		1923	
0.5 to 5	22.2	0.3	21.7	0.3		
5 to 20	51.4	1.7	50.2	2.1	32.0	1.2
20 to 100	78.9	7.4	79.0	9.8	39.0	7.0
100 to 500	93.1	21.8	94.1	29.2	90.2	22.8
500 to 1,000	96.4	32.1	97.1	41.3	94.9	33.9
1,000 and over	100.0	100.0	100.0	100.0	100.0	100.0
	1925					
5 to 20	30.1	1.0				
20 to 100	67.0	6.3				
100 to 500	89.4	21.6				
500 to 1,000	94.5	32.5				
1,000 and over	100.0	100.0				
	1929		1937		1939	
5 to 20	33.3	1.1	30.3	1.0	32.9	1.2
20 to 50	55.5	3.3	52.8	3.0	55.7	3.6
50 to 100	69.0	6.3	67.0	5.8	69.5	6.8
100 to 250	82.5	12.8	81.0	11.9	82.9	13.7
250 to 500	89.7	20.5	88.7	19.3	90.0	21.8
500 to 1,000	94.5	30.8	94.0	29.6	94.7	32.6
1,000 to 2,500	97.9	46.7	97.7	45.1	98.0	49.0
2,500 to 5,000	99.0	58.8	99.0	57.2	99.1	61.2
5,000 and over	100.0	100.0	100.0	100.0	100.0	100.0

Source: Table B-1.

[a] For comparability in coverage of industries.

of the third method yielded positively sloping curves, indicating that the geometric mean of total output is larger than the redefined midpoint. Positively sloping curves are, of course, inconsistent with the known interclass distribution. Therefore, the third method of linear interpolation is also inadequate.

Since no method of linear intraclass interpolation offered promise of plausible results, it was decided to abandon the attempt to eliminate any establishments which had an output below a certain level. There was at least one procedure by means of which a specified number of establishments and the corresponding total output could be removed, however, namely, through interpolation on smoothed Lorenz curves. That procedure was followed to find the aggregate output attributable to the 184,230 largest establishments in any year. In order to check the accuracy of the interpolated results, the minimum and maximum possible total outputs which could be assigned to the plants that were removed from the distributions were also calculated. The minimum is the product of the lower limit of a class interval times the number of establishments in that class which were removed; the maximum is the product of the average output in the class times the number removed. Let us elaborate by means of a concrete example.

Consider the situation in 1904. There were 213,466 establishments with outputs of $500 or more (see Table B-1). That number is to be reduced to 184,230 by removing the smallest 29,236. The 29,236 plants are 13.7 per cent of the total. From a smoothed Lorenz curve based on the distribution in Table B-2, we found that 0.3 per cent of an aggregate output of $14,255,515,000 was produced by the smallest 13.7 per cent of establishments. Therefore, the interpolated output of the smallest 29,236 plants was $42,767,000. That output lies between the minimum and the maximum possible outputs for these 29,236 plants, since the minimum is $14,618,000 (29,236 times $500) and the maximum is $72,330,000 (29,236 times $2,474). All adjustments of the outlined nature were made before the Lorenz distributions in Table B-4 were computed. The adjustments are presented in Table B-3.

TABLE B-3

Adjustments[a] in Data for Manufacturing Establishments Classified by Value of Products to Provide Coverage of Largest 184,230 Establishments: Census Years, 1904–1929

| | | Amounts Subtracted from Smallest Size Classes | | |
| | | Value of Products (thousand dollars) | | |
	Establishments	Minimum	Maximum	Interpolated
1904	29,236	14,618	72,330	42,767
1909	80,594	40,294	192,056	159,542
1914	84,220	42,112	201,803	186,221
1919	86,072	281,463	434,287	361,007
1921	63,914	186,791	247,123	203,566
1923	7,866	39,330	88,524	58,181
1929	22,433	112,165	249,253	135,988

[a] See text for explanation of adjustments.

TABLE B-4

Adjusted[a] Lorenz Distributions of 184,230 Largest Manufacturing Establishments Classified by Value of Products: Census Years, 1904–1939 (cumulative per cent)

Value of Products Class (thousand dollars)	Establishments	Value of Products		
		I[b]	II[c]	III[d]
		1904		
0.5 to 5	22.6	1.1	0.7	0.9
5 to 20	61.7	6.4	6.0	6.2
20 to 100	87.4	21.0	20.7	20.9
100 to 1,000	99.0	62.2	62.0	62.1
1,000 and over	100.0	100.0	100.0	100.0
		1909		
0.5 to 5	6.6	0.9	0.1	0.3
5 to 20	53.4	5.4	4.7	4.8
20 to 100	83.9	17.9	17.3	17.4
100 to 1,000	98.4	56.2	55.8	55.9
1,000 and over	100.0	100.0	100.0	100.0
		1914		
0.5 to 5	5.8	0.8	0.1	0.2
5 to 20	52.3	4.6	3.9	4.0
20 to 100	82.3	15.3	14.7	14.8
100 to 1,000	98.0	51.3	50.9	51.0
1,000 and over	100.0	100.0	100.0	100.0
		1919		
5 to 20	28.7	1.2	1.0	1.1
20 to 100	69.1	6.9	6.7	6.8
100 to 500	89.8	21.4	21.2	21.2
500 to 1,000	94.6	31.7	31.5	31.6
1,000 and over	100.0	100.0	100.0	100.0
		1921		
5 to 20	33.0	1.7	1.6	1.7
20 to 100	71.8	9.5	9.3	9.4
100 to 500	92.1	28.9	28.8	28.9
500 to 1,000	96.1	41.1	41.0	41.1
1,000 and over	100.0	100.0	100.0	100.0
		1923		
5 to 20	29.1	1.1	1.0	1.1
20 to 50	67.6	6.9	6.8	6.9
50 to 100	89.8	22.7	22.6	22.7
100 to 1,000	94.7	33.8	33.8	33.8
1,000 and over	100.0	100.0	100.0	100.0

(*continued*)

TABLE B-4 (*concluded*)

Value of Products Class (thousand dollars)	Establishments	Value of Products		
		I[b]	II[c]	III[d]
		1925[e]		
5 to 20	30.1			1.0
20 to 50	67.0			6.3
50 to 100	89.4			21.6
100 to 1,000	94.5			32.5
1,000 and over	100.0			100.0
		1929		
5 to 20	25.2	1.0	0.8	0.9
20 to 50	50.1	3.1	2.9	3.1
50 to 100	65.3	6.1	6.0	6.1
100 to 250	80.4	12.7	12.5	12.6
250 to 500	88.5	20.4	20.2	20.4
500 to 1,000	93.9	30.7	30.6	30.7
1,000 to 2,500	97.7	46.6	46.5	46.6
2,500 to 5,000	99.0	58.8	58.7	58.7
5,000 and over	100.0	100.0	100.0	100.0
		1937[f]		
5 to 20	30.3			1.0
20 to 50	52.8			3.0
50 to 100	67.0			5.8
100 to 250	81.0			11.9
250 to 500	88.7			19.3
500 to 1,000	94.0			29.6
1,000 to 2,500	97.7			45.1
2,500 to 5,000	99.0			57.2
5,000 and over	100.0			100.0
		1939		
5 to 20	32.9			1.2
20 to 50	55.7			3.6
50 to 100	69.5			6.8
100 to 250	82.9			13.7
250 to 500	90.0			21.8
500 to 1,000	94.7			32.6
1,000 to 2,500	98.0			49.0
2,500 to 5,000	99.1			61.2
5,000 and over	100.0			100.0

Source: Tables B-1 and B-3.

[a] For comparability in coverage of industries.

[b] Based on the minimum value of products subtracted from the smallest size classes (see Table B-3).

[c] Based on the maximum value of products subtracted from the smallest size classes (see Table B-3).

[d] Based on the interpolated value of products subtracted from the smallest size classes (see Table B-3).

[e] Includes only 183,877 establishments.

[f] Includes only 166,794 establishments.

THE EXTENT OF MONOPOLY, 1899 AND 1937

NATIONAL INCOME DATA

The procedure followed in estimating the extent of enterprise monopoly in 1899 is essentially the same as that used for 1937 and 1939. Dr. Robert Martin's statistics on income by industrial origin formed the basis of the estimate.[4] Table B-5 presents his statistics for 1899 and 1937. The particular

TABLE B-5

Proportional Distribution of National Income by Major Industry Division: 1899 and 1937

	Amount (thousand dollars)		Proportion	
	1899	1937	1899	1937
Agriculture	2,933	6,757	0.1892	0.0973
Mining	416	1,743	0.0268	0.0251
Construction	655	1,806	0.0422	0.0260
Manufacturing	2,714	16,629	0.1751	0.2395
Trade	2,578	8,414	0.1663	0.1212
Finance[a]	859	4,568	0.0554	0.0658
Transportation and communication	1,528	5,934	0.0986	0.0855
Electric light and power and gas	58	1,264	0.0037	0.0182
Services	1,745	7,130	0.1126	0.1027
Miscellaneous income[b]	1,013	3,608	0.0653	0.0520
Government and government enterprises	1,005	11,566	0.0648	0.1666
Total	15,504	69,419	1.0000	0.9999

Source: Robert F. Martin, *National Income in the United States, 1799–1938*, National Industrial Conference Board, New York, 1939, Tables 1, 16, 40, 43, and 45.

[a] This category includes Martin's "miscellaneous income of private origin" (see *ibid.*, p. 95, for the sources of these items of income).

[b] Corresponds to Martin's "miscellaneous private production income" (see *ibid.*, p. 57, for the sources of these items of income).

methods for apportioning income by origin within the broad industrial groups will be pointed out in the pertinent parts of the ensuing discussion.

We should note at this point that the Martin series is not strictly comparable with the new Department of Commerce series, on the basis of which the estimates of the extent of monopoly in 1937 and 1939 were computed. The two series overlap for the years 1929–1938. The change in our estimate of the extent of monopoly in 1937, which followed from basing it on the Martin series, was presented in Table 8. After discussing our estimation procedure for 1899, we shall return to this point and show the methods used for revising the estimate for 1937.

MONOPOLISTIC INDUSTRIES IN 1899

A list of highly concentrated industries in the period 1895–1904 for which some definite data exist is given in Table B-6. We assume that these industries were monopolistic in 1899. In addition to the list, we have classified banking as monopolistic in 1899 on the grounds of local monopoly, assuming that banking was at least as monopolistic in that year as in the 1930's. It was not always possible to find completely satisfactory production figures for each of the industries listed. Those who are interested in doing so may compare the listed industries with those for which estimates were made (see Tables B-2 through B-4).

MANUFACTURING

Sources of Data and Industrial Classification.   The major source of data on manufacturing industries in 1899 is the *Census of Manufactures: 1900.* That census actually presents data preponderantly for the calendar year 1899 but also for fiscal years including parts of 1899 and 1900.[5] A convenient summary of value added by industries is to be found in Solomon Fabricant's book on manufacturing output.[6] This summary was utilized as the source of value-added data.

Since Fabricant uses the industrial classification of the 1929 Census, we have done the same. The 1929 classification differs somewhat from that for 1939 and therefore introduces some ambiguity into comparisons of our estimates for industry groups in 1899 with those for groups in 1937. However, in general, no real problems are raised, since the main respect in which the 1929 classification differs from the 1939 classification is that the former is less detailed. The 1929 group "Textile products," for instance, comprises two 1939 groups: "Textile products" and "Apparel."

Apportionment of Income by Origin.   Martin's series does not assign income by origin to industrial classifications below the level of major industry divisions. The income originating in manufacturing cannot be apportioned among major industry groups (foods, beverages, etc.) on the basis of relative value added without considerable error, since overhead items, which are included in value added, differ substantially among industry groups. Fabricant gives estimates for certain census years of the ratio of income by origin to value added for some combined major industry groups.[7] The ratios differ rather widely among the combinations, varying in 1919, for instance, from 0.58 to 0.77. The ratio for any combined group varies, moreover, with the business cycle. The years nearest to 1899 which were in approximately the

TABLE B-6

List of Monopolistic Industries, by Industrial Divisions, in the Period 1895–1904, with Percentage of Output in the United States Controlled by Largest Firms, with Sources of Information

	U.S. Output Controlled by Largest Firms		Source of Information	
	Per Cent	No. of Firms	Source[a]	Pages
Mining				
Metal mining				
Copper	55–60	1	D	229
	33	1	A	17
	64	4	A	39–41
Iron ore	80	1	C	c
	85	1	A	202
	60	1	E	129
Anthracite mining	90[b]	6	G	53
	86[b]	4	G	53
Nonmetallic mining				
Asphalt	35–95[c]	1	A	295,306
	Low–95[c]	1	F	435–45
	85–95	1	C	cxxiii
Borates	100	1	C	cxvi
Gypsum	80	1	A	281
Manganese ore	56[d]	1	H	61–62
	74[d]	3	H	61–62
	76[d]	4	H	61–62
Mercury	16[d]	1	H	61–62
	52[d]	4	H	61–62
Marble	45[d]	2	H	61–62
	66	4	H	61–62
Tripoli, pumice, etc.	55[d]	3	H	65
Bauxite, fuller's earth	46[d]	4	H	65
Tungsten	100[d]	4	H	65
Uranium and vanadium	100[d]	3	H	65
Chromite	100[d]	1	H	65
Magnesite	100[d]	1	H	65
Molybdenum	100[d]	1	H	65
Titanium ore (rutile)	100[d]	1	H	65
Construction				
Building construction	Unknown	1	A	327–35
Manufacturing				
Foods				
Meat packing	"Bulk"	4	A	257–59
	50	4	E	151
Biscuits and crackers	70	1	A	260
Fruits and vegetables				
Canned fruits	40[e]	1	A	241
			K	474, 478

(continued)

TABLE B-6 (*continued*)

	U.S. Output Controlled by Largest Firms		Source of Information	
	Per Cent	No. of Firms	Source[a]	Pages
Canned milk	"Large"	1	A	239
Sugar refining	90	1	B	17–18
	57–90	1	A	64, 67
	67	1	E	148
Chewing gum	65	1	C	xviii
	85	1	A	220
Confectionery				
Caramels	100	1	C	xviii
	90	1	A	217
Candy	55[f]	1	A	261
Corn products				
Starch	85	1	C	cxii
	40–81[e]	1	E	102
Box starch	90	1	C	xviii
Glucose	45–81[e]	1	E	102
Baking powder	25	1	C	lxxiii, 382
	50	4	C	lxxiii, 382
	58–65	4	A	268
Ice	80[g]	1	A	228
Beverages				
Liquors, malt	100[h]	1	C	xviii
Malt	50[i]	1	A	294
Liquors, distilled	80–95	1	B	18
	60	1	A	246
Tobacco products				
Cigarettes	75	1	C	lxxiii
	90	1	A	96
Tobaccos	90	1	A	96
Plug tobacco	60	1	C	lxxiii
Snuff	80	1	E	140–41
Textile products				
Cotton goods				
Cotton duck	45–90	1	A	318, 321
Cotton thread	67	1	C	xviii
	50	1	A	235
Cotton yarn	20–40	1	A	317
Woolen and worsted goods	60	1	A	236
Cordage and twine	48–58	3	C	xvii
Felt goods, wool	60	1	A	221
Oilcloth	50	1	A	273
Leather products				
Leather	60–75	1	A	281
Sole leather	50	1	C	cxxi
Upper leather	75	1	A	226
Rubber products	55–65	2	C	xvii
Rubber shoes	70	1	A	xvii
	50	1	A	282
Rubber goods, other	40–60[j]	1	A	569
	25–100[j]	1	C	xli

(*continued*)

TABLE **B-6** (*continued*)

	U.S. Output Controlled by Largest Firms		Source of Information	
	Per Cent	No. of Firms	Source[a]	Pages
Paper products				
Paper and pulp	70–80	1	C	xviii, lxxxix
Newsprint	65–80	1	C	xvii–xviii
	60	1	A	253
Writing paper	55	1	A	237
Box- and straw-board	90	1	A	275
Bags, paper	80–95	1	A	273–74
Envelopes	50–60	1	A	279
Wallpaper	60	1	C	xviii
Printing and publishing				
Printing materials; type founding	77	1	A	235
Chemical products				
Chemicals, n.e.c.				
Heavy chemicals	70	1	A	248
Casein and milk sugar	70	1	A	242
Borax	100	1	C	cxvi
Cottonseed products	65	1	A	220
Linseed products	85–95	1	A	55, 59
Explosives	"Substantial"	k	G	306
Fertilizers				
Phosphates	60	1	A	326
Glue and gelatin	55	1	A	223
Paints and varnishes				
White lead; lead oxides	85–95	1	A	59
Salt	30–60	1	A	313
	67	1	F	211
	80–90[l]	1	C	xviii
Petroleum and coal products				
Petroleum refining	84	1	A	132
	80–95	1	B	18
	86	1	E	106
Stone, clay, and glass products				
Wall plaster and wallboard				
Gypsum	80	1	A	281
Pottery				
Terra cotta and dense tile fireproofing	65	1	A	263
Fire-brick	70	1	A	251
Vitrified sewer pipe	40[f]	1	A	232
Glass				
Table glassware	50–70	1	A	264
Plate glass	72–80	1	C	lviii
	100	4	C	lviii
Window glass	73	1	C	cxv
Forest products				
Furniture				
Public seating furniture	80	1	A	231
Matches	85	1	A	245

(*continued*)

TABLE **B-6** (*continued*)

	U.S. Output Controlled by Largest Firms		Source of Information	
	Per Cent	No. of Firms	Source[a]	Pages
Iron and steel products				
Blast-furnace products				
Pig iron	43	1	E	119
Steel-mill products	61	1	E	120
	65–75	1	C	xvii, xcix
Steel ingots and castings	66	1	E	119
Rails	60	1	E	119
Structural shapes	62	1	E	119
Plates and sheets	65	1	E	119
Black-plate	80	1	E	119
	96	1	B	18
Coated tin-mill products	73	1	E	119
Seamless tubes	83	1	E	119
Nails and spikes	68	1	E	119
	65–90	1	B	18
Steel springs				
Railway car and locomotive springs	95	1	A	268
Wire				
Smooth wire and rods	75–80	1	B	18
	78	1	E	119
Wirework				
Barbed-wire fencing	100	1	B	18
Woven wire fencing	100	1	B	18
Wrought pipe and tubes	57	1	E	119
Cast-iron pipe				
Soil pipe and fittings	80–95	1	A	242
Stoves and ranges				
Gas and oil ranges	"Moderate"	1	A	234
Tin cans and tinware	65–75	1	A	216
Heating apparatus				
Steam radiators	80	1	A	230
Plumbers' supplies				
Enameled ironware	80	1	A	272
Tools, other				
Steel shears	60	1	B	206
Nonferrous metal products				
Smelting and refining				
Copper	30[m]	1	A	16
	64	4	A	16, 39–41
Lead	85–100	1	C	97
	85–95	1	A	59
Secondary metals, nonprecious	100	2	C	97
Gold and silver	100	1	C	97
	85–95	1	A	59
Silverware	10	1	B	209
	40[n]	1	A	256
Plated ware	55–60	1	B	209
Stamped and enameled ware	55	1	A	263

(*continued*)

TABLE B-6 (*continued*)

	U.S. Output Controlled by Largest Firms		Source of Information	
	Per Cent	No. of Firms	Source[a]	Pages
Machinery				
Foundry and machine-shop products				
Pneumatic tube systems	87	1	A	229
Pneumatic tools; air compressors	80	1	A	243
Car wheels	20	1	A	262
Brake shoes	90	1	A	213
Airbrakes	o	1	A	284–85
Elevators	85	1	C	cxxvii
	65	1	A	226
Bobbins and shuttles	90	1	A	282
	85	1	C	cxiv
Shoe machinery	50	1	A	277
Lasting machines	100	1	G	280
Bottoming room machines	70	1	G	281
Welting and outside stitching machines	80	1	G	281
Heeling machines	70	1	G	281
Heavy steam-power machinery	80	1	A	257
Heavy machinery	50	1	A	210
Agricultural implements	70	1	A	252
	85	1	G	282–83
Seeding machines	90	1	A	231
Hand implements	80	1	A	222
Business machines				
Cash registers	95	1	G	287
Typewriters	75	1	A	274
Electrical machinery	90	2	A	249
Carbon products	87	1	A	261
Phonographs	80	1	A	223
Scales and balances	50	1	A	244
Sewing machines	45	1	G	298
	65	2	G	298
Transportation equipment				
Bicycles	65–70	1	F	252, 259
	65	1	C	cxxvi
Railroad cars	65	1	A	218
Sleeping cars	85	1	A	267
Locomotives	70	1	A	228
	100	2	G	285
Ships and boats	60[p]	1	A	233
	40–60	1	A	368
	35	1	G	480
Miscellaneous products				
Organs, pianos, etc.				
Aeolians, pianolas, organs	Unknown[q]	1	A	209

(*continued*)

TABLE B-6 (*concluded*)

	U.S. Output Controlled by Largest Firms		Source of Information	
	Per Cent	No. of Firms	Source[a]	Pages
Buttons				
Covered	85	1	A	275
Ivory	45	1	A	275
Photographic supplies				
Flexible photographic paper and Kodak supplies	100	1	C	193
Toys and games	70	1	A	205
Trade				
Wholesaling				
Illuminating oil	89	1	E	106
Transportation				
Steam railroads			A	431–50
Express	100	4	A	246–47
Pipelines, oil	84–96	1	E	106
Water transportation				
Atlantic steamship lines	40	1	A	107
Street railways	r	r	A	386–414
Communication				
Telephone	Very high	1	A	373–80
Telegraph	Very high	1	A	381–85
Electric light, power, and gas				
Electric light and power systems	90	2	A	249

[a] Sources cited are the following:

A: John Moody, *The Truth about the Trusts*, Moody Publishing Co., New York, 1904.

B: U.S. Industrial Commission, *Report of the Industrial Commission*, Vol. I, Government Printing Office, Washington, 1900.

C: *Ibid.*, Vol. XIII, 1901.

D: *Ibid.*, Vol. XIX, 1902.

E: Charles R. Van Hise, *Concentration and Control: A Solution of the Trust Problem in the United States*, The Macmillan Co., New York, 1914.

F: Arthur S. Dewing, *Corporate Promotions and Reorganizations*, Harvard University Press, Cambridge, 1914.

G: Harry W. Laidler, *Concentration of Control in American Industry*, Thomas Y. Crowell Co., New York, 1931.

H: U.S. Bureau of the Census, *Mines and Quarries, 1902*, Government Printing Office, Washington, 1905.

I: U.S. Census Office, *Twelfth Census of the United States, Taken in the Year 1900: Manufactures*, Part I, Washington, 1902.

K: *Ibid.*, Part IV.

[b] In 1912.   [c] Fluctuated over period.   [d] Estimated from frequency distributions of firms by output.   [e] Represents 65 per cent of all canning in California.   [f] Local areas.   [g] New York and New England markets.   [h] Local areas in Ohio and Pennsylvania.   [i] Percentage of total establishments controlled.   [j] Percentages differ with products.   [k] Trade Association.   [l] In market east of the Rockies.   [m] Fifteen per cent of world production.   [n] Includes silver-plated ware.   [o] Percentage not given but very high.   [p] Great Lakes region.   [q] Percentage probably high.   [r] Local monopolies.

TABLE B-7

Proportion of National Income Originating in Manufacturing Major Industry Groups: 1899

	Value Added[a] (million dollars) (1)	Ratio of Net Production to Value Added[b] (2)	Net Production[c] (million dollars) (3)	Proportion of	
				Net Production in Manufacturing[d] (4)	National Income[e] (5)
Foods	418.8	0.58	242.9	0.0758	0.0133
Beverages	289.1	0.58	167.7	0.0523	0.0092
Tobacco products	170.8	0.58	99.1	0.0309	0.0054
Textile products	710.6	0.72	511.6	0.1596	0.0279
Leather products	186.7	0.72	134.4	0.0419	0.0073
Rubber products	39.6	f	47.1[f]	0.0147	0.0026
Paper products	93.4	0.67	62.6	0.0195	0.0034
Printing and publishing	284.4	0.67	190.5	0.0594	0.0104
Chemical products	196.7	0.58	114.1	0.0356	0.0062
Petroleum and coal products	45.1	0.58	26.2	0.0082	0.0014
Stone, clay, and glass products	194.6	0.78	151.8	0.0474	0.0083
Forest products	534.8	0.78	417.1	0.1301	0.0228
Iron and steel products	427.8	0.70	299.5	0.0934	0.0164
Nonferrous products	221.9	0.70	155.3	0.0484	0.0085
Machinery	482.7	0.70	337.9	0.1054	0.0185
Transportation equipment	180.3	0.70	126.2	0.0394	0.0069
Miscellaneous	102.2	f	121.6[f]	0.0379	0.0066
Total	4,579.5	0.70	3,205.6	0.9999	0.1751

[a] Solomon Fabricant, *The Output of Manufacturing Industries, 1899–1937*, National Bureau of Economic Research, New York, 1940, pp. 608–39.

[b] *Ibid.*, p. 349. These ratios actually represent the ratio of net income originating to value added but, for reasons explained in the text, are used only to apportion income by origin among major industry groups and not to determine income originating in all manufacturing. The ratios are arithmetic averages of those for 1919 and 1923, years in about the same phase of the business cycle as 1899. See *ibid.*, p. 375.

[c] Col. 1 times col. 2. The data will not correspond exactly with income by origin. Note that "net production" for all manufacturing is $3,205.6 million, while Martin estimates income originating in manufacturing as $2,714 million (Martin, *National Income in the United States, 1799–1938*, pp. 58–59).

[d] Col. 3 divided by total net production (3,205.6).

[e] Col. 4 times 0.1751, the proportion of national income originating in manufacturing (see Table B-1).

[f] No separate ratios are available for these groups. The difference between total net production (3,205.6) and net production for all other groups (3,036.9) has been divided between these two groups. Division was made on the basis of value added, each being apportioned the same proportion of remaining net production as it had of the total value added in the two groups. The proportions were 0.2793 and 0.7207 for rubber products and miscellaneous industries, respectively.

same phase of the business cycle as 1899–1900 and for which Fabricant presents these ratios are 1919 and 1923.[8]

We have pursued the following procedure in estimating the income originating in major industry groups. Value added in a group was multiplied by the average of the ratios in the years 1919 and 1923 of income to value added, yielding what we have termed an estimate of "net production." The net-production figure is not exactly equal to income by origin, as is shown by the fact that total net production in manufacturing is $3,206 million, while Martin estimated total income as $2,714 million.[9] Consequently, the income originating in manufacturing ($2,714 million or 17.51 per cent of total national income) was apportioned among industry groups on the basis of relative net production. Such a procedure does not seem likely to produce any systematic bias in the results.

Income originating in an industry group was allocated to monopolistic industries in the manner explained on pp. 96–99. Basic data are given in Tables B-8 and B-9.

MINING

Sources of Data. Sources were outlined on p. 95. The Bureau of the Census conducted its first survey of mines and quarries in 1902. We have no information which is useful for deriving value added before that year. Barger and Schurr's summary of gross value of products for mineral industries has been used.[10]

Apportionment of Income by Origin. For reasons pointed out in the preceding paragraph, we have been forced to estimate the income originating in monopolistic mining industries on the basis of value-of-products data. Moreover, Martin does not break down his statistics on income for subdivisions of mining. Consequently, we have estimated the proportion of national income which originated in monopolistic mining industries by multiplying the proportion of national income originating in all mining (0.0268) by the proportion of total value of products in mining which was accounted for by monopolistic industries (0.4012). The resulting estimate is 1.08 per cent of national income.

The data in Table B-11 indicate that the value-of-products ratio would probably not deviate much from the value-added ratio, if known. In that table both value of products and value added for monopolistic mining industries are shown for 1902. The proportion of total value of products accounted for by monopolistic industries is 0.2567, while the proportion of value added is 0.2582.

TABLE B-8

Basic Data for Monopolistic Manufacturing Industries, by Major Industry Group: 1899

	Value Added (thousand dollars)		Ratio of (1) to (2) (3)	Proportion of National Income Originating in Monopolistic Industries[a] (4)
	Monopolistic Industries (1)	All Industries (2)		
Foods	190.4	418.8	0.4546	0.0060
Meat packing	102.8			
Bread and baking products[b]	16.9			
Fruits and vegetables, canned[b]	5.9			
Butter; cheese; milk, canned[b]	2.0			
Beet sugar	2.5			
Cane sugar, n.e.m.; cane-sugar refining	18.3			
Chewing gum; confectionery	25.5			
Corn products	9.3			
Baking powder	7.4			
Beverages	86.2	289.1	0.2982	0.0027
Malt	4.6			
Liquors, distilled	81.6			
Tobacco products	85.3	170.8	0.4994	0.0027
Cigarettes; cigars[b]	16.6			
Tobacco products, other	68.7			
Textile products	143.9	710.6	0.2025	0.0056
Cotton goods[b]	38.5			
Woolen goods	47.4			
Worsted goods	43.2			
Cordage and twine	11.2			
Felt goods	2.7			
Oilcloth	0.9			
Leather products	49.0	186.7	0.2625	0.0019
Leather	49.0			
Rubber products	39.6	39.6	1.0000	0.0026
Shoes, rubber	18.4			
Rubber goods, other	21.2			
Paper	66.3	93.4	0.7098	0.0024
Paper; pulp	56.8			
Bags, paper, n.e.m.	2.3			
Envelopes	2.6			
Wallpaper	4.6			
Printing and publishing	2.7	284.4	0.0095	0.0001
Printing materials, n.e.c.	0.7			
Type founding	2.0			

(*continued*)

TABLE B-8 (*continued*)

	Value Added (thousand dollars)		Ratio of (1) to (2) (3)	Proportion of National Income Originating in Monopolistic Industries[a] (4)
	Monopolistic Industries (1)	All Industries (2)		
Chemicals	47.8	196.7	0.2430	0.0015
Chemicals, n.e.c.; gases compressed; rayon[b]	7.1			
Cottonseed products	13.6			
Linseed products	2.8			
Fertilizers	15.7			
Glue and gelatin	1.6			
Paints and varnishes	2.4			
Salt	4.6			
Petroleum and coal products	21.1	45.1	0.4678	0.0007
Petroleum refining	21.1			
Stone, clay, and glass products	25.9	194.6	0.1331	0.0011
Pottery[b]	10.9			
Glass[b]	15.0			
Forest products	2.6	534.8	0.0049	0.0001
Matches	2.6			
Iron and steel products	336.1	427.8	0.7880	0.0129
Blast-furnaces products	75.3			
Steel-mill products	206.3			
Nails and spikes, n.e.m.	6.2			
Springs, steel, n.e.m.	2.7			
Wire, n.e.m.	2.4			
Wirework, n.e.c.	9.0			
Wrought pipe, n.e.m.	5.8			
Heating apparatus	11.9			
Plumbers' supplies, n.e.c.	7.5			
Tin cans and tinware, n.e.c.	10.0			
Nonferrous products	101.5	221.9	0.4574	0.0039
Copper	43.0			
Lead	31.3			
Secondary metals, precious	0.9			
Plated ware	6.7			
Silverware	7.7			
Stamped and enameled ware	11.9			
Machinery	200.0	482.7	0.4143	0.0077
Foundry and machine-shop products[b]	72.6			
Agricultural implements	57.3			
Business machines	4.8			
Typewriters; carbon paper	5.5			
Electrical machinery	43.0			

(*continued*)

TABLE B-8 (*concluded*)

	Value Added (thousand dollars)		Ratio of (1) to (2) (3)	Proportion of National Income Originating in Monopolistic Industries[a] (4)
	Monopolistic Industries (1)	All Industries (2)		
Phonographs	1.4			
Scales and balances	3.7			
Sewing machines	11.7			
Transportation equipment	103.3	180.3	0.5729	0.0040
Motorcycles and bicycles	15.1			
Cars, railroad, n.e.m.	32.1			
Locomotives, n.e.m.	15.0			
Ships and boats	41.1			
Miscellaneous products	2.8	102.2	0.0274	0.0002
Organs; pianos; organ and piano parts[b]	0.5			
Toys and games, n.e.c.	2.3			
Total, all industries	1505.5	4579.5		0.0561

Source: Fabricant, *The Output of Manufacturing Industries, 1899–1937*, pp. 608–39; and Tables B-7 and B-9.

[a] Proportion of national income originating in all industries times ratio in col. 3.

[b] Only parts of the noted industry are included (see Table B-9).

TABLE B-9

Computation of Value Added by Parts of Certain Manufacturing Industries: 1899

	Value of Products (thousand dollars)		Ratio of (1) to (2) (3)	Value Added (million dollars)	
	Parts of Industry (1)	Entire Industry (2)		Entire Industry (4)	Parts of Industry (5)
Bread and bakery products			0.2105[a]	80.3	16.9
Biscuits and crackers					
Fruits and vegetables, canned	11,590	56,668	0.2045	28.6	5.9
Canned fruits	11,590				
Butter, cheese, canned milk	11,889	130,783	0.0909	21.9	2.0
Canned milk	11,889				
Cigarettes and cigars			0.1633[a]	102.1	16.6
Cigarettes					
Cotton goods	81,277[b]	332,806	0.2442	157.8	38.5
Cotton duck	14,263				
Cotton thread	11,825				
Cotton yarn	55,189				
Chemicals, n.e.c.	17,334[c]	62,677	0.2766	25.6	7.1
Sodas	11,638				
Potashes	174				
Alums	2,447				
Coal-tar products	1,339				
Cyanides	1,596				
Casein	30				
Milk sugar	110				
Paints and varnishes	6,761[c]	69,562	0.0972	24.8	2.4
White lead	4,211				
Lead oxides	2,550				
Pottery, etc.	14,862[b]	44,263	0.3358	32.3	10.9
Fireproofing	1,665				
Fire brick	8,637				
Sewer pipe	4,560				
Glass	21,306	56,540	0.3768	39.8	15.0
Window glass	10,879[b]				
Plate glass	5,802[b]				
Tableware	2,618				
Jellies, tumblers, etc.	2,007				
Sheet-metal work, n.e.c.			0.3506[a]	28.5	10.0
Tin cans and tinware, n.e.c.					
Foundry and machine-shop products	143,770[d]	685,901[e]	0.2096	345.6	72.6
Pianos and organs	940[b]	41,120	0.0229	23.7	0.5
Player pianos, etc.	667				
Self-playing organs	273				

Source: *Twelfth Census of the United States, Taken in the Year 1900: Manufactures,* Parts I, IV, and V; Fabricant, *The Output of Manufacturing Industries, 1899–1937,* pp. 608–39.

(*continued*)

TABLE B-10

Basic Data for Monopolistic Mining Industries, by Major Industry Group: 1899

| | Value of Products (thousand dollars) | | Ratio of (1) to (2) (3) |
	Monopolistic Industries (1)	All Industries (2)	
Metal mining	106,916	189,057	0.5655
Bauxite	117		
Copper	70,263ᵃ		
Iron ore	34,646		
Manganese	435		
Mercury	1,453		
Molybdenum	1		
Titanium	1		
Anthracite mining	88,142	88,142	1.0000
*Nonmetal mining*ᵇ	41,056	58,713ᵇ	0.6993
Asphalt	554		
Borates	505		
Gypsum	752		
Stone	39,208		
Tripoli	37		
Total	236,114	588,543	0.4012

Source: Harold Barger and S. H. Schurr, *The Mining Industries, 1899–1939: A Study of Output, Employment and Productivity*, National Bureau of Economic Research, New York, 1944, pp. 305–9.

ᵃ Estimated as 0.4612 of the values of all nonferrous mining products, that ratio obtaining in 1909, which is the earliest year for which copper data are available.

ᵇ Barger and Schurr's "Nonmetals" total less the summed value of "coal" and "petroleum and natural gases."

NOTES TO TABLE B-9 (*concluded*)

ᵃ Ratio of value added for part to value added for entire industry for first year after 1899 in which value added was reported separately (*ibid.*, pp. 608–39).

ᵇ Value of products for establishments classified in the industry.

ᶜ Value of products for establishments classified in the industry group to which this industry belongs.

ᵈ This figure represents the total value of products of the 81 establishments in this industry, each with a value of products exceeding $1,000,000 in 1905, taken from *Census of Manufactures: 1905*, Part I, p. 509. No other estimate is available for the many commodities in this heterogeneous industry which were considered as monopolized. See Table B-6 for a list of these commodities.

ᵉ Total value of products in 1905.

TABLE B-11

Data for Monopolistic Mining Industries: 1902 (thousand dollars)

	Value Added[a]	Value of Products
Bauxite	88	128
Copper	39,906	51,178
Iron ore	56,034	65,465
Manganese	160	177
Mercury	1,205	1,550
Anthracite mining	63,027	76,174
Asphalt	205	237
Borates	2,170	2,384
Gypsum	1,341	2,089
Marble	4,218	5,044
Tripoli	53	55
Total, above industries	168,407	204,481
Total, all mining	652,333	796,826

Source: *Mines and Quarries, 1902*, p. 45.

[a] Computed by subtracting from value of products the following items: (1) "contract work" and (2) "cost of supplies and materials."

FINANCE

Commercial banking was considered to be subject to local monopolies in 1899. Investment banking was also classified as monopolistic. The estimate for the percentage of national income originating in banking was taken from Simon Kuznets' revision of W. I. King's income-by-origin statistics for the period 1909–1919.[11] According to these statistics, the percentages attributable to banking were 1.2 in 1909, 1.3 from 1910 through 1915, 1.2 in 1916, and 1.1 from 1917 through 1919. There does not seem to be any indication of trend upward or downward. It is pertinent to point out that the Department of Commerce national income series shows the percentage in 1937 and 1939 as 1.2.[12] Since no significant trend was observable, we assumed that the percentage in 1899 was the same as that in 1909, that is, 1.2.

TRANSPORTATION AND COMMUNICATION

All sectors of these areas were considered monopolistic, with the exception of water transportation. The percentage of national income originating in water transportation was taken as King's revised estimate for 1909. His estimates, as revised by Kuznets, showed 0.8 per cent from 1909 through 1912, 0.7 for 1913 and 1914, 0.8 for 1915 and 1916, 0.9 for 1917 and 1918, and 1.2 for 1919.[13] Since there was no substantial trend up to the war years, we assumed 0.8 to be the percentage of national income which originated in water transportation in 1899.

REVISION OF THE 1937 ESTIMATE OF THE EXTENT OF MONOPOLY

Because the general method which has been used here for determining the income originating in monopolistic industries has involved the apportionment of the known income from the major industrial division which included the monopolistic industries, the use of different national income series in any year is likely to yield different estimates. That is, the estimates will probably differ if the national income series show different proportions of national income as originating in the same broadly defined industrial divisions. We note from the data in Table B-12 that the proportions of national income which are assigned to broad industrial classifications are not the same

TABLE B-12

Proportional Distribution of National Income by Industrial Origin from Martin and Department of Commerce Series: 1937

	Department of Commerce	Martin
Agriculture	0.0985	0.0973
Mining	0.0264	0.0251
Construction	0.0274	0.0260
Manufacturing	0.2622	0.2395
Trade	0.1621	0.1212
Finance	0.1079	0.0658
Transportation and communication	0.0749	0.0855
Public utilities	0.0234	0.0182
Services	0.1093	0.1027
Government and government enterprises	0.1059	0.1666
Miscellaneous	0.0020	0.0520

Source: Tables 2 and B-5.

in the Department of Commerce and in the Martin data for 1937. The largest discrepancies occur in the proportions assigned to manufacturing and government.

Our estimates of the income originating in monopolistic industries were adjusted to the Martin data as follows: For mining, construction, transportation, communication, and services we multiplied the percentage of national income which Martin attributed to the division by the proportion of production in the division which our original estimates showed as originating in monopolistic industries. For instance, we estimated earlier that monopolistic mining industries accounted for 0.269 of all mining production in 1937 (0.71 out of 2.64 per cent of national income). Therefore, we multiplied the 2.51 per cent of national income which Martin attributed to mining by 0.269, getting 0.68 per cent of national income as originating in monopolistic mining industries.

For manufacturing the adjustments were carried one step further. The percentages of national income attributable to manufacturing major industry groups were recomputed on the basis of the method we used for 1899[14] (see Table B-12). The procedure explained in the preceding paragraph was then applied at the industry group level.

For finance the revised percentage of national income originating among insurance carriers was likewise computed by the method we explained in the second paragraph above. But we retained the Department of Commerce estimate for banking, since our estimate for 1899 was also made independently of the Martin series.

For agriculture and trade we computed the percentage of national income in the same way as was done in our Tables A-14 and A-15, substituting Martin's total national income ($69,419 million) for that of the Department of Commerce ($73,627 million).

A revision was also made in the definition of monopoly used for 1937, in order to make it similar to the definition used for 1899.[15] The revision required a recalculation of the extent of monopoly in manufacturing. Under the second definition of monopoly used for 1937 (see pp. 48–49), we included the manufacturing industries in Tables A-3, A-4, A-6, and A-7. Under the first definition of monopoly used for 1937 (see pp. 24–25), we included the manufacturing industries in Tables A-3 through A-6 minus those in Table A-7. The difference in results under the two definitions is shown in columns 6 and 7 of Table B-13.

TABLE B-13

Proportion of National Income Originating in Manufacturing Major

	Value Added[a] (million dollars) (1)	Ratio of Net Production to Value Added[b] (2)
Foods	3,370.8	0.52
Tobacco products	325.1	0.52
Textile products	1,786.3	0.64
Apparel	1,243.7	0.64
Lumber	633.8	0.64
Furniture	636.3	0.64
Paper	862.9	0.62
Printing and publishing	1,786.6	0.62
Chemicals	1,776.2	0.58
Petroleum and coal products	619.5	0.58
Rubber products	368.8	h
Leather products	583.8	0.64
Stone, clay, and glass products	890.3	0.64
Iron and steel products	3,389.0	0.68
Nonferrous products	845.8	0.68
Electrical machinery	1,102.1	0.68
Machinery	2,331.6	0.68
Automobiles	1,581.9	0.68
Transportation equipment	404.6	0.68
Miscellaneous products	634.7	h
Total	25,173.5	0.65

See text for an explanation of the method used.

[a] *Census of Manufactures: 1939*, Vol. II.

[b] Fabricant, *The Output of Manufacturing Industries, 1899–1937*, p. 349.

[c] Col. 1 times col. 2.

[d] Col. 3 divided by total net production in manufacturing.

[e] Col. 4 times 0.2395, the proportion of national income originating in manufacturing according to the Martin national income data (see Table B-5).

[f] Col. 5 times the proportion of production in each group originating in monopolistic industries as defined in Chapter 2. The latter proportions were derived from Table A-10.

Industry Groups, Computed on Basis of Martin National Income Data: 1937

Net Production[e] (million dollars) (3)	Proportion of Total Net Production in Manufacturing[d] (4)	Proportion of National Income Originating in		
		All Industries[e] (5)	Monopolistic Industries	
			Estimate I[f] (6)	Estimate II[g] (7)
1,752.8	0.1071	0.0257	0.0128	0.0063
169.1	0.0103	0.0025	0.0019	0.0019
1,143.2	0.0699	0.0167	0.0022	0.0018
796.0	0.0486	0.0116	0.0001	0.0001
405.6	0.0248	0.0059	0.0012	
407.2	0.0249	0.0060	0.0008	0.0004
535.0	0.0327	0.0078	0.0003	0.0003
1,107.7	0.0677	0.0162		
1,030.2	0.0630	0.0151	0.0078	0.0051
359.3	0.0220	0.0053	0.0042	
424.8	0.0260	0.0062	0.0006	0.0042
373.6	0.0228	0.0055	0.0001	0.0003
569.8	0.0348	0.0083	0.0060	0.0021
2,304.5	0.1408	0.3337	0.0133	0.0123
575.1	0.0351	0.0084	0.0039	0.0034
749.4	0.0458	0.0110	0.0089	0.0004
1,585.5	0.0969	0.0232	0.0051	0.0059
1,075.7	0.0657	0.0157	0.0156	0.0156
275.1	0.0168	0.0040	0.0028	0.0028
723.2	0.0442	0.0106	0.0041	0.0041
16,362.8	0.9999	0.2394	0.0917	0.0671

[g] Col. 5 times the proportion of production in each group originating in monopolistic industries as redefined in Chapter 3. The latter proportions were derived from Tables A-3 through A-6 (see text, Appendix B).

[h] No separate ratios are available for these groups. The difference between total net production (16,362.8) and net production for all other groups (15,214.8) has been divided between these groups. The division was made on the basis of value added, each group being apportioned the same proportion of the remaining net production as it had of the total value added in the two groups. The proportions were 0.3675 and 0.6325 for rubber products and miscellaneous products, respectively.

Basic Data on Extent of Monopoly: 1954 and 1958

INTRODUCTION

Government and individual industry studies were among the sources used to determine the nature of industrial competitiveness in the 1950's. However, there were no directly relevant multi-industry studies comparable to those prepared during the 1930's. Consequently, the following description of the classification methodology is necessarily more detailed than that presented in Appendices A and B for the earlier years. The classifications are described by major industrial division in the following nine sections. Each section includes a brief description of the type of industrial activity (indicated by reference to the Standard Industrial Classification, SIC), a description of the standards applied, and an indication of the difficulties encountered in applying these criteria.

I. CLASSIFICATION OF MANUFACTURING INDUSTRIES BY COMPETITIVE STATUS

As mentioned in Chapter 5, manufacturing division data are compiled on both product and industry bases for the twenty major industry groups comprising the manufacturing division of the Standard Industrial Classification (SIC):

The manufacturing division includes those establishments engaged in the mechanical or chemical transformation of inorganic or organic substances into new products and usually described as plants, factories, or mills, which characteristically use power-driven machines and materials-handling equipment. Establishments engaged in assembling component parts of manufactured products are also considered manufacturing if the new product is neither a structure nor other fixed improvement.[1]

EFFECT OF INDUSTRY RECLASSIFICATION

Despite two changes in the SIC classification definitions, the overall scope of the manufacturing division has remained comparable since 1937. However, these industrial reclassifications are important factors in this study because they affect such measures of industrial structure as concentration ratios. Because industrial structure is one aspect of effective monopoly, concentration ratios (indicating the share of output provided by the four largest companies in each industry) were utilized in classifying manufacturing industries and products in each census year studied. Consequently, any influence that might weaken the comparability of the data or analysis raises some concern because that influence could also weaken the conclusions reached from an analysis of such data. However, it is believed that these SIC changes have not seriously affected either the comparability of the data or the analytic results. This question of comparability is described at greater length in Appendix D, which also includes a discussion of Lorenz and other statistical comparisons.

DETERMINATION OF HIGHLY CONCENTRATED INDUSTRIES

In 1958, the manufacturing division originated $103,817 million, or 28.26 per cent of national income. In order to assess the importance of the highly concentrated manufacturing industries, estimates of absolute concentration have been compiled. These estimates are presented in Tables C-1 through C-4; they were derived from three statistical measures which were applied originally by Means, Thorp, and Crowder in the mid-1930's. Two of these measures are based on industry data, while the third is derived from product data. Under one approach, an industry is considered concentrated if four companies account for two-thirds or more of its shipments; the second considers any similar concentration ratios one-half or more as identifying a highly concentrated industry. The third approach considers production to be highly concentrated if four companies account for three-quarters or more of the output of a product. The number of companies and minimum ratio are determined by convenience, availability, and the need to set some minimum levels suitable for general applicability to all industries. No particular reasons dictate the choice of these specific values, although use of the more limited product definitions should be compensated, in part, by higher ratios than those applied to the industry measures.

Direct 1939–1958 comparisons are provided in Chapter 5 for modified two-digit SIC major industry groups. Each comparison is based on four-digit SIC industry data, but direct four-digit industry comparisons are

TABLE C-1

Basic Data for Manufactured Products with Concentration Ratios of 3/4 or Larger in 1954, by Major Industry Group and Industry

	SIC	Value of Shipments for Concentrated Products as Per Cent of Total Value	Value Added for Concentrated Products as Per Cent of Total Value Added	Per Cent of National Income Originating in Concentrated Products
Food and kindred products	20		7.500	0.198
Concentrated milk	2023	49.573		
Special dairy products	2025	80.154		
Canned fruits and vegetables	2033	19.821		
Cereal breakfast foods	2043	95.699		
Chewing gum	2073	97.117		
Leavening compounds	2091	98.706		
Corn wet milling products	2094	87.902		
Flavorings	2095	52.125		
Food preparations, n.e.c.	2099	3.781		
Tobacco manufactures	21		72.642	0.167
Cigarettes	2111	98.961		
Textile mill products	22		3.569	0.046
Scouring and combing mill products[a]	2211	96.674		
Thread	2223	29.028		
Wool carpets and rugs[b]	2271	18.540		
Hard surface floor coverings	2274	87.938		
Apparel and related products	23		0.992	0.013
Housefurnishings, n.e.c.	2392	29.355		
Lumber and wood products except furniture	24		0.172	0.002
Cooperage	2445	25.369		
Paper and allied products	26		3.802	0.042
Pulp	2611	11.279		
Paper coating and glazing	2641	23.938		
Pulp goods, pressed and molded	2694	106.956		
Chemicals and allied products	28		20.888	0.455
Alkalies and chlorine	2812	31.682		
Inorganic chemicals, n.e.c.	2819	13.261		
Cyclic (coal-tar) crudes	2821	113.314		
Plastics materials	2823	25.285		
Synthetic fibers	2825	96.890		

(*continued*)

TABLE C-1 (*continued*)

	SIC	Value of Shipments for Concentrated Products as Per Cent of Total Value	Value Added for Concentrated Products as Per Cent of Total Value Added	Per Cent of National Income Originating in Concentrated Products
Organic chemicals, n.e.c.	2829	1.222		
Medicinal chemicals	2833	3.410		
Soap and glycerin	2841	32.240		
Cleaning and polishing products	2842	90.016		
Inorganic color pigments	2852	64.436		
Softwood distillation	2862	69.684		
Linseed oil mill products	2882	104.525		
Toilet preparations	2893	20.805		
Carbon black	2895	3.333		
Compressed and liquified gases	2896	111.950		
Salt	2898	99.587		
Rubber products	30		39.069	0.180
Tires and inner tubes	3011	88.065		
Leather and leather products	31		1.590	0.007
Industrial leather belting	3121	74.598		
Stone, clay, and glass products	32		14.128	0.147
Flat glass	3211	134.754		
Gypsum products	3272	97.286		
Asbestos products	3292	21.857		
Minerals: ground or treated	3295	3.449		
Primary metal industries	33		16.671	0.467
Steel mill products[b]	3312	22.083		
Primary copper[b]	3331	88.120		
Primary lead[b]	3332	75.290		
Primary zinc	3333	8.885		
Primary aluminium	3334	76.936		
Primary nonferrous metals, n.e.c.	3339	159.487		
Aluminum rolling and drawing	3352	48.063		
Rolling and drawing, n.e.c.	3359	4.205		
Wiredrawing (excluding wire products)	3392	1.751		
Fabricated metal products	34		10.021	0.217
Tin caps and other tinware	3411	98.086		
Cutlery	3421	39.959		

(*continued*)

TABLE C-1 (*continued*)

	SIC	Value of Shipments for Concentrated Products as Per Cent of Total Value	Value Added for Concentrated Products as Per Cent of Total Value Added	Per Cent of National Income Originating in Concentrated Products
Files	3424	104.089		
Hardware, n.e.c.	3429	2.511		
Boiler shop products	3443	23.361		
Metal stampings	3463	4.541		
Metal barrels, drums, and pails	3491	1.838		
Safes and vaults	3492	84.861		
Machinery (except electrical)	35		6.857	0.221
Steam engines and turbines	3511	70.505		
Internal combustion engines	3519	21.726		
Tractors	3521	39.443		
Metalworking machinery	3542	2.907		
Office and store machines, n.e.c.	3579	17.268		
Sewing machines	3583	95.950		
Refrigeration machinery[b]	3585	7.232		
Ball and roller bearings	3593	46.250		
Electrical machinery	36		22.257	0.435
Carbon and graphite products	3612	103.161		
Electric measuring instruments	3613	20.334		
Motors and generators	3614	5.860		
Transformers	3615	75.699		
Insulated wire and cable	3631	76.893		
Engine electrical equipment	3641	9.188		
Electric lamps (bulbs)	3651	94.885		
Electronic tubes	3662	43.004		
Telephone and telegraph equipment	3664	94.776		
Communication equipment, n.e.c.	3669	39.425		
Storage batteries	3691	19.129		
Primary batteries	3692	96.795		
Electrical products, n.e.c.	3699	60.571		
Transportation equipment	37		43.394	1.746
Motor vehicles and parts[b]	3717	92.121		
Aircraft propellers[b]	3723	90.917		
Locomotives and parts	3741	85.264		
Railroad and street cars	3742	68.195		
Motorcycles and bicycles	3751	17.047		

(*continued*)

TABLE C-1 (*concluded*)

	SIC	Value of Shipments for Concentrated Products as Per Cent of Total Value	Value Added for Concentrated Products as Per Cent of Total Value Added	Per Cent of National Income Originating in Concentrated Products
Instruments and related products	38		19.935	0.128
Mechanical measuring instruments	3821	9.500		
Surgical appliances and supplies	3842	22.474		
Photographic equipment	3861	43.326		
Watches and clocks	3871	49.907		
Miscellaneous manufactures	39		0.891	0.006
Organs	3932	129.407		
Cork products[a]	3982	100.145		
Miscellaneous products, n.e.c.	3999	7.072		

The five-digit products are grouped by four-digit industry "families" of products. Except as noted below, the four-digit classifications used in this table include all underlying five-digit products. However, in many instances, some products within a four-digit grouping will have concentration ratios of 3/4 or more, while other products within the same grouping will have lower concentration ratios. Thus, the following list indicates the four-digit groups in which only some product lines were concentrated in 1954; the list also includes the names and SIC numbers of the concentrated products within each four-digit class.

Four-Digit SIC	Concentrated Products within Each Four-Digit Class
2023	Canned milk, 20232.
2025	Process cheese and related products, 20252.
2033	Canned baby foods, 20336;[a] Canned soups and poultry products, 20337.
2091	Baking powder, 20911; Yeast, 20912.
2094	Corn sirup, sugar, and starches, 20941; Dextrin, 20943; Corn oil, 20944; Wet-process corn byproducts, 20945.
2095	Beverage bases, except sirups, 20952; Flavoring sirups, soft drink, 20953.
2099	Desserts, ready-to-mix, except ice cream mix, 20991.
2223	Thread for use in the home, 22231.
2271	Carpets and rug-weaving yarns, wool, 22712.
2274	Lineoleum, 22741; Asphalted-felt-base floor and wall covering, and supported plastic floor and wall covering, 22742 and 22743.
2392	Towels and wash cloths, woven, 23923.
2445	Slack cooperage, 24451.
2611	Special alpha and dissolving wood pulp, 26111; Soda wood pulp, 26116.
2641	Pressure-sensitive tapes, including plastics, 26414.[a]
2812	Sodium carbonate (soda ash), 28122[a]; Other alkalies, 28124.
2819	Aluminum compounds, 28194; Inorganic chemicals, reagent and high-purity grades, 28196.
2823	Cellulose plastics materials, 28231; Vulcanized fiber, 28232; Regenerated cellulosic products, except rayon, 28233.[a]

NOTES TO TABLE C-1 (*continued*)

2825	Acetate yarn, 28251; Rayon yarn, viscose and cupramonium process, 28252; Noncellulosic synthetic fibers, except glass, 28253.[a]
2829	Industrial ethyl alcohol, natural, 28291.
2833	Botanical products, 28320.
2841	Soaps, except specialty, packaged, 28411.
2842	Synthetic organic detergents, packaged, 28421.
2852	White opaque pigments, 28521.
2893	Dentifrices, including mouthwashes and gargles, 28933.
2895	Other blacks, except carbon and charcoal, 28932.
2896	Elemental, 28961; Acetylene, 28962; Carbon dioxide, 28963.
3121	Leather packings, and oil and grease retainers, 31212.
3211	Sheet (window) glass, 32111; Plate glass, 32112; Laminated glass, including safety glass, 32311.
3292	Asbestos-cement sheets and wallboards, 32925; Other asbestos and asbestos-cement products, 32926.
3295	Natural graphite, ground refined or blended, 32953.
3312	Steel ingots, 33121; Steel plates, 33123; Tin, terme, plate and black plate, 33125; Structural shapes and pilings, 33126; Other steel mill shapes and forms, 33129.
3331	Copper smelter products, 33311; Refined unalloyed copper, 33312.
3332	Lead smelter products, 33321; Refined unalloyed lead, 33322.
3333	Zinc residues and other zinc smelter products, 3331.
3339	Precious metals, 33392; Other nonferrous metals, smelter or refined, 33391 and 33393.
3352	Aluminum plate and sheet, 33521.
3359	Magnesium mill products, rolled, drawn, extended, 33591.[a]
3392	Other nonferrous metal wire, 33924.
3411	Metal cans, 34111; Fluid milk-shipping containers, metal, 34112; Other tinware, 34113.
3421	Razor blades and razors, except electric, 34212.
3429	Vacuum bottles and jugs, 34293.
3443	Power boilers, over 15 psi, parts and attachments, 34433.
3463	Crowns, 34636.
3491	All other metal barrels, including beer barrels, 34913.
3511	Steam and hydraulic turbine generator-set units, 35112.
3519	Gas engines, except gas turbines, 35193; Outboard motors, 35195; Other internal combustion engines, 35196.
3521	Contractors' off-highway wheel-type tractor, 35212; Tracklaying-type tractors, 35214; Parts and attachments for tracklaying-type tractors, 35218.
3542	Forging machines, except presses, 35423.
3579	Coin-operated amusement machines and mechanisms, 35752.
3583	Household sewing machines, 35831; Industrial sewing machines, except shoe stitching, 35832; Parts and attachments for sewing machines, 35833.
3585	Compressors and compressor units, refrigerators, 35854.
3593	Roller bearings, complete, 35932.
3613	Integrating instruments, electric, 36131.
3614	Land transport motors, generators and control equipment, 36145.
3615	Power and distribution transformers, 36152; Transformer parts and supplies, 36153.
3631	Communication wire and cable, 36311.
3641	Ignition harness and cable sets, 36411.
3662	Other cathode ray tubes, 36622; Radio receiving-type tubes, 36623.

(*continued*)

NOTES TO TABLE C-1 (*concluded*)

3669	Railway signals, electric, 36692.
3691	Storage batteries, except SLI type, 36912.
3699	Lamp components, 36991; Electrical hearing aids, 36992.
3717	Passenger cars, knocked down or assembled, 37171; Truck tractor, truck chassis and trucks, 37172; Motor coaches, except trolley buses, 37173.
3741	Locomotives, new railroad service types, 37411;[a] Locomotives, switching type, 37412; Locomotives, industrial switching and mining types, 37413;[a] parts for locomotives, for sale separately, 37414; Rebuilt locomotives, 37415.
3742	Passenger trains, new, 37421; Freight train cars, new, 37422; Street, rapid transit, interurban cars, 37423; Rebuilt passenger and freight train cars, 37425.
3751	Motorcycles, motorbikes, scooters, and parts, 37511.
3821	Motor-vehicle instruments, except electric, 38214.
3842	Sanitary napkins and tampons, 38421.
3861	Photographic film and plates, silver halide type, 38615; Photographic paper and cloth, silver halide type, 38616.
3871	Watches, domestic movements, jeweled lever type, 38712; Watches, domestic movements, pin lever type, 38713;[a] Watches, imported movements, all types, 38714.
3999	Other chemical fire-extinguishing equipment, 39992.

Source: U.S. Congress, Senate, *Concentration in American Industry; 1954,* 85th Cong., 1st Sess., Government Printing Office, Washington, Bureau of the Census, *Census of Manufactures, 1954,* Government Printing Office, Washington; U.S. Department of Commerce, Office of Business Economics, *U.S. Income and Output, a Supplement to the Survey of Current Business, 1958,* Government Printing Office, Washington, Table I-10, pp. 130–31.

[a] No concentration ratio provided, but data indicate substantial concentration.

[b] Since no value-of-shipments data have been provided for the four-digit industries because of duplication in reuse of products within these industries, these figures constitute an estimate required for subsequent allocation of value added by manufacture.

unfeasible because of the post-1939 SIC changes described in Appendix D. Despite these changes, the two-digit major industry group data for 1954 and 1958 have been arranged in a manner comparable to that available for 1939. This was achieved by combining several of the two-digit major industry groups in each year as in Table 20, but only 16 comparisons are available for the detailed 1939–1958 period. Some industries were omitted in one of the years, but such exclusion has rather minor effects on the comparisons, especially in view of the large differences in the importance of the highly concentrated industries.

The significance of the highly concentrated industries and products is indicated by the share of national income originating in these sectors. However, national income data are available only on a two-digit industry basis and not for the narrower industry or product classifications. Thus, the industry or product contributions to national income must be allocated from other data. In this study, industry contributions were allocated from a ratio of the value added by manufacture in the highly concentrated industries to the value added for each two-digit major industry group. National

TABLE C-2

Basic Data for Manufactured Products with Concentration Ratios of 3/4 or Larger in 1958, by Major Industry Group and Industry

	1957 SIC	Value of Shipments for Concentrated Products as Per Cent of Total Value	Value Added for Concentrated Products as Per Cent of Total Value Added	Per Cent of National Income Originating in Concentrated Products
Food and kindred products	20		6.456	0.146
Condensed and evaporated milk	2023	42.903		
Canned specialties	2032	31.234		
Cereal breakfast foods	20430	97.221		
Biscuit and crackers	2052	35.664		
Chocolate and cocoa products	2072	66.748		
Chewing gum and chewing gum base	20730	94.927		
Flavorings	2087	42.402		
Vegetable oil mills, n.e.c.	2093	46.372		
Food preparations, n.e.c.	2099	6.454		
Tobacco products	21		78.870	0.186
Cigarettes	21110	98.937		
Textile mill products	22		1.157	0.007
Synthetic broad-woven fabrics and related products	2221	5.343		
Wool fabrics and related products	2231	2.921		
Thread	2284	33.899		
Apparel and related products	23		1.101	0.015
Trimmings and stitchings	2398	37.177		
Paper and allied products	26		7.101	0.099
Paper coating and glazing	2641	22.782		
Pressed and molded pulp goods	2646	102.070		
Paper and board products, n.e.c.	2649	9.324		
Sanitary food containers	2654	63.195		
Building paper and board	2661	19.993		
Printing and publishing	27		1.150	0.018
Books, publishing and printing	2731	14.789		
Chemicals and allied products	28		17.663	0.392
Alkalies and chlorine	2812	25.921		
Industrial gases	2813	47.726		

(continued)

TABLE C-2 (*continued*)

	1957 SIC	Value of Shipments for Concentrated Products as Per Cent of Total Value	Value Added for Concentrated Products as Per Cent of Total Value Added	Per Cent of National Income Originating in Concentrated Products
Cyclic (coal-tar) crudes	28140	90.035		
Inorganic pigments	2816	55.519		
Industrial inorganic chemicals, n.e.c.	2819	10.332		
Plastics materials	2821	21.565		
Cellulosic man-made fibers	2823	80.645		
Synthetic organic fibers, noncellulosic[a]	28240	108.713		
Soap and other detergents	2841	50.295		
Toilet preparations	2844	18.678		
Gum and wood chemicals	2861	41.738		
Carbon black (channel and furnace process only)	28950	99.671		
Chemicals preparations, n.e.c.	2899	12.305		
Rubber and plastics products	30		2.591	0.013
Tires and inner tubes	3011	7.194		
Stone, clay, and glass products	32		14.018	0.144
Flat glass	3211	76.203		
Pressed and blown glass, n.e.c., from other glass produced in the same establishment	3229	66.100		
Gypsum products	3275	93.056		
Abrasive products	3291	7.911		
Asbestos products	3292	60.800		
Primary metal industries	33		8.885	0.211
Blast furnaces and steel mills[b]	3312	0.943		
Gray iron castings	3321	10.295		
Primary copper[b]	3331	100.000		
Primary lead[c]	3332			
Primary zinc[b]	3333	12.360		
Primary aluminum	3334	100.262		
Aluminum rolling and drawing	3352	60.418		
Nonferrous wire drawing, etc.	3357	3.525		
Fabricated metal products	34		10.588	0.222
Metal cans	34110	96.598		
Cutlery	3421	45.023		
Hardware, n.e.c.	3429	3.053		

(*continued*)

TABLE C-2 (*continued*)

	1957 SIC	Value of Shipments for Concentrated Products as Per Cent of Total Value	Value Added for Concentrated Products as Per Cent of Total Value Added	Per Cent of National Income Originating in Concentrated Products
Boilershop products	3443	24.524		
Metal stampings	3461	5.268		
Safes and vaults	34920	76.693		
Machinery, except electrical	35		13.061	0.393
Steam engines and turbines	3511	50.893		
Internal combustion engines	3519	17.122		
Construction machinery	3531	37.593		
Metal-cutting machine tools	3541	3.457		
Ball and roller bearings	3562	41.456		
Computing and related machines	3571	93.551		
Typewriters and parts	35720	79.168		
Electrical machinery	36		21.006	0.454
Electric measuring instruments	3611	13.186		
Transformers	3612	78.271		
Switchgear and switch-boards	3613	24.068		
Motors and generators	3621	3.760		
Carbon and graphite products	36240	101.222		
Electrical housewares and fans	3634	9.675		
Sewing machines[a]	36360	89.398		
Electric lamps	36410	94.271		
Telephone, telegraph apparatus[b]	3661	99.388		
Electron tubes, receiving type	36710	88.170		
Primary batteries, dry and wet	36920	98.165		
Engine electric equipment	3694	49.112		
Transportation equipment	37		52.946	1.024
Motor vehicles and parts[b]	3717	99.295		
Aircraft	3721	15.350		
Aircraft engines and parts	3722	39.858		
Aircraft propellers and parts	37230	68.171		
Ship building and repairing	3731	27.142		

(*continued*)

TABLE C-2 (*concluded*)

	1957 SIC	Value of Shipments for Concentrated Products as Per Cent of Total Value	Value Added for Concentrated Products as Per Cent of Total Value Added	Per Cent of National Income Originating in Concentrated Products
Locomotives and parts	3741	87.149		
Railroad and street cars	3742	20.306		
Instruments and related products	38		14.691	0.095
Mechanical measuring devices	3821	9.739		
Photographic equipment	3861	43.155		
Watches and clocks	3871	25.477		
Miscellaneous manufacturing	39		2.065	0.014
Hard-surface floor coverings	3982	82.837		
Miscellaneous products, n.e.c.	3999	10.926		

The five-digit products are grouped by four-digit industry "families" of products. Except as noted below, the four-digit classifications used in this table include all underlying five-digit products. However, in many instances, some products within a four-digit grouping will have concentration ratios of 3/4 or more, while other products within the same grouping will have lower concentration ratios. Thus, the following list indicates the four-digit groups in which only some product lines were concentrated in 1958; the list also includes the names and SIC numbers of the concentrated products within each four-digit class.

Four-Digit SIC	Concentrated Products within Each Four-Digit Class
2023	Canned milk, 20232.
2032	Canned baby foods (except meat), 20321; Other canned specialities, 20324.
2052	Biscuits, crackers, and pretzels, 20521.
2072	Confectionery-type chocolate, made in chocolate plants, 20722; Other chocolate and cocoa products, made in chocolate plants, 20728.
2087	Flavoring sirups, soft drinks, 20873.
2093	Linseed oil, 20931; Vegetable oils (other than cottonseed, soybean, and linseed), 20932.
2099	Desserts (ready-to-mix), 20991; Baking powder and yeast, 20994.
2221	Finished blankets, 22219.
2231	Finished wool yarns, tops, or raw stock not spun or combed at some establishment, 22311.
2284	Finished thread for use in the home, 22841; Unfinished thread, 22843.
2398	Automobile and furniture trimmings, 23981.
2641	Pressure-sensitive tape, 26414.
2646	Bituminous fiber pipe and conduits, 26461; Other pressed and molded pulp goods, 26462.
2649	Sanitary napkins and tampons, 26494.

(continued)

NOTES TO TABLE C-2 (*continued*)

2654	Milk and other beverage cartons, 26541; Cups and liquid-tight food containers, 26542.
2661	Hard-pressed wood fiber board, 26613.
2731	Subscription reference, 27312.
2812	Sodium carbonate, 28122;[a] Other alkalies, 28124.
2813	Acetelyne, 28132;[a] Carbon dioxide, 28133.
2816	Titanium pigments, 28161.[a]
2819	Aluminum oxide and other aluminum compounds, 28195 and 28196.
2821	Cellulose plastics materials, except from scrap, 28211;[a] Regenerated cellulosic products, except rayon, 28212.
2823	Acetate yarn, 28231; Rayon yarn, viscose and cuprammonium process, 28232.
2841	Synthetic organic detergents, packaged, 28415.
2844	Dentifrices, including mouthwashes, gargles, and rinses, 28444.
2861	Softwood distillation products, 28611.
2899	Salt, 28991.
3011	Other pneumatic tires and solid tires, 30113.
3211	Sheet (window) glass, 32111; Plate glass and other flat glass, 32112 and 32114.[a]
3229	Lighting and electronic glassware, 32292; Glass fiber, 32293; Other pressed and blown glassware, 32294.
3275	Gypsum building materials, 32751; Other gypsum products, 32752.
3291	Nonmetallic artificial mixed grains, powders, and flour abrasives, 32911.
3292	Asphalt floor tiles, 32925; Vinyl asbestos floor tile, 32926; Asbestos textiles and other asbestos and asbestos cement products, 32927.
3312	Open die or smith forgings (open-frame hammer or press) produced in steel mills, 32129.
3321	Molds for heavy steel ingots, 33211.
3331	Copper smelter products, 33311; Refined copper made by primary copper refiners, 33312.
3332	Lead smelter products, 33321;[a] Refined lead made by primary lead refiners, 33323.
3333	Zinc residues and other zinc smelter products, 33331.
3334	Aluminum-base alloys (pig, ingot, shot, etc.) made by primary aluminum refiners, 33341;[a] Refined unalloyed aluminum, 33342.
3352	Aluminum and aluminum-base alloy wire (including ACSR) made in aluminum rolling mills, 33521; Aluminum plate and sheet (including foil stock), 33522;[a] Plain aluminum foil, 33523; Rolled aluminum rod, bar, and structural shapes, 33524.
3357	Aluminum and aluminum-base alloy wire (including ACSR) except that made in aluminum rolling mills, 33571.[a]
3421	Razor blades and razors, except electric, 34212.[a]
3429	Vacuum and insulated bottles, jugs, and chests, 34293.
3443	Steel power boilers, parts and attachments (over 15 psi steam working pressure), 34433.
3461	Stamped and spun hospital utensils and cooking and kitchen household utensils, aluminum, 34614.
3511	Steam, gas, and hydraulic generator set units and parts, 35111.
3519	Gas engines (except gas turbines), 35193; Outboard motors, 35195.
3531	Contractors' off-highway wheel tractors, 35311; Tracklaying-type tractors, 35312; Parts and attachments for tracklaying and contractors' off-highway wheel tractors, 35313; Integrated tractor shovel loaders, 35317.
3541	Gear cutting and finishing machines, 35413.
3562	Roller bearings, complete, 35622.
3571	Computing and related machines, including cash registers, 35711 and 35712

(*continued*)

NOTES TO TABLE C-2 (*concluded*)

3611	Integrating instruments, electrical, 36111.
3612	Power and distribution transformers, 36122; Power regulators, boosters, and reactors, other transformers, and transformer parts, 36123.
3613	Circuit breakers, 36132; Fuses and fuse equipment, 36134.
3621	Land transportation motors, generators, and control equipment, 36213.
3634	Electric razors and dry shavers, 36342.[a]
3661	Telephone switching and switchboard equipment, 36611;[a] Other telephone and telegraph (wire) apparatus equipment and components, 36612.
3694	Battery-charging generators, 36942; Cranking motors, 36943; Spark plugs, 36944.[a]
3717	Passenger cars, knocked down or assembled, 37171; Truck tractor, truck chassis, and trucks (chassis of own manufacture), 37172; motor coaches (except trolley buses) and fire department equipment (chassis of own manufacture), 37173.
3721	Complete personal, commercial transport and utility-type aircraft, 37212 and 37213.
3722	Aircraft engines for U.S. military customers and all missile engines and aircraft engines for other than U.S. military customers, 37221 and 37222.
3731	Self-propelled ships, nonmilitary, new construction, 37313.
3741	Locomotive, railroad services and switching types, 37411; Other new locomotives, 37412; Parts for locomotives and rebuilt locomotives, 37413.
3742	Passenger train cars, new, 37421.[a]
3821	Motor vehicle instruments except electric, 38214.
3861	Photographic sensitized film and plates, 38615; Sensitized photographic paper and cloth, silver halide type, 38616.
3871	Watches with domestic movements and parts for all clocks and watches, 38715.
3982	Linoleum, 39821; Asphalt-felt-base and supporting plastic floor covering, 39822.
3999	Coin-operated amusement machines, 39992.

Source: U.S. Congress, Senate, *Concentration Ratios in American Industry, 1958*, 87th Cong., 2d Sess., Government Printing Office, Washington, 1962, Part I, Tables 4 and 5; U.S. Department of Commerce, Office of Business Economics, *Survey of Current Business*, XLII (July 1962), Table 7, p. 11.

[a] No concentration ratio is provided, but data indicate substantial concentration.

[b] Estimate based on data which include considerable duplication; value of shipments is not provided. This estimate is required for subsequent allocation of value added by manufacture.

[c] No data are provided, and estimates are not possible as necessary information has been withheld to avoid disclosing figures for individual companies.

income contributions from the highly concentrated product lines were allocated in two steps. A ratio (of the value of shipments of the heavily concentrated products to the value of shipments of all products in the primary four-digit industry group) was used to apportion value added by manufacturing to the heavily concentrated *product lines*, and the final apportionment of national income was achieved in the same manner as with the heavily concentrated *industries*. These computations are found in Tables C-1 through C-8; the results are described below.

Also, in 1958 the industry concentration data were presented on a 1945 SIC basis, whereas the product concentration data were presented on the

TABLE C-3

Basic Data for Manufacturing Industries with Concentration Ratios of 2/3 or Larger in 1954 and 1958, by Major Industry Group

	SIC	Value Added for Concentrated Industries as Per Cent of Total Value Added		Per Cent of National Income Originating in Concentrated Industries	
		1954	1958	1954	1958
Food and kindred products	20	10.219	7.118	0.269	0.182
Tobacco manufactures	21	73.405	79.717	0.165	0.191
Textile mill products	22	2.308	3.939	0.029	0.042
Lumber and wood products, except furniture	24		0.255		0.002
Paper and allied products	26	0.555	0.873	0.006	0.009
Chemicals and allied products	28	25.674	19.044	0.537	0.411
Rubber products	30	51.143	50.009	0.235	0.245
Leather and leather products	31	2.132	1.948	0.009	0.007
Stone, clay, and glass products	32	18.616	9.890	0.194	0.099
Primary metal industries	33	10.467	10.774	0.266	0.267
Fabricated metal products	34	7.807	8.037	0.175	0.168
Machinery, except electrical	35	13.358	17.896	0.431	0.517
Electrical machinery, equipment, and supplies	36	17.680	18.043	0.367	0.390
Transportation equipment	37	46.017	44.961	1.851	0.870
Miscellaneous manufacturing industries	39	1.993	2.034	0.014	0.014
Total manufactures				4.548	3.414

The following industries (with SIC) include products represented in the above major industry group data:

20 Cereal breakfast food, 2043; Flour mixes, 2045; Biscuit and crackers,[a] 2052; Cane-sugar refining, 2062; Chocolate and cocoa products, 2072; Chewing gum, 2073; Leavening compounds, 2091; Corn wet milling, 2094.

21 Cigarettes, 2111.

22 Finishing wool textiles,[b] 2216; Thread mills,[b] 2223; Hard-surfaced floor coverings, 2274; Wool-felt hats and hat bodies, 2282.

24 Excelsior mills,[b] 2425; Cigar boxes,[b,c] 2443.

26 Pulp goods, pressed and molded, 2694.

28 Sulfuric acid, 2811; Alkalies and chlorine,[a] 2812; Cyclic (coal-tar) crudes, 2821; Synthetic fibers, 2825; Explosives, 2826; Medicinal chemicals, including botanicals,[a] 2833; Soap and glycerin, 2841; Inorganic color pigments, 2852; Hardwood distillation, 2861; Softwood distillation, 2862; Linseed oil mills, 2882; Vegetable oil mills, n.e.c.,[b] 2884; Fatty acids, 2887; Essential oils,[b] 2892; Carbon black, 2895; Compressed and liquefied gases, 2896; Salt, 2898.

30 Tires and inner tubes, 3011; Rubber footwear,[a] 3021; Reclaimed rubber, 3031.

31 Industrial leather belting, 3121.

(*continued*)

NOTES TO TABLE C-3 (*concluded*)

32   Flat glass, 3211; Pressed and blown glass,[a] 3229; Gypsum products, 3272.
33   Electrometallurgical products, 3313; Primary copper, 3331; Primary lead,[c] 3332; Primary aluminum,[c] 3334; Primary nonferrous metals, n.e.c.,[a] 3339; Aluminum rolling and drawing, 3352.
34   Tin cans and other tinware, 3411; Files,[c] 3424; Safes and vaults, 3492; Metal foil,[a] 3497.
35   Steam engines and turbines, 3511; Tractors, 3521; Mechanical stokers, 3568; Computing and related machines, 3571; Typewriters, 3572; Domestic laundry equipment, 3581; Sewing machines,[c] 3583; Vacuum cleaners,[b] 3584.
36   Carbon and graphite equipment, 3612; Transformers, 3615; Electric lamps (bulbs), 3651; Phonograph records, 3663; Telephone and telegraph equipment, 3664; Primary batteries, 3692.
37   Motor vehicles and parts, 3717; Aircraft propellers, 3723; Locomotives and parts, 3741.
39   Organs, 3932; Piano and organ parts, 3933; Cork products, 3982; Matches,[a] 3983; Tobacco pipes,[b] 3996.

Source: *U.S. Income and Output, a Supplement to the Survey of Current Business, 1958*, Table I-10, pp. 130–131; *Survey of Current Business*, XLII (July 1962), Table 7, p. 11; *Concentration in American Industry: 1954*, Table 42; *Concentration Ratios in American Industry, 1958*, Part I, Tables 2 and 7 (Part 2); *Census of Manufactures: 1954*, Vol. I; *Summary Statistics*, Chapter III, Table 1.

  [a] 1954 only.
  [b] 1958 only.
  [c] Concentration ratio in 1958 withheld to avoid disclosure for individual companies, but data indicate sufficiently high concentration for inclusion in this table.

newest 1957 SIC basis. However, by tracing the SIC changes, the data in Table C-6 have been placed on the same basis as the industry data in Tables C-3 and C-4.

Manufacturing industries contributed 24.73 per cent of national income in 1939, 30.17 per cent in 1954, and 28.26 per cent in 1958. This increase occurred mainly at the expense of the agriculture, mining, and transportation sectors, which showed relatively large declines, and to a lesser extent at the expense of the finance and communications sectors, whose share of national income declined slightly during this period. The increased importance of the manufacturing sector was accompanied by an increased importance of highly concentrated manufacturing industries and product lines. In 1939 these highly concentrated industries accounted for 6.7 per cent of national income, while in 1954 and 1958 they accounted for 9.5 and 8.6 per cent, respectively. Detailed figures are presented in Table C-8. These estimates include all *industries* with concentration ratios of 1/2 or over and also *products* with concentration ratios of 3/4 or more. Nutter considered only products valued at $10 million or more; these 1939 figures are adopted in this study. However, the post-1939 products were selected without regard to a minimum total value; consequently, some highly concentrated products have been included despite values under $10 million. In addition, the products data

TABLE C-4

Basic Data for Manufacturing Industries with Concentration Ratios of 1/2 to 2/3 in 1954 and 1958, by Major Industry Group

		Value Added for Concentrated Industries as Per Cent of Total Value Added		Per Cent of National Income Originating in Concentrated Industries	
	SIC	1954	1958	1954	1958
Food and kindred products	20	9.112	11.137	0.240	0.284
Tobacco manufactures	21	8.677	20.283	0.022	0.048
Textile mill products	22	3.489	1.872	0.044	0.020
Apparel and related products	23	0.405	2.002	0.005	0.024
Lumber and wood products, except furniture	24	0.384	0.196	0.004	0.001
Furniture and fixtures	25	2.208	4.033	0.011	0.019
Paper and allied products	26	1.624	1.351	0.018	0.015
Chemicals and allied products	28	19.091	22.605	0.399	0.488
Products of petroleum and coal	29	15.375	1.067	0.188	0.011
Rubber products	30		6.362		0.031
Stone, clay, and glass products	32	32.042	35.822	0.334	0.358
Primary metal industries	33	57.439	54.268	1.463	1.345
Fabricated metal products	34	2.784	2.737	0.062	0.057
Machinery, except electrical	35	6.593	5.422	0.213	0.157
Electrical machinery, equipment, and supplies	36	31.272	14.449	0.649	0.312
Transportation equipment	37	12.968	36.378	0.522	1.215
Instruments and related products	38	52.369	42.557	0.337	0.274
Miscellaneous manufacturing industries	39	5.729	9.371	0.041	0.066
Total				4.552	4.725

The following industries (with SIC) include products represented in the above major industry group data:

20 Concentrated milk, 2023; Special dairy products, 2025; Cured fish, 2032; Biscuits and crackers,[b] 2052; Beet sugar, 2063; Malt,[a] 2083; Distilled liquor, 2085; Shortening and cooking oils,[a] 2092; Margarine,[b] 2093; Flavorings, 2095.

21 Cigars,[b] 2121; Chewing and smoking tobacco, 2131.

22 Scouring and combing plants, 2211; Thread mills,[a] 2223; Knit glove mills, 2255; Knitting mills, n.e.c.,[a] 2259; Fur-felt hats and hat bodies, 2281; Straw hats, 2283; Hatters' fur, 2284.

23 Work shirts, 2328; Suspenders and garters, 2383; Trimming and art goods,[b] 2396.

24 Excelsior mills,[a] 2425; Rattan and willow ware, 2442.

25 Household furniture, n.e.c.,[a] 2519; Professional furniture,[b] 2532; Window shades, 2562; Furniture and fixtures, n.e.c.,[a] 2599.

(*continued*)

NOTES TO TABLE C-4 (*concluded*)

26 Fiber cans, tubes, drums, etc., 2674.
28 Alkalies and chlorine,[b] 2812; Intermediate and organic colors, 2822; Synthetic rubber, 2824; Organic chemicals, n.e.c., 2829; Medicinal chemicals, including botanicals,[b] 2833; Gum naval stores, 2863; Tanning and dying materials,[b] 2865; Vegetable oil mills, n.e.c.,[a] 2884; Printing ink, 2891; Essential oils,[a] 2892.
29 Beehive coke ovens,[a] 2931; Byproduct coke ovens,[a] 2932; Petroleum and coal products, n.e.c., 2999.
30 Rubber footwear,[b] 3021.
32 Glass containers, 3221; Pressed and blown glass, n.e.c.,[b] 3229; Products of purchased glass,[a] 3231; Vitreous plumbing fixtures, 3261; Vitreous-china food utensils, 3262; China decorating for the trade, 3265; Mineral wool, 3275; Abrasive products, 3291; Asbestos products, 3292; Nonclay refractories, 3297.
33 Blast furnaces,[a] 3311; Steel works and rolling mills, 3312;[a] Blast furnaces and steel mills,[b] 3312; Malleable iron foundries,[a] 3322; Primary zinc, 3333; Primary non-ferrous metals, n.e.c.,[b] 3339; Copper rolling and drawing,[a] 3351; Rolling and drawing, n.e.c.,[a] 3359.
34 Cutlery,[b] 3421; Hand saws and saw blades,[a] 3425; Metal barrels, drums, and pails,[a] 3491; Steel springs,[a] 3493; Collapsible tubes, 3496; Metal foil,[b] 3497.
35 Elevators and escalators, 3562; Industrial trucks and tractors, 3565; Scales and balances,[a] 3576; Laundry and dry-cleaning machinery, 3582; Vacuum cleaners,[a] 3584; Measuring and dispensing pumps, 3586; Ball and roller bearings, 3593.
36 Motors and generators,[a] 3614; Electrical appliances,[a] 3621; Engine electrical equipment, 3641; Electronic tubes, 3662; Communication equipment, n.e.c.,[a] 3669; Storage batteries, 3691; X-ray and therapeutic apparatus, 3693.
37 Truck trailers, 3715; Aircraft,[b] 3721; Aircraft engines, 3722; Railroad and street cars, 3742; Motorcycles and bicycles, 3751.
38 Scientific instruments,[a] 3811; Optical instruments and lenses,[a] 3831; Surgical appliances and supplies,[b] 3842; Ophthalmic goods, 3851; Photographic equipment, 3861; Watchcases, 3872.[b]
39 Silverware and plated ware, 3914; Pianos, 3931; Pens and mechanical pencils, 3951; Lead pencils and crayons,[b] 3952; Matches,[b] 3983; Fireworks and pyrotechnics, 3985; Tobacco pipes,[a] 3996; Soda fountain and bar equipment, 3997.
Source: The same as those for Table C-3.
[a] 1954 only.   [b] 1958 only.

have not been corrected for the post-1939 price changes. For these two reasons, the post-1939 estimates are slightly higher than warranted on a strictly comparable basis.

In 1939, the 54 industries with concentration ratios of 2/3 or larger accounted for roughly 16 per cent of manufacturing output and 3.8 per cent of national income; these industries constituted about 19 per cent of all manufacturing industries. In 1954, 64 industries, or 14 per cent of the manufacturing industries, accounted for approximately 15 per cent of manufacturing output and 4.5 per cent of national income. In 1958, 64 similarly concentrated industries, or 12 per cent of the total, provided 14 per cent of manufacturing output and 3.4 per cent of national income.

In 1939, the 42 industries with concentration ratios of 1/2 to 2/3 constituted about 15 per cent of manufacturing industries and accounted for 5 per cent of manufacturing output and 1.3 per cent of national income. In 1954, 81 similarly concentrated industries, or 18 per cent of manufacturing industries, accounted for 15 per cent of manufacture and 4.6 per cent of national income. For 1958, 73 manufacturing industries with similar concentration

TABLE C-5

Basic Data for Manufacturing Industries Classified as Monopolistic but Not among Those with Concentration Ratios of 1/2 or Larger in 1954 and 1958, by Major Industry Group

	SIC[a]	Value Added for Monopolistic Industries as Per Cent of Total Value Added		Per Cent of National Income Originating in Monopolistic Industries	
		1954	1958	1954	1958
Food and kindred products	20	15.907	16.364	0.419	0.418
Printing and publishing	27	34.228	31.895	0.523	0.496
Petroleum and coal products	29	73.621	84.057	0.901	0.841
Electrical machinery	36	14.722	18.160	0.305	0.392
Total				2.148	2.147

The following industries (with SIC) include products represented in the above major industry group data:
20   Ice cream and ices, 2024; Bread and related products, 2051.
27   Newspapers, 2711.
29   Petroleum refining, 2911.
36   Electric measuring instruments, 3613;[b] Electric control apparatus, 3616;[c] Electric industrial apparatus, 3619;[d] Insulated wire and cable, 3631.[e]

Source: *U.S. Income and Output, A Supplement to the Survey of Current Business, 1958,* Table I-10; *Survey of Current Business,* XLII (July 1962), Table 7, p. 11; *Census of Manufactures: 1954; Concentration Ratios in American Industry, 1958,* Part I, Table 2, pp. 10-42, Table 7, pp. 386–451.

[a] The 1945 SIC code groupings are used to maintain comparability with other industry tables for 1958. Unless otherwise indicated by footnotes, the 1954 and 1958 SIC numbers and classifications remained unchanged.

[b] Excludes SIC 36131, included elsewhere. SIC 36132 and SIC 36133 provide $274,063,000 or 78.9 per cent of the $347,154,000 value of shipments in the SIC 3613 product class group in 1954. In 1958 these establishments were reclassified in SIC 3611. These data exclude SIC 36111, included elsewhere. SIC 36112, SIC 36113, and SIC 36110 provide $498,846,000 or 84.9 per cent of the $587,755,000 value of shipments in the SIC 3611 product class group.

[c] In 1958 these establishments were reclassified into the new SIC 3613 and SIC 3622.

[d] In 1958 these establishments were reclassified to form about 50 per cent of SIC 3629 and about 25 per cent of SIC 3567.

[e] Excludes SIC 36311, included elsewhere. SIC 36312 provides the remaining $778,322,000 or 75.8 per cent of the $1,026,695,000 in the SIC 3631 product class group. In 1958 these establishments were reclassified to provide about 65 per cent of SIC 3357.

TABLE C-6

Basic Data for Manufactured Products with Concentration Ratios of 3/4 or Larger in 1954 and 1958 Not Included among Industries in Tables C-3 and C-4, by Major Industry Group

	SIC[a]	Value Added for Concentrated Products as Per Cent of Total Value Added		Per Cent of National Income Originating in Concentrated Products	
		1954	1958	1954	1958
Food and kindred products	20	1.635	1.143	0.043	0.029
Textile mill products	22	0.662	0.196	0.008	0.002
Apparel and related products	23	0.992	1.111	0.013	0.013
Paper and allied products	26	3.208	7.085	0.036	0.076
Printing and publishing	27		1.155		0.018
Chemicals and allied products	28	6.739	7.599	0.141	0.164
Stone, clay, and glass products	32	0.081		0.001	
Primary metal industries	33	0.087	0.313	0.002	0.008
Fabricated metal products	34	3.187	2.892	0.071	0.061
Machinery, except electrical	35	1.667	0.840	0.054	0.024
Electrical machinery	36	2.323	2.734	0.048	0.059
Transportation equipment	37		1.682		0.033
Instruments and related products	38	1.301	3.010	0.008	0.019
Miscellaneous manufactures	39	0.196		0.001	
Total				0.426	0.506

The following industries (with SIC) include products represented in the above major industry group data:

20 Canned specialties, 2032;[e] Canned fruits and vegetables, 2033;[b] Food preparations, n.e.c., 2099.[d]

22 Wool carpets, rugs, 2211;[b] Wool fabrics and related products, 2231.[e]

23 House furnishings, n.e.c., 2392;[b] Trimmings and stitchings, 2398.[e]

26 Pulp mills, 2611;[b] Paper coating and glazing, 2641;[d] Sanitary food containers, 2654;[e] Building paper and board mills, 2661.[e]

27 Books, publishing and printing, 2731.[e]

28 Inorganic chemicals, n.e.c., 2819;[d] Plastic materials, 2823;[b] Plastic materials, 2821;[e] Soap and other detergents, 2841;[e] Cleaning and polishing products, 2842;[b] Toilet preparations, 2844;[e] Toilet preparations, 2893.[b]

32 Minerals: ground or treated, 3295.[b]

33 Secondary nonferrous metals, 3341;[e] Wire drawing, 3392.[b]

34 Cutlery, 3421;[b] Hardware, n.e.c., 3429;[d] Boilershop products, 3443;[d] Metal stampings, 3461;[e] Metal stampings, 3463.[b]

35 Internal combustion engines, 3519;[d] Metal-cutting machine tools, 3541;[e] Metal-working machinery, 3542;[b] Office and store machinery, 3579;[b] Refrigeration machinery, 3585;[b] Miscellaneous products, n.e.c., 3999.[e]

(continued)

NOTES TO TABLE C-6 (*concluded*)

36 Electric measuring instruments, 3611;[c] Switchgear and switchboards, 3613;[c] Electric measuring chart, 3613;[b] Motors and generators, 3621;[c] Insulated wire and cable, 3631;[b] Electric housewear and fans, 3634;[c] Electrical products, n.e.c., 3699.[b]
37 Ship building and repairing, 3731.[c]
38 Mechanical measuring instruments, 3821;[b] Surgical appliances and supplies, 3842;[b] Watches and clocks, 3871;[d] Mechanical measuring devices, 3821.[c]
39 Miscellaneous products, n.e.c., 3999.[b]

Source: The same as those for Tables C-1 and C-2.

[a] The SIC listed is the product identification used in Tables C-1 and C-2. The 1958 products have been grouped by 1954 major industry groups in order to maintain comparability with the industry concentration data for 1958.

[b] 1954 only.

[c] 1958 only.

[d] The same industry name and SIC number were used in both 1954 and 1958.

TABLE C-7

Basic Data for Concentrated Products and Industries in Tables C-3 through C-6, Classified as Competitive in 1954 and 1958, by Major Industry Group

	SIC	Value Added for Competitive Industries as Per Cent of Total Value Added		Per Cent of National Income Originating in Competitive Industries	
		1954	1958	1954	1958
Food and kindred products	20	0.882	0.815	0.023	0.021
Paper and allied products	26	1.246		0.014	
Chemicals and allied products	28	0.225	0.108	0.005	0.002
Rubber products	30	5.622	6.362	0.026	0.031
Stone, clay, and glass products	32	0.947	0.872	0.010	0.010
Machinery, except electrical	35	1.685	1.602	0.054	0.046
Total				0.132	0.110

The following industries (with SIC) include products represented in the above major industry group data:
20 Cured fish, 2032.
26 Pulp,[a] 2611.
28 Vegetable oil mills, n.e.c., 2884.
30 Rubber footwear, 3021.
32 Vitreous-china food utensils, 3262.
35 Typewriters, 3572; Sewing machines, 3583.

Source: U.S. Bureau of the Census, *U.S. Commodity Exports and Imports as Related to Output, 1958,* Government Printing Office, Washington, 1962; Tables C-3 through C-6.

[a] Only part of industry omitted.

ratios, or 17 per cent of these industries, provided 16 per cent of manufacturing output and 4.7 per cent of national income.

In 1939, the 121 census products showing concentration ratios of at least 3/4 accounted for 2.9 per cent of national income and about 12 per cent of manufacturing output, while in 1954 the 141 products with this ratio accounted for 4.4 per cent of national income and 14 per cent of industrial production. In 1958, the 130 similarly concentrated census products represented 15 per cent of manufacturing output and 3.4 per cent of national income.

These figures indicate concentrations of domestic manufacturing output, but they do not measure the extent of effective monopoly in the domestic economy. The reason is that concentration is a structural phenomenon, while effective monopoly is far more behavioral in nature. Clearly, the procedures applicable to a structural study are not equally suited to a behavioral study. However, measures of concentration can be used as the basis of a measure of effective monopoly.[2] Effective manufacturing monopolies include the highly concentrated industries and products *plus* other industries believed to be effectively monopolistic, while highly concentrated industries are excluded if grounds exist for denying their effectively monopolistic nature.

MANUFACTURING INDUSTRIES WITH CONCENTRATION RATIOS UNDER 50 PER CENT

The newspaper industry has been included in the monopolistic sector because of the growth of newspaper chains, a decrease in the number of newspapers, and the decline of multipaper communities. These trends, which have reduced local market competition, have been depicted in data presented by T. J. Kreps.[3] In 1958 there were 1,762 cities with daily newspapers, but only 76 of these cities had competing dailies. Competitive dailies did not exist in 14 states, and competitive Sunday papers were absent from 30 states. The number of daily newspapers has shown a steady decline since 1916, even though daily circulation has more than doubled. Similarly, noncompetitive trends are shown by data for newspaper chains, which have been increasing in numbers and scope. It is estimated that about 40 per cent of newspaper circulation was "noncompetitive" from other newspapers in 1958. The decline in number of newspapers can be attributed to such basic and valid conditions as capital requirements, operating inefficiencies, and greatly increased interindustry competition; all of these are described in Kreps' study of the newspaper industry. Because local monopoly is a feature of newspaper publishing and because oligopoly or oligopsony characterizes related industries and activities, the newspaper industry has been classified as effectively monopolistic.

TABLE C-8

Percentage of National Income Originating in All Manufacturing Industries 1954, and 1958

	Industries with		
	2/3 or Larger		
	1939[a]	1954[b]	1958[b]
Food and kindred products	0.31	0.269	0.182
Tobacco products	0.27	0.165	0.191
Textile products	0.02	0.029	0.042
Apparel and related products	0.00	0.000	0.000
Furniture and lumber (combined)	0.02	0.000	0.002
Paper and allied products	0.00	0.006	0.009
Printing and publishing	0.00	0.000	0.000
Chemicals and allied products	0.39	0.537	0.411
Petroleum and coal products	0.00	0.000	0.000
Rubber products	0.24	0.235	0.245
Leather and leather goods	0.00	0.009	0.007
Stone, clay, and glass	0.08	0.194	0.099
Iron and steel, and nonferrous, and instruments and miscellaneous (combined)	0.50	0.455	0.449
Electrical machinery	0.00	0.367	0.390
Machinery, except electrical	0.27	0.431	0.517
Automobile and transportation equipment (combined)	1.74	1.851	0.870
Total	3.84	4.548	3.414

	Subtotals for Concentrated Industries and Products		
	1939	1954	1958
Food and kindred products	0.78	0.552	0.495
Tobacco products	0.32	0.187	0.239
Textile products	0.20	0.081	0.064
Apparel and related products	0.01	0.018	0.037
Furniture and lumber (combined)	0.11	0.015	0.022
Paper and allied products	0.03	0.060	0.100
Printing and publishing	0.00	0.000	0.018
Chemicals and allied products	0.52	1.077	1.063
Petroleum and coal products	0.00	0.188	0.011
Rubber products	0.24	0.235	0.276
Leather and leather goods	0.02	0.009	0.007
Stone, clay, and glass	0.21	0.529	0.457
Iron and steel, and nonferrous, and instruments and miscellaneous (combined)	1.72	2.440	2.279
Electrical machinery	0.02	1.064	0.761
Machinery, except electrical	0.51	0.698	0.698
Automobile and transportation equipment (combined)	2.21	2.373	2.118
Total	6.73	9.526	8.645

Concentration Ratios of			Products, not Included in Concentrated Industries, with Concentration Ratios of 3/4 or Larger		
1/2 to 2/3					
1939[a]	1954[c]	1958[c]	1939[a]	1954[d]	1958[d]
0.41	0.240	0.284	0.06	0.043	0.029
0.05	0.022	0.048	0.00	0.000	0.000
0.12	0.044	0.020	0.06	0.008	0.002
0.01	0.005	0.024	0.00	0.013	0.013
0.03	0.015	0.020	0.06	0.000	0.000
0.01	0.018	0.015	0.02	0.036	0.076
0.00	0.000	0.000	0.00	0.000	0.018
0.03	0.399	0.488	0.10	0.141	0.164
0.00	0.188	0.011	0.00	0.000	0.000
0.00	0.000	0.031	0.00	0.000	0.000
0.00	0.000	0.000	0.02	0.000	0.000
0.09	0.334	0.358	0.04	0.001	0.000
0.34	1.903	1.742	0.88	0.082	0.088
0.00	0.649	0.312	0.02	0.048	0.059
0.04	0.213	0.157	0.20	0.054	0.024
0.18	0.522	1.215	0.12	0.000	0.033
1.31	4.552	4.725	1.58	0.426	0.506

Industries with Concentration Ratios Smaller than 1/2 but Classified as Effectively Monopolistic			Industries Classified as Competitive but Included with Concentrated Industries		
1939[a]	1954[e]	1958[e]	1939[a]	1954[f]	1958[f]
0.80	0.419	0.418	0.00	0.023	0.021
0.00	0.000	0.000	0.00	0.000	0.000
0.04	0.000	0.000	0.01	0.000	0.000
0.00	0.000	0.000	0.00	0.000	0.000
0.18	0.000	0.000	0.02	0.000	0.000
0.02	0.000	0.000	0.01	0.014	0.000
0.00	0.523	0.496	0.00	0.000	0.000
0.31	0.000	0.000	0.00	0.005	0.002
0.51	0.901	0.841	0.00	0.000	0.000
0.00	0.000	0.000	0.22	0.026	0.031
0.00	0.000	0.000	0.01	0.000	0.000
0.46	0.000	0.000	0.00	0.010	0.010
0.17	0.000	0.000	0.00	0.000	0.000
0.91	0.305	0.392	0.00	0.054	0.046
0.01	0.000	0.000	0.08	0.000	0.000
0.00	0.000	0.000	0.00	0.000	0.000
3.41	2.148	2.147	0.35	0.132	0.110

(continued)

TABLE C-8 (*concluded*)

	Total Percentage of National Income Originating in Effectively Monopolistic Industries		
	1939	1954	1958
Food and kindred products	1.58	0.948	0.892
Tobacco products	0.32	0.187	0.239
Textile products	0.23	0.081	0.064
Apparel and related products	0.01	0.018	0.037
Furniture and lumber (combined)	0.27	0.015	0.022
Paper and allied products	0.04	0.046	0.100
Printing and publishing	0.00	0.523	0.514
Chemicals and allied products	0.83	1.072	1.061
Petroleum and coal products	0.51	1.089	0.852
Rubber products	0.02	0.209	0.245
Leather and leather goods	0.01	0.009	0.007
Stone, clay, and glass	0.67	0.519	0.447
Iron and steel, and nonferrous, and instruments and miscellaneous (combined)	1.89	2.440	2.279
Electrical machinery	0.93	1.315	1.107
Machinery, except electrical	0.44	0.698	0.698
Automobile and transportation equipment (combined)	2.04	2.373	2.118
Total	9.79	11.542	10.682

[a] Table A-10. [b] Table C-3. [c] Table C-4. [d] Table C-6. [e] Table C-5. [f] Table C-7.

Several electrical equipment industries have been included in the effectively monopolistic sector on the basis of Federal grand jury price-fixing indictments and either guilty or *nolo contendre* pleas at the subsequent trials. Because the issues have received such wide publicity, they are not discussed in detail here. Collusive behavior characterizes the following industries: electrical measuring instruments; electric control apparatus; electrical industrial apparatus, n.e.c.; and insulated wire and cable.

The effectively monopolistic sector embraces industries in which the relevant market dimensions are local or regional rather than national. Concentrations ratios for these smaller markets have been prepared for only a limited number of industries. For 1958 only, the census has provided concentration ratios for states and regions for 29 manufacturing industries.[4] Analysis of these limited statistics indicated that, of the 782 different state-wide concentration ratios provided, only 13 were less than the industry's national concentration ratio, whereas 289 were 21–40 points higher and 305 were higher by more than 40 points.[5] In the manufacturing industries the national classifications were directed first at the structural aspects and then at the behavioral qualifications. Several criteria have been established for the very limited number of industries which are characterized by regional markets and for which structural data are available. These standards are concentrated local markets structures typified by heavy concentration, and a trend toward local market noncompetitive behavior or evidence of scale or other barriers to entry into the local markets. On these bases, the following industries have been included in the effectively monopolistic sector: ice cream and ices, bread and related products, and petroleum refining.

HEAVILY CONCENTRATED INDUSTRIES AND PRODUCTS OMITTED FROM ESTIMATES OF EFFECTIVE MONOPOLY

To this point, we have attempted to identify effectively monopolistic industries through an examination of both structural and behavioral characteristics. Structural considerations are utilized because of a strong presumption that, other things being equal, the more concentrated industries provide less room for the free play of competitive forces, and their markets are more likely to be characterized by noncompetitive behavior and characteristics.

Since the structural measures are applied only with the realization that structural monopoly may accompany workably competitive behavior, we must identify the industries in which this occurs. For the 1939 period, the work of the Temporary National Economic Committee was most valuable in providing this identification, but no comparable subsequent industrial examination is available for the late 1950's. Thus, other means must be used to identify the industries in which concentrated conditions are tempered by competitive factors. Since alternative supply sources are a prime factor in reducing monopoly power, available import statistics have been used to indicate the extent to which imports meet domestic demand. Table C-7 lists the major groups in which heavily concentrated industries or products are believed to be characterized by workably competitive conditions because of high levels of imports. The level at which imports become a significant factor will vary by industry, and although the importance of potential imports cannot be measured directly, some minimum level must be set if a detailed industry analysis is precluded. For present purposes it was presumed that a sufficiently high level of imports to effect a competitive classification existed when imports totaled 25 per cent of domestic production.

II. CLASSIFICATION OF TRADE AND SERVICE INDUSTRIES BY COMPETITIVE STATUS

The wholesale trade sector provided $21,442 million or 5.84 per cent of the national income in 1958. This sector included eight industry groups and many manufacturing industries. The 1942 SIC includes an establishment in the wholesale trade category if:

... its predominant activity is marketing merchandise to retailers, to industrial users, or to other wholesalers, whether or not it is engaged in auxiliary manufacturing or retailing. For the most part, establishments are classified as a whole and no attempt is made to split the business. The volume of business done by wholesale establishments does not represent the total wholesale business as it excludes wholesaling done by establishments classified elsewhere, but, on the other hand, it includes the retailing, manufacturing, and other incidental activities of wholesalers.[1]

In 1958, $39,694 million, or 10.80 per cent of national income, originated in retail trade. This division included 15 major industry groups and many different industries. The retail trade category included:

... establishments engaged in selling merchandise for personal or household consumption and rendering services incidental to the sale of goods. For the purposes of this classification, it is necessary to include each establishment as a particular group on the basis of the activity from which it derives the principal part of its gross receipts. Many retail establishments sell such a wide range of articles that they cannot be classified on the basis of commodity sales; in such cases, establishments are classified on the basis of usual trade designations such as drug stores, cigar stores, etc.[2]

In 1958, $41,908 million, or 11.41 per cent of the national income, originated in the service industries. The service division covered 11 industry sectors within the 1942 major service industry groups. This division, broadly defined, included:

... heterogeneous group of establishments which are primarily engaged in rendering services to individuals and business establishments and which are not classified in other industrial divisions. Included in this division are hotels and other lodging places; establishments providing personal, business, repair, and amusement services; medical, legal, engineering, and other professional services; educational institutions; non-profit membership organizations; and other miscellaneous services, as distinguished from trade establishments, whose principal source of revenue is the sale of merchandise.[3]

Despite their heterogeneous functions and coverage, these three divisions—wholesale trade, retail trade, and service—are considered together, because they share many common characteristics. Also, market characteristics considered relevant to the trade and service industries are minor in the evaluation of other industries.

Examination of employment size data for trade and service industries in 1958 reveals no large national concentration. However, many state and regional monopolies are indicated when a 1/2 or greater concentration ratio is applied as the test. Although these concentration ratios indicate many regional monopolies, these industries may encounter effective competition from other industries. Trade and service industries should be classified on the basis of noncompetitive behavior rather than local concentration ratios; this reflects the predominantly local orientation of companies in these industries as contrasted to others. The trade and service industries generally involve local markets, which include only a few companies. The limited number of intraindustry competitors may be economically justified for any of several reasons, including lack of demand, interindustry competition, or interproduct competition. The essential factor, for purposes of this report, is whether concentration of economic power, or monopolistic profits and power, exists in any of these industries; if such conditions exist, the industry cannot be assigned to the competitive sector.

Nutter classified only one service (motion pictures) and two trade (milk distribution and new automobile distribution) industries as monopolistic for the year 1939. The motion picture industry was so classified because of the dominance of eight leading producers in the production and distribution of movies. This dominance was achieved and maintained through a policy of co-operation and noncompetitive behavior. Milk distribution was considered monopolistic, because the industry was dominated by a few large companies which frequently exercised control over price, employees, and producers (including the milk-marketing co-operatives). Milk prices showed remarkable stability, and distributor profits frequently were very large. In addition, the distributors' margins generally were greater and more stable than the prices received by the farmers. Local health regulations, high weight and bulk relative to value, and specialized transportation requirements limit the geographic milk supply. Wilcox thought that new car marketing was noncompetitive, although used car stocks, trade-in allowances, and other competitive factors were present. These were less important than the domination by the manufacturers[4] of distributor franchises, operations, and policies.

The problem of classifying the service and trade industries in 1958 is difficult to resolve satisfactorily. It is beyond the scope of this study to analyze separately each industry or even each industry group. The procedure selected involves the examination of each industry classified as monopolistic in 1939 and also of those industries which economists and "expert" witnesses considered noncompetitive. This approach permits coverage of the most significant trade and service industries, and its flexibility allows a later examination of individual industries or industry groups.

In 1958, the motion picture industry seemed to be competitive, especially as compared to 1939. A 1948 antitrust decision divorced the production units and theaters of previously integrated companies; the same decision placed film rental practices on a more competitive basis.[5] Furthermore, television has grown to provide a new and successfully competitive medium of entertainment. The movie producers have met this challenge in several ways: by filming television shows, by selling old films for televised showing, and by investing in television stations and networks. This last strategy seems particularly ominous for future competition. The movie industry also has encountered new competition from foreign movies and from independent domestic producers. Consequently, the movie industry can be included in the competitive classification for 1958.

The dominance of a few large milk companies, which has been described, has been the subject of complaints in a number of local markets. Also, the use of secret subsidiary "fighting companies," local regulations that limit the regional supply, rebates, and other practices have limited competition in many local milk distribution markets. Several states prohibit price discrimination by milk dealers, and milk farmers have been permitted to form co-operative selling organizations to secure higher prices through more effective bargaining power. Many of the industry's local and regional markets are characterized by similar patterns of restrictive behavior. In 1955, the Borden-Bowman dairy conspiracy in Chicago was described by A. McDonald of the National Farmers Union, who admitted however, that he knew of no similar cases in other localities.[6] The fluid milk and other products have had a long history of regional noncompetitive behavior at the processing and distribution levels. In the latter part of the 1950's, milk price-fixing indictments and suits were filed in several fluid milk markets, including Miami and Key West, Florida; Reno and Las Vegas, Nevada; Washington, D.C.; Baltimore, Maryland; Toledo, Ohio; and Minneapolis, Minnesota.[7] In addition, several Congressional hearings have been devoted to the competitive problems of small business in the dairy industries.[8] The increased number of acquisitions by the few large national dairy food manufacturers have provided them with an important degree of vertical integration and local market leverage. Because this form of continued growth may permit this small number of national dairy companies to increase economic domination of local markets, these acquisitions have been of growing concern. Between January 1, 1951, and mid-1953, Borden acquired 10 dairy companies and Foremost Dairy Company acquired 43 companies by merger.

Willard F. Mueller and others have testified regarding the degree of concentration and the forms of competition in the dairy industries. The decline of independent fluid milk distributors and the importance of mergers in the development of the large milk companies also were discussed. Mueller maintained that about 12 fluid milk distributors exist in an average city, with the largest distributor supplying about 34 per cent of the market compared to about 75 per cent for the four largest companies. Although he denied that returns to scale existed for large plants and companies, he admitted that a company's power in any one local market is increased by its product and geographical scope. Mueller also stated that the ice cream industry was more concentrated locally than even the fluid milk industry.[9]

The post-1939 share of national income originating in the fluid milk distribution sector has been derived in a manner comparable to the 1939 estimates, except that the later estimates are based on pounds of milk sold for fluid milk and cream consumption, whereas the product of per capita consumption and population were used in 1939. The retail price margin is used as an estimate of national income originating in fluid milk retail distribution, and the farmer's price as an estimate of national income originating

TABLE C-9
Basic Data for the Retailing of New Automobiles: 1939, 1954, and 1958

	Wholesale Sales[a] (thousand dollars)	Ratio of Retail Margin to Wholesale Sales[b]	Value Added in Retailing[c] (thousand dollars)	Percentage of National Income Originating in Retailing[d]
1939	2,260,018	0.250	565,004	0.78
1939		0.218[e]	492,684	0.68
1939[f]	2,318,857	0.218	505,511	0.70
1954	9,878,113	0.250	2,469,528	0.82
1954		0.218[e]	2,153,429	0.71
1958	12,873,140	0.250	3,218,285	0.88
1958		0.218[e]	2,806,345	0.76

[a] Automobile Manufacturers' Association, *Automobile Facts and Figures*, Automobile Manufacturers' Association, Detroit, 1961; passenger cars, motor trucks, and buses are included, but this source provides 1939 data that differs from the sales values used by Nutter.
[b] See Appendices A and C for methodology.
[c] Wholesale value times ratio of retail margin to wholesale sales.
[d] Value added in retailing divided by the total national income.
[e] Ratio used by Nutter on the basis of a 17.9 per cent retail margin.
[f] Table A-14.

in fluid milk production. Although this procedure was designed to maintain comparability with estimates for 1939, it appears that these estimates may be too large. Fluid milk distribution was included in the *1954 Census of Manufactures*, where it provided just over 10 per cent of value added in the food and kindred products major industry group. The national income estimate for fluid milk distribution bears a much larger relation to national income in the food groups; hence it appears that the data utilized for methodological comparability in this paper may not be properly representative. This industry was classified as noncompetitive in 1954 and 1958.

New automobile distribution still is concentrated, but manufacturers no longer enjoy the absolute powers which they exercised in the 1930's. The Automobile Dealer-Franchise Act of 1956 was designed to restore some

balance in the manufacturer-distributor relationship by requiring the manufacturer to act in good faith in dealing with distributors.[10] More important,
perhaps, there seems to be a trend toward separation or at least limitation of
the duties and obligations which manufacturers can require from their
distributors. Since 1939, the distributor's compulsory use of a manufacturer's credit subsidiary has been prohibited. The restrictive use of only
those parts and accessories produced by the automobile manufacturer also
seems to have been limited by the courts; the Standard Stations decision
appears to prohibit certain distributor restrictions.[11] However, other
noncompetitive practices, such as sales quotas, may still exist to restrict
competition. The use of exclusive dealerships that limit a distributor to
only one line of new cars seems to have facilitated the dominance of the
manufacturers. The most important type of competition has involved
distributors of different makes of cars, but even here the use of common
used-car lists is a restrictive factor. Also, manufacturers' policies and
opinions would seem to have a strong influence on the type of competition
between distributors of different makes of cars. The industry is classified as
noncompetitive in 1958.

The automobile distributors' contribution to the national income cannot
be estimated in a manner comparable to that for 1939. Neither data for the
retail value of automobile sales nor reliable data of retail sales margins are
any longer published. However, one industry source believes the markup is
between 15 and 20 per cent of the wholesale price.[12] Catalogue, or recom-
mended selling, prices are not useful in determining retail margins, because
these prices are seldom, if ever, adhered to by the dealers. The 20 per cent
markup has been used to determine the amount of national income originating in the automobile distribution industry.

By 1958, many of the service and trade industries experienced some degree
of increased concentration. The increased concentration and its competitive
effects have been most noticeable in the food-retailing industry, which has
been studied by the FTC.[13] The large retailing units have expanded greatly
in importance, and vertical integration as well as horizontal expansion has
promoted the decline of the small retail units. In 1948, retail food stores
independent of any chain, co-operative, or other wholesale or retail organization accounted for 50 per cent of total food sales, but this share declined to
about 30 per cent in 1958. From 1939 to 1958, the total number of food
stores declined from 560,000 to 225,000; from 1948 to 1958, the number of
single-unit food stores declined by 90,000–100,000 units. However, the
growth of large food retailers on a regional and national level has not been
accompanied by a monopolistic power in the food markets. It appears that
effective competition has resulted between corporate chains and the voluntary
associations of retailers that have developed.

III. CLASSIFICATION OF GOVERNMENT AND REST-OF-WORLD CONTRIBUTIONS TO NATIONAL INCOME

In 1958, $46,618 million, or 12.69 per cent, of national income was provided by state, local, and federal governments and the enterprises operated by these governments. These enterprises, listed in the 1954 *National Income Supplement to the Survey of Current Business*, include federal agencies of a regulatory as well as a business nature, such as the Public Housing Administration. The state and local enterprises include ". . . state workmen's compensation funds, and business-type activities involving significant amounts and accounted for as enterprises, mainly alcoholic beverage monopolies; water, electric, gas and transit systems, housing authorities; highway toll facilities; ports and terminals; and airports."[1] The entire government division has been included in the government classification.

In 1958, the rest of the world contributed $2,099 million, or 0.57 per cent, of our national income. This division includes ". . . foreign countries, United States territories and possessions, and international organizations."[2] This division has not been included in any sector, primarily for lack of knowledge of the specific contributors involved.

IV. CLASSIFICATION OF FINANCE, INSURANCE, AND REAL ESTATE INDUSTRIES BY COMPETITIVE STATUS

In 1958, national income originating in the finance, insurance, and real estate division totaled $37,555 million, or 10.22 per cent, of the total. Differences between industrial classifications used in the national income accounts and those listed in the SIC manual are described in the following discussion of the relevant industry groups. However, two additional problems exist in the classification of this industrial division.

The first problem is the evaluation of public regulatory agencies, their powers, practices, and effectiveness. The finance, insurance, and real estate industries generally operate under greater restrictions than most other industries. However, the mere presence of government regulatory agencies does not automatically provide a unique pattern of competitive industry behavior. The type of regulation, its form, and its effect on business practices must be evaluated when determining the industry's competitive status.

A second problem is comparing the relative importance of interindustry versus intraindustry competition. Evaluation of intraindustry competition requires a determination of the relevant market(s), while evaluation of interindustry competition involves greater analysis of product competition as well as the relevant market patterns.

These two problems arise in the classification of other industrial divisions, and both are complicated by an absence of adequate data to allocate each industry on a comparable basis. These data were available in the mining division, where value added in mining enabled the allocation of national income to each contributing industry. In the finance, insurance, and real estate division the lack of data precludes an allocation of national income, even on the industry group basis. For this reason, the classifications are presented on a major industry group basis along with an explanation of reasonable alternative classifications. Separate industry allocations of national income are avoided, because no common means are available for such a statistical allocation.

In 1939 only the banking and insurance carriers were included in the monopoly classification; all others were classified as competitive. In 1958, three major industry groups have been included in the workably competitive class: security and commodity brokers, dealers, and exchanges; insurance agents and combination offices; and real estate. The others have been considered concentrated and effectively monopolistic. No industry groups are allocated to the government-regulated class, but it is likely that individual industries should be so classified. Although some degree of government regulation (entry, practices, etc.) affects all of these sectors, the prevalence and results of this regulation vary greatly by industry.

SECURITY AND COMMODITY BROKERS, DEALERS, AND EXCHANGES

The security and commodity brokers, dealers, and exchanges industry group includes "offices of brokers, dealers, and exchanges dealing in securities and commodities; concerns furnishing quotation services; and offices of investment advisers." In 1958, this group accounted for $638 million, or 1.7 per cent, of all national income originating in the finance, insurance, and real estate division. The securities group seems to be composed primarily of nonmonopolistic industries. Those industries that might be considered as concentrated or structurally monopolistic are under the jurisdiction of the Federal Securities and Exchange Commission. In general, this major industry group is regulated by various state and federal authorities. However, the large number of profit-seeking companies indicates strong rivalry for much of the available business, and the group has been included in the competitive sector.

INSURANCE AGENTS, BROKERS, AND SERVICES

Insurance agents, brokers, and services are a separate major industry group but are not subclassified by group or industry. This sector includes:

... agents primarily representing one or more insurance carriers, or brokers not representing any particular carriers, primarily engaged as independent contractors in the sale or placement of insurance contracts with carriers, but not employees of the insurance carriers they represent. This industry also includes independent organizations concerned with insurance services.[1]

Agents generally are regulated by, or registered with, a state agency. The industry members have no monopoly power, but their prices are determined by the companies whose policies they police. In 1958, $2,181 million, or 5.8 per cent, of the finance division's contribution to national income originated in this sector.

REAL ESTATE

The real estate sector includes establishments of owners, lessors, and lessees of real property, as well as developers, agents, brokers, etc. This major industry group includes six groups with a total of 23 industries. The available data for the SIC real estate industries do not permit statistical analysis of concentration. The real estate group provided 63.5 per cent of the $37,555 million in national income that originated in the finance division in 1958; this share amounted to $23,835 million. No data are offered to support this classification, because no census or other compilations have been found to measure and allocate the amount of national income originating in each of the real estate industries. However, the SIC descriptions of each industry indicate that the markets and participants are so numerous that competition probably typifies industrial behavior in the real estate sector.

BANKING

The 1942 SIC and the 1957 banking major industry groups include the following five component industry groups: Federal Reserve banks, commercial and stock savings banks, trust companies not engaged in deposit banking, and establishments performing functions closely related to banking. However, the 1942 SIC also includes "inactive banks and banks in the process of liquidation," which are not included in the 1957 SIC. The contribution of this group to national income is believed to be negligible. In 1958, $5,929 million in national income, or 15.8 per cent of the finance division's contributions, originated in the banking sector.

The Federal Reserve banking group includes the twelve Federal Reserve banks and their branches. Because the Federal Reserve is a quasi-governmental agency, it should be classified in the government category. However, no means seem to be available for allocating the share of national income originating in this industry group.

The commercial banking industry has experienced many changes during the past 40 years, and the decline of independent banks is shown in Table C-10. The great decline during the first part of this period reflects the

TABLE C-10
Number of Commercial Banks

1920	30,444
1929	24,287
1934	15,518
1940	14,477
1949	14,156
1959	13,444

Source: U.S. Congress, House, 86th Cong., 2nd Sess., Select Committee on Small Business, Staff Report, *Banking Concentration and Small Business*, Committee print, 1960, p. 3.

TABLE C-11
Percentage Share of Bank Deposits Held by 100 Largest Commercial Banks, 1929–1959

1929	41.9
1934	53.6
1940	45.7
1949	45.5
1959	45.6

Source: *Banking Concentration and Small Business*, p. 3.

excessive number of banks and the more severe form of competition, which together drove many weak banks out of existence.

The traditional dominance of a relatively few large banks is reflected in other commercial bank statistics. In 1959, over half of the domestic commercial banks had less than $10 million in deposits and over 30 per cent had less than $2 million. In contrast, several banks had assets of several billion dollars.[2] The large variations in size reflect the differences in relevant market characteristics, such as customer types and services offered. The data in Table C-11 show the concentration of deposits held by the largest commercial banks. Normally, these relatively small market shares would indicate a definite lack of concentration in this industry. However, the data and the conclusion presuppose a national market, and this assumption is questionable in reference to the commercial banking industry.

At least three types of bank market areas can be identified; all are determined in the spatial sense by the community area served and in the functional sense by the type of customer served. The national market is the largest and includes all domestic banks. Previous data illustrated the lack of concentration in the national market, but the national market concept has a limited applicability. Only a relatively few customers have the credit rating or financial needs to tap the national market. Similarly, only a few banks are sufficiently large to service correspondents or customers of national standing. The national market affects only indirectly the vast number of domestic commercial banks and customers.

The local markets, which include most banks and bank customers, are the direct contrast, in scope and number size, of the national market. Local market banks are limited by size to meeting the needs of local depositors and customers and are insignificant factors for national banking purposes.

TABLE C-12

Percentage of Total Assets Owned by Largest Banks in Principal Financial Centers: 1955

	4 Largest Banks	2 Largest Banks	Largest Bank
New York	60	41.8	22.0
Providence	98	93.2	57.7
Pittsburgh	87	79.2	61.0
Minneapolis	87	76.0	39.7
Cleveland	97	72.3	74.7
Boston	83	71.6	52.2
Chicago	84	66.9	34.1
Detroit	90	65.9	46.5
Dallas	84	64.9	32.8
Atlanta	92	63.9	33.2
Richmond	84	55.9	33.2
Kansas City	75	53.7	34.3
St. Louis	68	53.5	28.0
Baltimore	77	44.9	24.0
Philadelphia	69	44.6	24.7
Washington	60	43.0	26.3

Source: U.S. Congress, Senate, *Corporate Mergers and Acquisitions*, 85th Cong., 1st Sess., 1957, Senate Report No. 132, p. 66.

The local banks service a customer whose credit need is small, whose credit rating is highest at the local level, and whose direct financial interests are centered on local activities. Concentration ratios generally are high on a local market basis, even for the major financial centers; this is illustrated by Table C-12.

A third intermediate regional market was described by D. A. Alhadeff in his study of the California banking system.[3] This regional market would include banks too small for the national market but sufficiently large to serve customers with a credit rating and needs that exceed local levels, although falling short of national standing. No concentration data are available for regional markets, which are defined with even less precision than the local and national markets.

Mergers have increased sharply in recent years, but their competitive effect is uncertain. Intraregional mergers generally affect only the regional market, while local mergers may increase competition by eliminating weak banks and strengthening the survivors. The development of branch banking and bank holding companies has further concentrated the assets and policies of commercial banks. The Select Committee on Small Business of the U.S. House of Representatives has found a tendency for concentration to be the highest in states where branch banking is least restricted.[4] Nationally, bank branches increased from 1934 to 1959 although the number of banks declined. Branch banking and bank holding company development in the United States has depended on state law, and the prevalence of each system varies with the banking statutes of the individual state. Mergers, branches, and holding companies all tend to further reduce the degree of independence in our commercial banking system. Dr. Alhadeff concluded that the numerical decline in banks has increased their effective concentration only in the intermediate market, although some operating efficiencies also occurred as a result of the increased development of branches and bank holding companies.[5]

Little price competition exists in commercial banking markets, but competition in other areas is allegedly quite strong. Other financial industries also tend to avoid price competition. This avoidance may be quite understandable in the light of past history when bank standards were lower, but the absence is regretted as limiting consumer opportunities. Some new strong competition has developed from other financial institutions, but these are specialized and do not offer the broad range of services—especially demand deposit services—found in commercial banking. These other financial industries include institutions specializing in one or a very limited number of services. Even commercial banks specialize in providing money through demand deposits in short-term business credit. The other financial institutions are regulated by specialized agencies and are classified into industries according to their financial characteristics. All of these industries compete with commercial banks to some extent, but their individual efforts seem far less important than the sum of their interindustry competition. Also, the commercial banks provide less competition to each of these industries than the industries offer to the commercial banks. At one time, the commercial banks were the prime source of several types of financial services now provided primarily by nonbanking institutions. The commercial banks still offer many services also provided by the other, specialized groups, but generally do so under less favorable conditions and regulations than the specialized institutions. Interest rates, reserve requirements, taxation, and other items seem to be regulated more severely in commercial banking than in other financial industries.

Most specialized institutions are included in the nonbanking major industry groups, but savings banks are included as a separate industry group within the banking major industry group. Mutual savings banks are found primarily in the eastern states. At the end of 1959, there were 518 mutual savings banks with 448 branches and $38,527 million in assets, compared to $273,309 million in assets for all 14,004 commercial and stock savings banks, nondeposit trust companies, and mutual savings banks.[6] For mutual savings banks entry and operations seem to be even more strictly regulated than for commercial banks, and maximum limits are generally set on the size of each depositor's account. Savings bank investments generally are limited to only the highest class of bonds and mortgages. Similarly, savings banks are restricted in the type of loans they can grant; these restrictions are presumably imposed in the interests of safety. Although savings banks compete for savings funds with other financial institutions, this competition has become intense only in recent years. Because the entry and operations of mutual savings banks are so highly restricted, the group is considered as noncompetitive during the period studied.

Trust companies not engaged in deposit banking constitute another banking group; this includes companies engaged in the fiduciary business but not regularly engaged in deposit banking. There were 55 such banks with 10 branches at the end of 1959. These 55 banks had assets of $210 million, or less than 0.1 per cent of all bank and trust company assets.[7]

The final banking industry group includes establishments performing functions closely related to banking: foreign exchange establishments, check cashing agencies and currency exchanges, and institutions carrying on other specialized banking functions.

INSURANCE CARRIERS

In 1958, insurance carriers originated $4,128 million, or 11.0 per cent, of all national income originating in the finance, insurance, and real estate division industry groups. Twenty insurance industries are listed in the 1942 SIC classification. The life insurance group seems to be the most important of the industry groups, each of which represents a separate type of insurance. Insurance companies are regulated almost entirely by state agencies, and much of the relevant literature is devoted to the rate bureaus and risk-sharing pools that, together with lax state regulation, have served for the elimination of price competition.

Although concentration of life insurance companies declined between 1940 and 1960, the concentration ratios still are higher than for other insurance groups. Table C-13 indicates data for two measures of life insurance concentration. Between the end of 1940 and the end of 1960, the number of life insurance companies increased from 444 to 1,455.

TABLE C-13

Year-End Share of Insurance in Force for Legal Reserve
Life Companies, and Share of Assets Held by Largest
Companies (per cent)

	Share of Insurance in Force		
	1940	1950	1960
10 largest companies	68.3	62.7	56.9
50 largest companies	90.4	86.2	81.1
100 largest companies	95.8	93.5	89.7

	Share of Assets Held by Largest Companies			
	1940	1950	1955	1960
Largest company	17.6	n.a.	15.2	n.a
4 largest companies	49.9	n.a.	44.8	n.a.
10 largest companies	70.2	66.8	64.6	61.8
50 largest companies	n.a.	91.4	n.a.	87.3

n.a. Not available.
    Source: Simon Whitney, *Antitrust Policies*, The Twentieth
Century Fund, New York, 1958, Vol. II, p. 379; Institute of Life
Insurance, mimeograph release.

Simon Whitney concluded that only slight price competition exists in the
life insurance industry; however, nonprice competition appears very important. Because the life insurance companies use common mortality
tables, life insurance policies have been sold at "approximately the identical
rate without the need of formal cooperation."[8] The life insurance industry
has developed without the formal rate-making and risk-sharing bureaus
found in other insurance industries; this reportedly reflects the common
mortality tables, uniform costs, and identical methods for computing reserves.

Until the South-Eastern Underwriters decision by the United States
Supreme Court in June 1944, insurance was not considered as commerce, and
insurance industries were exempt from federal and most state antitrust prose-
cution.[9] Only a minimum of state regulation existed, and state enforcement of rate regulation was erratic. After the 1944 decision, Congress
provided three years for the states to enact regulatory insurance laws and
authorized federal regulation only in the absence of state laws. Because
most states were averse to unrestrained rate competition, the pre-existing
private rate-making bureaus were retained but placed under tighter supervision.

The development of model statutes provided a common framework for
state laws. Ocean marine insurance was exempt from regulation because of

foreign competition and the individual requirements for each policy. Fire, marine, surety, and casualty rates were the primary ones covered, because these generally had been set by the private rate-making bureaus. Accident and health policy rates have been covered in many subsequent state statutes. The new regulatory laws provided for rate deviation by bureau members, and, according to Whitney, the increased frequency and significance of these deviations may provide strong price competition. Nonprice competition apparently has been a significant factor in many of these insurance industries.

TABLE C-14

Share of Year-End Assets Held by Largest
Fire and Casualty Companies (per cent)

	1939	1955
Largest company	2.6	2.9
4 largest companies	9.4	9.4
10 largest companies	18.1	19.6

Source; Whitney, *Antitrust Policies*, Vol. II, p. 379

Whitney's apparent satisfaction with the post-1944 insurance developments is based on the abolition of several collusive price-setting practices and the value of generally co-operative rate-making that avoids the previously experienced dangers of unregulated rate competition.[10]

A rather different attitude is apparent in the reports of the Senate Antitrust and Monopoly Subcommittee of the Committee on the Judiciary, which cover several aspects of the insurance industry.[11] These reports have been critical of developments in the fire and casualty, as well as marine and aviation insurance industries. The subcommittee has indicated general dissatisfaction with the lack of rate competition, the discriminatory tactics of reinsurance groups, and the inadequacy of state regulation.

Although the fire and casualty insurance groups are much less concentrated (Table C-14) than the life insurance groups, the subcommittee reported that excessive state rate regulation had discouraged the development of a competitive fire and casualty insurance industry. Witnesses indicated the greater competitiveness of the newer casualty (especially automotive insurance) over fire and allied lines. Inland marine insurance was found to reflect the same factors as fire insurance. The subcommittee complained that private rate bureaus were too often accepted as of paramount importance by state authorities. Also, it was reported that many rating organizations, advisory bureaus, and important insurance companies maintained mutual officers and directors. The rating bureaus frequently are used in active efforts to defeat rate competition by complaining as aggrieved parties in court or administrative proceedings and thus placing heavy burdens of litigation on rate cutters.

Domestic marine insurance is underwritten mainly by one syndicate of chiefly American companies, although one firm serves as the primary writer. This underwriting pool arrangement spreads the risks among many companies and presumably permits small firms to write insurance that otherwise would exceed their means. The American Hull Insurance Syndicate reportedly writes about 95 per cent of all hull business in the United States.[12] This concentration is the monopoly power that raises the domestic rates over those obtainable overseas. Restricted syndicate membership and enforced identical rates have resulted from this monopoly which prevents companies from competing on a price basis for new policies. Aviation insurance was considered to be as noncompetitive as the ocean marine industry, and for similar reasons.

Health insurance was written by 819 companies in 1960, compared to 514 in 1952; the number of monoline companies offering health insurance rose from 25 to 38. Over half of the insurers were life insurance companies. In addition, 78 Blue Cross plans, 69 Blue Shield plans, and more than 300 independent plans offered health protection in 1960.[13] Concentration data are not available, but in recent years many of these plans were required to secure state approval of their rates.

Data have not been obtained for accident, surety, title, and other insurance companies. The national income accounts are based on the 1942 SIC, which included in the insurance major industry group all those financial-obligation insurance companies that insured banks and similar associations; data are not included for these companies. Because data cannot be derived for each of the SIC industries, national income is not allocated by insurance industry groups. It is believed that the significant portions of the insurance sector have been characterized by noncompetitive behavior.

FINANCE, N.E.C.

The finance, n.e.c., sector of the national income accounts includes four of the 1942 SIC major industry groups: credit agencies other than banks— long term; credit agencies other than banks—short term; investment trusts and companies and holding and investment-holding companies; and finance, n.e.c. In 1958, these four major industry groups contributed $844 million, or 2.2 per cent, of the national income originating in the finance, insurance, and real estate division and included 50 industries of many shades of competitive behavior. The classification of these industries requires the evaluation of both interindustry and intraindustry competition as well as of varying degrees of government regulation. No one set of data is available for use in apportioning the total national income produced by these industries. Consequently, a single classification must be applied to this catchall group, and it has been placed in the effectively monopolistic sector.

V. CLASSIFICATION OF CONTRACT CONSTRUCTION INDUSTRIES BY COMPETITIVE STATUS

The contract construction division of the national income accounts consists of major industry groups 16 and 17 of the 1942 SIC. These two construction groups include general contractors and special-trade contractors (subcontractors). The division includes only contractors and subcontractors who

TABLE C-15
Number of Contract Construction Companies

1939	199,400
1947	268,100
1954	416,700
1958	467,600

Source: U.S. Department of Commerce, Office of Business Economics, *Business Statistics*, Government Printing Office, Washington, 1959, p. 26.

perform on a contract basis for others. Those who perform these functions for their own account are included in the real estate division. The three broad types of construction work covered are building construction, engineering projects, and special-trade construction. In 1958, $19,870 million, or 5.41 per cent, of national income originated in this division, which includes six general contract and eighteen subcontract industries. The industries are analyzed on a division basis, because none of the available data yields a satisfactory breakdown.

In 1939 this division was classified as effectively monopolistic, because several elements combined to restrain the free course of trade. The dominance of a few large contractors appears not to have been a serious factor in the 1939 classification. Wilcox stated: "Competition in the construction industry in many urban areas has been restrained by the activities of dealers in the various building materials, by the operations of rings of subcontractors or, less frequently, general contractors and by the practices of trade unions."[1]

The data in Table C-15 indicate the increase in contract construction companies during the period studied. Some domestic concentration data published by *Architectural Forum* magazine include the value of new construction put into place for each of the 100 largest general building contractors.[2] The list of companies and the values of construction are limited to general building contract construction. All heavy construction is omitted from consideration, as is all construction for a company's own account; home builders reportedly provide most of the latter type of construction. The list's greatest defect is that many companies which failed to provide data are omitted even though they are likely to be larger than some of the companies included. However, their omission probably results in only minor percentage differences, since the 100 largest companies listed in 1958 accounted for $2.7 billion, or 6.5 per cent, of new general construction. This share of production is small on the national level, but it appears that local or regional markets may be the most appropriate outlets for some construction industries. If regional markets are to be considered, these large companies quite probably would assume increased relative importance.

In 1959, the residential construction industry market structure was found to be substantially competitive by Carl Brehm, who relied in part on a 1949 study by the Bureau of Labor Statistics; this study apparently was the most recent statistical investigation of the home building industry.[3] The industry's basic characteristics in 1958 are believed similar to those of 1949. Rather free entry with low capital requirements still exists, although the presence and effect of restrictive agreements (in materials and labor, by producers, unions, and subcontractors) are uncertain. Secondary boycotts, union shops, and other activities by organized labor have restricted the free adjustment of some facets of the construction industry. However, it would seem that collusion or other noncompetitive behavior in the supply of building materials should be considered in the appropriate trade sector. A monopolistic building-materials supply industry may restrict the contractor's freedom, but it does not normally result in monopolistic contracting power.

In 1949 the major markets accounted for 80 per cent of new housing. Each of these markets generally has a large number of commerical builders and provides a structure that makes an administered price almost impossible to enforce by a contractor's group. The BLS study included both contract construction and construction for the builder's own account, but the same factors are relevant to both groups. The small contractors generally are custom builders, while the larger builders are more concerned with housing developments and may not be included in the contract construction industry. The relative importance of both owner and part-time builders helps to prevent the large builders from restricting the market.

The relative breakdown of general contractors versus subcontractors is not known. However, the SIC descriptions indicate that the subcontractors may be so specialized that interindustry competition is erratic. It is not known what degree of intraindustry competition exists. Brehm mentioned that competitive bids for subcontracts may be rather infrequent, because the large contractors may rely on personal relationships to assign the subcontracts and will use the closed bids only as a periodic check that the prices are in line with those of other subcontractors.

VI. CLASSIFICATION OF AGRICULTURE, FORESTRIES, AND FISHERIES INDUSTRIES BY COMPETITIVE STATUS

In 1958, $18,338 million, or 4.99 per cent, of all national income originated in agriculture, forestries, and fisheries. This division includes the farming sector and the agricultural services, forestry, and fisheries sector. The former sector is comprised of six SIC major industry groups, while the latter covers almost all of three major industry groups.

Of all the industries in this division, Nutter designated only fluid milk production as monopolistic; Wilcox stated that fluid milk production was fundamentally cartelized, like contract construction. The same basic patterns exist today since the marketing organizations still are operating as the farmer's central milk-selling agency in many of the most important milk-marketing areas. Between 1939 and 1958, government participation increased steadily on both federal and state levels. By 1959 roughly 40 per cent of wholesale milk sales were transacted under 77 federal milk-marketing orders, with 186,000 farmers delivering 36 billion pounds of milk under these orders in 1958.[1] It is estimated that an additional 16 or 17 billion pounds are affected by milk laws in the 18 states that have some regulation over the price of fluid milk in intrastate commerce. Indirect effects of this regulation may be felt in still other milk sales. The fluid milk-producing industry still is considered noncompetitive, but for 1954 and 1958 it is included in the government-supervised rather than in the effectively monopolistic sector. The determination of national income originating by fluid milk producers in 1954 and 1958 is considered in the trade sector, where estimates also were derived for national income originating in the milk distribution industry of the trade sector.

It is believed that no other farm products are so widely affected by these special agricultural provisions. Many products are affected by government price support programs, but these programs do not have the monopolistic effects that are considered in this study. The farm industries traditionally have been composed of many small producers, none having control over the market. Despite the recent trend toward larger farming units, the increase

TABLE C-16

Basic Data for Production and Distribution of Fluid Milk: 1939, 1954,

	Fluid Use of Milk Sold by Farmers (million pounds)	Farm Price (cents per pound)
1939	33,056ᵉ	2.29
1939		
1954	47,526	4.77
1958	52,954	4.91

Source: U.S. Department of Agriculture, Agricultural Marketing Service, *The Dairy Situation;* production data from DS-210, May 1950, p. 56, and DS-277, April 1960, p. 20; price data from DS-276, February 1960, p. 22.

ᵃ Fluid milk times farm price.

ᵇ Fluid milk times retail margin.

ᶜ Value added in production divided by total national income.

in concentration has not been sufficiently large to warrant a noncompetitive designation.

VII. CLASSIFICATION OF TRANSPORTATION INDUSTRIES BY COMPETITIVE STATUS

The national income accounts include a transportation division subdivided into seven sectors, as compared to the SIC manual, which includes nine major industry groups within the transportation division. Despite the difference in subclassification, the transportation divisions of the two series are identical in scope. It is doubly difficult to classify the transportation industries by competitive status, because the analysis must allow for both interindustry and intraindustry competition. In transportation, unlike most other areas of industrial activity, interindustry competition is as important as intraindustry competition.

The seven transportation sectors originated $16,429 million, or about 4.47 per cent, of our 1958 national income, with over 41.5 per cent of this contribution provided by the railroad sector. The transportation division includes some of the largest as well as the smallest of domestic companies and both regulated and unregulated industries. Entry, operations, and rates of transportation industries are heavily regulated by state, local, and federal authorities. The economic regulatory agencies generally attempt to eliminate the alleged dangers of unrestricted competition that may result from large fixed investments or ease of entry into a transportation division. However, not all transportation companies are regulated, and exemptions from economic regulation have been granted in each of the transportation sectors. Private and 1958

Retail Margin (cents per pound)	Value Added (million dollars)		Percentage of National Income Originating in	
	Production[a]	Distribution[b]	Production[e]	Distribution[d]
3.07	757	1,015	1.04[f]	1.38
			0.96[f]	0.75[f]
5.50	2,267	2,616	0.75	0.86
6.33	2,600	3,352	0.71	0.91

[d] Value added in distribution divided by total national income.

[e] From DS-210 and probably higher than the level that would be comparable to data from DS-277.

[f] Table A-14. Differences from the preceding 1939 figures reflect differences in the data and methods used in the two studies.

carriers are always exempt from economic regulations, whereas most common carriers are strictly regulated and contract carriers are regulated to a lesser degree.

Although the railroads once possessed a decided monopolistic advantage in transportation, no mode of transportation now exercises a similarly dominant position. Of course, each form of transportation enjoys an advantage in particular types of service; these specialized advantages must exist for a transportation industry to develop. Competition between different modes of transportation stems from these advantages and is increased by the many jurisdictional authorities and by exemptions from regulation. According to E. Williams:

... Analysis of transportation markets under present conditions indicates a high degree of competition, although that competition is not of equal force for all types of traffic and, as between types of transportation, remains weak for some types of service. Over an increasing range of the business, however, the opportunity to substitute unregulated transportation is becoming the ultimate regulator of what common carriers can charge and of the character of service they must render if they desire to retain the traffic.[1]

The transportation function can often be performed by several modes and by two or more classes of service within each mode. Thus, the problem seems to involve a twofold analysis; one portion is an evaluation of each transportation sector, and the other is an evaluation of intermodal competition.

RAILROADS

The railroad sector includes all railroads that are regulated by the Interstate Commerce Commission: line-haul railroads and switching and terminal companies, as well as railway express services and sleeping and other passenger car services. The sector is identical to the railroad major industry group of the 1942 SIC, and in 1958 provided $6,824 million, or 41.5 per cent, of the national income originating in the transportation division. The total scope of the ICC regulation dictates that this industry be placed in the government-supervised sector. Aside from this regulation, the railroads engage in vigorous intraindustry nonprice competition with other modes of transportation. In recent years, mergers and joint action have characterized the industry, and it is likely that concentration will continue as a means of improving the financial and competitive status of the railroads.

LOCAL AND HIGHWAY PASSENGER TRANSPORTATION

The local and highway passenger transportation sector includes all of the 1942 SIC major industry groups 73 and 74 except for the fixed facilities for the highway passenger transportation industry group. This sector includes street, suburban, and interurban railways, local and nonlocal bus lines, taxicabs, and miscellaneous passenger transportation, n.e.c. Many of the companies operate with exclusive franchises granted by regulatory agencies. The excluded group represents the companies operating fixed facilities, such as passenger terminals, that are used by the companies doing the actual transportation; this group is included in the services to transportation sector, and most of its operations probably are regulated by local, state, or federal agencies. ICC-regulated railroads are excluded, but ICC-regulated bus lines are included in this sector. This sector does not include highway transportation that is a secondary aspect of other transportation companies and is not provided by a separate company. In 1958 this sector provided $1,430 million, or 8.7 per cent, of the national income originating in the transportation division. This sector includes some companies that are not common carriers, and whose rates or entry, or operating conditions, are not determined by statute; since their contribution to national income cannot be identified, but probably is minute, the entire section has been included in the government-supervised sector.

HIGHWAY FREIGHT TRANSPORTATION AND WAREHOUSING

The highway freight transportation and warehousing sector includes all of the major industry groups 75 and 79 of the 1942 SIC—local trucking, non-local common carrier and contract carriers, fixed freight-handling facilities, and various warehousing and storage industries. In 1958 this sector produced \$4,911 million, or 29.9 per cent, of the national income originating in the transportation division. Private trucking generally is local, but surveys indicate that, in 1955, 46.6 per cent of all truck ton-miles on main rural roads was provided by private trucking.[2] Private trucking is not a part of this industry sector, but it is an important competitive factor. Although most trucking firms are small, many are large, and the vast majority of trucking companies are state regulated. In 1958, there were 13,640 motor freight carriers regulated by the State of California, while the ICC regulated 15,510 common and 2,329 contract carriers at the end of 1957.[3] The trucking industry is characterized by ease of entry and doubtful returns to scale. Particular types of trucking are exempt from economic regulation. The industry has been classified as government supervised, even though a considerable portion (i.e., local carriers) would be classified as competitive because of lack of effective regulation, ease of entry, and the actual or potential use of private carriage. An important factor in this case is the influence of government regulation on the decision of many businesses to own or rent their own truck transportation or to hire a public or private carrier.

WATER TRANSPORTATION

The water transportation sector is identical to the 1942 SIC water transportation major industry group 76 except for the exclusion of industry group 766, services incidental to water transportation, which has been included in the services allied to transportation sector. In 1958 this sector provided \$949 million, or 5.8 per cent, of the national income originating in transportation. Five industry groups, comprised of 12 industries, are included in this sector. Ocean-borne transportation is a regulated industry group with an exemption from the antitrust laws which permits joint rate making through shipping conferences.

Coastline and intercoastal transportation by common and contract carriers is regulated by the Federal Maritime Board (commerce between the continental United States, Alaska, Hawaii, and foreign countries) and the Interstate Commerce Commission (domestic water commerce). However, the exceptions to this regulation seem so numerous that the ICC has estimated its jurisdiction as covering only about 10 per cent of domestic water commerce.[4] This complaint pertains also to the ICC's power to regulate two other water transportation industry groups, Great Lakes transportation and transportation on rivers and canals, both including companies and industries regulated by the ICC. The local water transportation industry group seems to include industries generally exempt from federal regulation. Most of the water transportation sector participants seem to be regulated in some degree, although the regulation generally is ineffective. The national income contribution could be prorated by tonnage or value of shipments, and each sector classified, but it seems best to include it in the supervised sector and to keep in mind the borderline nature of this general classification.

AIR TRANSPORTATION

The air transportation (common carrier) sector consists of one of the three SIC transportation industry groups. The other two groups are included in the services allied to transportation sector. These companies (both certificated and noncertificated) are devoted primarily to mail, express, freight, or passenger transportation by air. The other two industry groups are flying (except common carrier) and airports and flying fields. In 1958, the air transportation sector provided $994 million, or about 6 per cent, of the national income originating in transportation. The Civil Aeronautics Board has jurisdiction over those intrastate operations that are related to safety measures, but the states still have the power to regulate the intrastate economic aspects of the airlines. All routes, schedules, certificates, and exemptions are granted by the CAB. Because entry, service, and rates are so thoroughly regulated, the industry has been included in the government-supervised sector. However, this regulation has been criticized as having created a monopoly situation in which the airlines can set common rates to be approved by the regulators, who perpetuate this monopoly by obstructing the smaller airlines.[5] Private and contract service air operations are regulated by the CAB only on safety matters.

PIPELINE TRANSPORTATION

The pipeline transportation sector is identical to major industry group 78 of the 1942 SIC. It includes only companies engaged in the transportation of petroleum and of gasoline by pipeline for hire. In 1958 this industry provided $322 million, or 2.0 per cent, of the national income originating in the transportation sector. Nutter retained Wilcox's effectively monopolistic designation for the year 1939, because the degree of government regulation was believed to be nominal. The industry is classified in the government-supervised sector for 1958, primarily because a consent decree arising from a 1941 Justice Department suit has since limited the dividends payable to a shipper-owner by a pipeline to 7 per cent of the stockholder's share of the total valuation of the pipeline (not only the equity). The restriction seems to limit the chief benefit to a shipper-owner. Pipelines are more expensive than ocean tankers, and it would seem that in normal times independent shippers have at least one competitive mode of transportation available.

SERVICES ALLIED TO TRANSPORTATION

The services allied to transportation sector has SIC major industry group 80 as its basic counterpart, although it also includes those SIC industry groups omitted from the previous transportation sectors. These industries include companies and services that are essential for successful transportation but are not engaged in actual transportation. In 1958 this sector provided $999 million, or 6.1 per cent, of the national income originating in the transportation division. An industry breakdown indicates that industry 80 includes companies furnishing such services incidental to transportation as forwarding, packing and crating, arranging for transportation, stockyards, railroad car rentals, fixed facilities for highway passenger travel, piers and docks, stevedoring, canal operation, flying (excluding common carriers), airports, and flying fields. A detailed classification has not been attempted, because the varied and catchall nature of this group would require a detailed analysis of each industry. In addition, a common measure of comparison would be required in order to allocate national income on a proper basis. Because so many facets of government regulation affect these industries directly as well as indirectly, they have been classified, with the rest of the transportation division, as government-supervised.

Regulation of entry, services, and rates has been the basis of our domestic transportation network. The regulated transportation policy is designed ideally to achieve a controlled competition that respects the interests of both shippers and carriers. However, the policy has often involved conflicting programs. Entry has been drastically limited in the air and railroad industries. In 1940 a pronouncement of rate policy provided that no rates would be kept high simply to protect another form of transportation; this was reiterated in 1958. However, there is no base useful in determining transportation rates on a common cost basis. Only railroads and pipelines pay for the construction and maintenance of their own rights of ways; user costs for other forms of transportation often are partially covered by public authorities, thus enabling carriers utilizing these subsidized facilities to cover their total costs with a lower rate. An added complication is nonregulated trucking, which does not need ICC rate approval; this group includes exempt carriers, contract carriers, and private carriers. Also, some motor carriers have failed to register with the ICC as required.

Although many of the aforementioned industry sectors have local components, it seems necessary and advisable to consider interindustry

TABLE C-17
Distribution of Intercity Freight Ton-Miles (per cent)

	Steam and Electric Railroads	Motor Trucks	Oil Pipelines	Inland Waterways, Including Great Lakes	Air Carriers
1940	61.30	10.03	9.58	19.08	
1946	66.61	9.07	10.59	13.72	0.01
1954	49.50	19.09	15.94	15.50	0.03
1958	46.31	20.47	17.51	15.66	0.48

Source: U.S. Congress, Senate, 87 Cong., 1st Sess., Committee on Interstate and Foreign Commerce, Report No. 445, *National Transportation Policy*, Government Printing Office, Washington, p. 1961; U.S. Interstate Commerce Commission, *73rd Annual Report*, Government Printing Office, Washington, 1959, p. 11, for 1958 data.

competition on a nonlocal basis. The problem is similar to that experienced in the banking sector, where several markets apparently exist.

Table C-17 indicates the changing percentage pattern of intercity transportation as measured by ton-miles. It does not show shifts in revenue, which may be higher per ton-mile for trucks than for railroads, but the table indicates the relatively increasing popularity of nonrail means of freight transportation. Similar patterns are evident for intercity passenger transportation, as shown in Table C-18.

The interindustry competitive influences arise whenever rates are established or changed, and their effect can be seen in comparable transport data. Discussions of transportation policy devote considerable attention to this interindustry competition. Except for the broad government regulation, imperfect as it may be, the transportation division would be classified as workably competitive; the interindustry competition seems sufficient to preclude an effectively monopolistic designation. However, government regulation is so extensive that the division is included in the government-supervised classification.

TABLE C-18
Distribution of Intercity Passenger-Miles (million miles)

	Public Carriers				Private Vehicles			Total Intercity
	Rail	Air	Bus	Total	Auto	Air	Total	
1940	19,773	1,052	9,800	30,625	245,751	212	245,963	276,588
1947	39,921	6,081	23,948	69,950	273,958	980	273,938	343,888
1953	26,905	15,734	24,946	67,585	529,194	1,696	530,819	598,404
1959	17,522	29,976	22,530	70,028	663,685	2,800	666,485	736,513

Source: *National Transportation Policy*, p. 336, 1961.

VIII. CLASSIFICATION OF MINING INDUSTRIES BY COMPETITIVE STATUS

CLASSIFICATION PROCEDURE UTILIZED

Table C-19 presents the value added by mining and the amount of national income originating in each mining industry for 1954 and 1958. The industries are arranged by major industry groups as listed in the *Census of Minerals, 1954*. The national income originating in each such group is listed and apportioned by industry and the degree of competition existing in that industry. The apportionment of national income for each major industry group is based on value added in mining for each industry. In some instances, industry groups rather than industries are listed.

Flexible standards are necessary in classifying mining industries, since the available data are not uniform or equally comprehensive. Because concentration ratios are not available for each mining industry, the determination of competitiveness must often be based on an analysis of conditions in the industry. Where concentration ratios are available, a level of 1/2 or more for the four largest companies has been accepted as indicative of the industry's effective structural monopolization. Where concentration ratios are not available, industries are considered effectively competitive if no one producer or no limited group of producers accounts for a major share of total product output. Industries have been classified as effectively monopolistic where one or a few companies account for significant portions of the output or where a large captive market apparently has precluded the existence of a competitive commercial market. Allocations based on each industry's particular characteristics necessarily require flexible standards that vary with the industry examined. In 1954 the mining division provided $4,923 million, or 1.63 per cent, of national income. In 1958 the division originated $5,435 million, or 1.48 per cent, of national income.

METAL MINING

Iron Ore. Iron ore mining is classified as an effectively monopolistic industry. Iron ore mines are highly integrated with iron and steel producers by direct ownership of major mines and by large annual ore purchase commitments that often follow the same pattern from year to year. Integrated domestic iron and steel producers control between 70 and 80 per cent of the domestic iron-mining industry. Many of these domestic producers also have holdings in foreign iron ore mines, and imported ores account for about 25 per cent of domestic iron ore consumption.[1] In view of large

TABLE C-19
Basic Data for Mining Industries: 1954 and 1958

	Value Added in Mining		National Income (million dollars)			
	Thousand Dollars	Per Cent	Total	Monopolistic Sector	Competitive Sector	Government Sector
			1954			
Metal mining	1,075,519	100.000	766.0	661.9	78.9	25.2
Iron ores	435,668	40.508	310.3	310.3		
Copper ores	334,876	31.136	238.5			
Lead and zinc ores	107,409	9.987	76.5		76.5	
Gold and silver ores	35,354	3.287	25.2			25.2
Bauxite	12,827	1.193	9.1	9.1		
Ferro-alloys except vanadium	107,399	9.986	76.5	76.5		
Metal mining contract services	26,703	2.483	19.0	19.0		
Miscellaneous metal ores	15,283	1.421	10.9	8.5	2.4	
Anthracite mining	196,835	100.000	161.0		161.0	
Bituminous coal and lignite mining	1,418,384	100.000	1,133.0		1,133.0	
Crude petroleum and natural gas extraction	7,673,694	100.000	2,182.0		2,182.0	
Crude petroleum and natural gas	6,555,115	85.424	1,864.0		1,864.0	
Oil and gas field contract services	1,118,544	14.576	318.0		318.0	
Nonmetallic minerals (except fuels) mining	1,181,986	100.000	681.0	228.2	452.8	
Dimension stone	15,155	1.282	8.7		8.7	
Crushed and broken stone	337,611	28.563	194.5		194.5	
Sand and gravel	356,729	30.180	205.5		205.5	
Clay, ceramic, and refractory minerals	78,449	6.637	45.2	18.8	26.3	
Natural abrasives, except sand	3,681	0.311	2.1		2.1	
Chemical and fertilizer mineral mining	340,520	28.809	196.2	190.5	5.7	
Nonmetallic minerals (except fuels) contract services	4,884	0.413	2.8	2.8		
Miscellaneous non-metallic minerals (except fuels)	44,957	3.804	25.9	15.9	10.0	
Total	11,546,418		4,923.0	890.1	4,007.7	25.2

(*continued*)

TABLE C-19 (*concluded*)

	Value Added in Mining		National Income (million dollars)			
	Thousand Dollars	Per Cent	Total	Monopolistic Sector	Competitive Sector	Government Sector
			1958			
Metal mining	1,187,327	100.000	757.0	685.8	47.0	24.2
Iron ores	500,232	42.131	318.9	318.9		
Copper ores	266,485	22.444	169.9	169.9		
Lead and zinc ores	73,679	6.205	47.0		47.0	
Gold and silver ores	37,896	3.192	24.2			24.2
Bauxite	15,430	1.300	9.8	9.8		
Ferro-alloys except vanadium	74,255	6.254	47.3	47.3		
Metal mining contract services	22,862	1.926	14.6	14.6		
Miscellaneous metal ores	196,488	16.549	125.3	125.3		
Anthracite mining	164,489	100.000	146.0		146.0	
Bituminous coal and lignite mining	1,609,964	100.000	1,221.0		1,221.0	
Crude petroleum and natural gas extraction	9,035,289	100.000	2,561.0		2,561.0	
Crude petroleum and natural gas	7,927,502	87.739	2,247.0		2,247.0	
Oil and gas field contract services	1,107,787	12.261	314.0		314.0	
Nonmetallic minerals (except fuels) mining	1,683,904	100.000	751.0	176.4	574.4	
Dimension stone	67,131	3.987	29.9		29.9	
Crushed and broken stone	562,435	33.401	250.8		250.8	
Sand and gravel	498,864	29.566	222.0		222.0	
Clay, ceramic, and refractory minerals	128,954	7.658	57.5	35.6	21.9	
Natural abrasives, except sand[a]						
Chemical and fertilizer mineral mining	335,153	19.903	149.5	111.7	37.7	
Nonmetallic minerals (except fuels) contract services	6,217	0.369	2.8	2.8		
Miscellaneous non-metallic minerals (except fuels)	86,150	5.116	38.4	26.3	12.1	
Total	13,680,993		5,435.0	862.2	4,549.4	24.2

Source: U.S. Department of Commerce, Bureau of the Census, *Census of Minerals, 1954,* Vol. I; *Summary Volume,* Government Printing Office, Washington, Table 2, pp. A-6, A-7; *Census of Minerals, 1958,* Vol. I; *Summary Volume,* Table 2, pp. 1–8, 1–9; *A Supplement to the Survey of Current Business, 1958,* Table I-10, pp. 130–131; *Survey of Current Business,* XLII (July 1962), Table 7, p. 11.

[a] Included in miscellaneous minerals.

fluctuations in production, iron ore prices have been unusually stable, but free entry into the iron-mining industry apparently does not exist. In 1954 the six largest establishments produced an average value added in mining that was 243 times greater than that for the 16 smallest establishments. Whitney has stated that iron ore control ceased being a serious monopoly issue when the United States Steel Company began selling iron ore to its steel-producing competitors and when this company's share of domestic iron ore shipments began declining.[2] However, it appears that a large, competitive market does not exist. Hence, iron ore mining is classified as a concentrated and effectively noncompetitive industry.

Copper. Copper activity is largely controlled by four large, completely integrated companies. The two largest companies account for about 55 per cent of domestic copper ore output, and the third largest provides another 12 per cent; the six largest copper companies produce over 80 per cent of domestic copper ore. Similarly, the five largest mines provide about 52 per cent of domestic copper ore, while the 10 largest produce about 76 per cent.[3] Refined copper prices have fluctuated rather widely during this period. Efforts to stabilize copper supplies and prices have had only limited success because of strikes at copper-consuming manufacturing establishments, increased production by smaller producers, and the greater availability of scrap copper. Also, low-grade mines require high production to cover costs, and some countries need large sales because copper is their primary dollar or cash export. Most of the costs of finished copper allegedly reflect mining costs rather than, as with steel or aluminum, processing.[4] Copper imports generally provide over a third of the available copper supplies, but net imports fluctuate widely. Because the domestic mines are so concentrated and integrated, the copper-mining industry is included in the noncompetitive sector, despite the fluctuating prices.

Lead and Zinc. The lead and zinc ore mining industries are believed to be workably competitive. Although six mines provided over half of the lead ores in 1954, there are many domestic mining companies, plus significant quantities of imports and secondary supplies of the two metals. In 1958 the five largest producers supplied over half of all domestic lead ore, but domestic mining accounted for only 26 per cent of our total lead supply.[5] The availability of lead imports and secondary lead may largely determine the price of lead ore, and the custom smelters depend on imports for over a third of their ore and concentrates. Domestic lead mines have higher costs than foreign mines and cannot meet domestic demand, but lead and zinc import quotas were enacted in 1958. New domestic lead resources are not being discovered to replace the current mines, and many of the largest companies have lead mines in other countries.[6] About 40 per cent of our domestic lead comes from Missouri, where roughly 90 per cent of this portion is produced by the St. Joseph Lead Company's straight lead mines. Bunker Hill is "the major miner" in Idaho, which contributes 20–25 per cent of domestic lead ores; and the United States Smelting, Refining, and Mining Company is the major producer in Utah, where 15 per cent of the domestic lead ores is produced.[7] It was reported that the major producers also refine other producers' lead ores on a toll or custom basis;[8] this seems to be a common practice in many mining industries. Although lead and zinc are often derived from common ore, lead output is declining whereas zinc output seems to be holding its own; about 48 per cent of domestic lead ores consists of lead-zinc combinations. Average lead prices and deliveries of refined lead have both declined in recent years. Lead prices, normally quite steady, showed unusual activity in 1958 and 1959.

The structure of the zinc industry is similar to that of the lead industry. The eight largest zinc-mining companies provide over 75 per cent of domestic output, but in 1954–1958 only 48 per cent of our zinc supply was derived from domestic mine output.[9] The zinc extractors do not seem as concentrated as the lead miners. Although large integrated companies predominate, their importance may be regionally centered about their mines. In 1960 the three leading zinc mines produced 23 per cent of domestic zinc, while the six largest mines provided 37 per cent and the top 25 mines yielded 80 per cent of domestic zinc ores.[10] Zinc prices have fluctuated since 1946, but they seem to have changed less frequently in recent years. About 500 companies participate in various stages of the zinc extractive industry. Smelters have been the principal group hurt by zinc import quotas, which provide up to half of our domestic supplies.

Both the lead- and zinc-mining industries have been included in the competitive sector. This classification reflects the importance of imports and secondary metal supplies, as well as the apparent lack of excessive concentration of domestic mining activity.

Gold and Silver. In 1958 the two largest mines produced about half of domestic gold ore; the 25 largest mines accounted for 88 per cent of domestic gold production. One of the two largest mines was a lode gold mine, while the other produced gold as a by-product of copper mining.[11] Five mines supplied 47 per cent of our domestic output in 1960. Homestake is the major domestic gold producer; its straight gold mines provide 32 per cent of gold production compared to 43 per cent for all domestic straight gold mines. Mounting costs and constant prices have reduced the profits of major gold producers. Copper mines provide 32 per cent of domestic gold, placers provide 19 per cent, and the base metal mines provide the rest.

From 1939 to date, gold prices have been determined by the government, the largest purchaser.

The 25 largest silver-producing mines accounted for 85 per cent of domestic silver ore production.[12] About 60 per cent of our domestic silver is produced as a by-product. The largest single mine provides between one-sixth and one-seventh of all domestic silver production. Until recently, the government has supported its official silver price by selling its free silver reserves to increase the silver supply and maintain low silver prices. This practice has been halted because of the depletion of free silver reserves, and silver prices have been fluctuating. However, less than 30 per cent of American silver is derived from mines that are devoted primarily to producing silver. Copper mines and "complex ores" each provide a third, while the rest is produced from other ores and from placers. American Smelting and Refining Company (ASARCO) is the world's largest silver miner (7 per cent) on a combined domestic and foreign mine basis. As the largest refiner, ASARCO also refines 40 per cent of the world's silver; American Metal Climax is the second largest refiner. Because the government's price role is so important, these two industries have been included in the government-supervised sector.

Bauxite. Bauxite has been classified as an effectively monopolistic industry, although 80 per cent of our consumption is imported. Of the 12 companies mining bauxite in the United States, six are very small producers for specialty users. Six of 25 establishments provided just over 83 per cent of this industry's value added in mining in 1954.[13] The two leading domestic producers are Alcoa and Reynolds, both located in Arkansas, where 97 per cent of our domestic bauxite seems to originate in mines that are owned and controlled by the large domestic aluminum producers. The absence of an open market price in the United States has been attributed to the heavy captive production:

The price of bauxite sold on the open market is largely based on alumina content and impurities present. As most bauxite is either consumed by the mining companies and their affiliates or purchased under long-term contracts, average quoted prices are not a reflection of a strongly competitive market, but are largely nominal.[14]

Because vertical integration is so important and price competition is absent, bauxite has been included in the monopolistic sector. A free competitive market is not indicated by the aforementioned conditions.

Ferro-Alloy Ores except Vanadium. The ferro-alloy ores, except for the vanadium group, are considered effectively monopolistic. The Union Carbide Corporation reportedly is the largest domestic producer of ferro-alloys, other major producers being the Vanadium Corporation, Pittsburgh

Metallurgical, and Molybdenum Corporation.[15] Each of the ferro-alloy industries is examined separately.

Anaconda and Manganese, Inc., are the two largest domestic manganese producers, but the United States is the world's largest manganese importer, importing 85 per cent of its supply.[16] Nevada is the largest producing state, followed by Arizona with many small mines and by Montana, where Anaconda provides most of the output. Domestic ore price depends on import price, a third of which usually reflects ocean freight charges, but government stockpile contracts generally were provided at prices much higher than the market price. The *1960 Minerals Yearbook* describes published price quotations as nominal.[17] Transportation charges from the western producing states also are a limiting competitive factor. Bethlehem Steel Corporation, United States Steel Company, and Union Carbide Metals Corporation reportedly are the major producers of manganese ferroalloys and allegedly have the largest holdings in foreign mines.[18] Other manganese ore consumers also produce or import foreign ores. In view of these production and price conditions, it seems unlikely that a free competitive market exists here; the industry is classified as concentrated.

The United States is, by far, the world's largest producer of molybdenum. The American Metal Climax (AMC) Company, our largest producer, supplies ore from the only domestic mine operated primarily for molybdenum; the company provides about two-thirds of domestic output and has the largest known reserves. Kennicott Copper Company is the second largest producer, with roughly a third of AMC's output.[19] The United States exports molybdenum and provides about 85 per cent of the world's production. The price of molybdenum has remained stable for years at a time, and the only changes have been increases. AMC apparently determines the price. Data for ferro-alloy ores, n.e.c., are combined with the molybdenum data by the Census Bureau, but it would seem that few, if any, of these minerals are produced under workably competitive domestic conditions. The industry includes chromium, nickel, and columbium, and the combined data have been included in the effectively monopolistic sector.

Metal-Mining Contract Services. The metal-mining contract services industry includes "establishments primarily engaged in performing contract services for the metal-mining industries, such as prospecting, mine exploration, and development work, including the removal of overburden, sinking shafts, and diamond drilling."[20] This includes about a third of all metal-mining contract services. Hauling services, contract constructions, and contract services performed by the non-metal-mining contract service industries probably account for the remaining contract service payments by the metal-mining industries. In 1954, 68 per cent of the establishments included in this industry had fewer than 10 employees and received less than 7 per cent of the receipts for services. The seven largest establishments received 65 per cent of these receipts. This pattern of concentration is even more noticeable when the 114 establishments are treated on a regional basis. Contract service companies were not included in this industry when they had complete responsibility for the mine's operation; in such instances they were included as mine operators. The *Census of Minerals, 1954* states that these establishments seem concentrated on the basis of industries, states, and type of work performed; they are included in the noncompetitive sector in this study.[21]

Miscellaneous Metal Ores. The miscellaneous metal ores industry group includes both effectively monopolistic and workably competitive elements. Mercury ore mining seems to be a workably competitive industry. About 22 mines produced about 97 per cent of domestic mercury in 1958 while the remaining output was provided by approximately 80 other mines.[22] In 1960, six out of 75 mines provided 85 per cent of domestic output.[23] Only one mine producer is integrated, and imports have provided between 17 and 50 per cent of domestic consumption in recent years. Prices generally show a fair degree of fluctuation and probably depend to a large extent on foreign production. Because imports are so important, it is doubtful that domestic producers can control either the price or the quantity of mercury. This industry is included in the workably competitive sector.

Titanium ore imports of ilmenite and, relative to domestic supply, rutile are important factors in domestic supply. Domestic producers seem to be at least moderately integrated. Only a few domestic companies with 10 establishments exist, and some are joint ventures for captive purposes. Census data for this industry include data for 47 establishments in the metallic minerals, n.e.c., industry. Of the 57 mining establishments listed for the combined industry in 1954, the four largest provided almost 90 per cent of the value added in mining.[24] In 1957 a substantial cutback in the military application of titanium resulted in a large price decline and an alleged overcapacity in domestic facilities, but this latter situation seems to have been overcome.[25] The *1960 Minerals Yearbook* lists four rutile and six ilmenite producers but provides no size comparisons. Ilmenite prices have remained rather stable, but rutile prices have declined in recent years. Virtually all ilmenite has been used for titanium pigments, while rutile has been employed for welding rod casting; rutile imports have increased in recent years and have been used in metal making. End product prices have reflected the costs of raw materials; titanium sponge and mill products have generally declined in price, while pigment prices have risen. The industry and the combined data are classified as noncompetitive.

Uranium-radium-vanadium ore mining comprises another unique industry. No radium ores are mined in the United States, and vanadium ore usually is produced as a coproduct of uranium. Vanadium is processed into one of three different grades at eight domestic plants. Union Carbide Company and Vanadium Corporation of America are reportedly the leading miners and concentrators. About 89 per cent of domestic uranium shipments is provided by 8 per cent of 35 domestic shippers.[26] Because the federal government is the sole uranium purchaser, and the Atomic Energy Commission establishes the price, the industry is included in the government-supervised sector.

ANTHRACITE COAL MINING

Anthracite mining is the second of the five major mining industry groups. In 1958, 16 companies produced 67 per cent of domestic anthracite, and the 15 largest mines provided a third of the value added in anthracite coal mining.[27] Demand for anthracite coal has been declining since the 1930's, and overcapacity has led to cutthroat competition in the past. Nonunion coal production has aggravated the situation, especially since a major portion of such coal is mined illegally from the property of unionized companies. Domestic anthracite is found only in Pennsylvania, which regulates its sale, resale, and shipment. Anthracite production is regulated by a commission representing producers, labor, and the public. The commission was formed in 1940 to replace a privately operated quota system that had been declared illegal. In 1956 the commission was reorganized to curb the widespread evasion that had limited its effectiveness. There is no compulsory adherence to the quotas established by the commission, and no penalties are imposed for violations.[28] No antitrust suits have been brought against the commission, probably because it is state sponsored and because unrestrained competition would be far more injurious to the industry. Because the commission has been ineffective as a cartel, the anthracite-mining industry has been included, with some misgivings, in the workably competitive sector.

The anthracite contract services, except for the stripping industry, accounted for almost $1 million in receipts during 1954, compared to $42 million in receipts by the anthracite stripping contract services industry and $249 million in net shipments by the anthracite-mining industry. The non-stripping services industry included 13 establishments controlled by 13 operating companies, and less than half of the value added in anthracite coal mining and the value of shipments was provided by the largest five establishments. Concentration was even less evident in the larger stripping contract services industry, where 132 establishments were operated by 131 operating companies in 1954. The three largest establishments provided just over a sixth of the value of shipments and the value added in mining in the anthracite stripping contract services industry in 1954. Both of these service industries have been included in the workably competitive sector.

BITUMINOUS COAL AND LIGNITE MINING

Bituminous coal and lignite mining is the third of the five major mine industry groups. The bituminous-coal-mining industry is composed primarily of single mine companies, the largest accounting for 8 per cent of the output. Although 9 per cent of the industry's firms provided 77 per cent of the output in 1960, about 15 per cent was captively produced.[29] Bituminous deposits are scattered about the country, and, although several industry associations exist, there is no government regulation. Lignite mining is a smaller and relatively local industry for which no company or industry data are readily available. In 1954 about 80 per cent of the establishments had only three or fewer employees and only one had over 100 employees. The United States imports an amount equal to about 82 per cent of its domestic output, but low concentration, overcapacity, price cutting, and strong competition from substitutes have featured the industry's most recent stages. A post-1939 series of mergers has increased concentration and offers strong hope of a cure for this sick industry. Between 1950 and 1961, the total annual share of the largest 15 producers of bituminous and lignite rose from 21.2 to 39.8 per cent of domestic production; concurrently, captive production has been declining in relative importance.

The bituminous-coal- and lignite-mining contract services industry has a coverage similar to the anthracite-mining contract service industries. This industry has received only about a third of all contract service payments by the bituminous coal miners; the other two-thirds apparently went to the contract construction of new capital equipment. In 1954, the four largest establishments provided just under one-seventh of the value of shipments and one-sixth of the value added in mining. There were 132 establishments in this industry, and in some areas it was difficult to determine the degree of concentration. This major industry group has been included in the workably competitive sector.

CRUDE PETROLEUM AND NATURAL GAS EXTRACTION

Crude petroleum and natural gas extraction comprise the fourth of the five major mining industry groups. Both of these industries involve many producing wells and companies, but differences as well as similarities exist in their operating and structural characteristics.

Twenty major integrated oil companies provide approximately half of our domestic net crude oil. Most of these companies purchase about half of their crude oil requirements for refinery runs, but both crude oil imports and domestic extraction are limited by legal provisions. Prices are published for each type of crude oil, and differentials are provided for quality and location. These prices are published by the refiners but may vary after incentives or other contract terms determined by the crude oil supplier and refiner. A crude oil producer generally must sell his oil locally, unless a public pipeline is available, but Whitney concluded that the major companies lacked the power to determine an arbitrary crude oil price.[30]

Although the Federal Power Commission regulates the price of natural gas, it has been criticized for failing to protect the consumer, for neglecting to provide precedents in future price negotiation, and for involving long delays in setting price considerations.[31] Monthly production and importation of crude oil are legally regulated, but there are no domestic production limits for natural gas. Although pipelines are regulated as common carriers, natural gas pipelines are owned by the purchasers and are not regulated. The public utility nature of natural gas also differentiates this industry from the crude oil industry, because a gas distributor is required to provide continuous service and cannot withdraw unilaterally from a market. These differences are reflected in price negotiations, where the natural gas extractors, and not the purchasers, reportedly enjoy the superior bargaining power.[32] The Federal Power Commission may deny high initial prices to the pipeline-distributor, but escalator or most favored customer clauses may provide for subsequent price increases. Also, extractors may evade price regulation by selling an entire gas field at once, or by withholding the gas from the market until the price rises. An estimated 50 per cent of all uncommitted domestic natural gas reserves is controlled by the four largest oil and natural gas companies, with the next four companies holding an additional 18 per cent. The crude petroleum and natural gas group has been considered workably competitive. Prices are not determined by a few parties, and output does not appear concentrated. Government regulation still seems to leave room for significant individual initiative.

The oil and gas field contract services industry group includes three industries that have become increasingly important in oil and gas extraction. For example, in 1954 this service industry group provided 42 per cent of all employment in the oil and gas extraction major industry group, as contrasted with 23 per cent in 1939. The services also provided 73 per cent of all wells drilled by the oil and gas extractive group in 1954, as compared with 62 per cent in 1939. In 1954 the three service industries provided about 15 per cent of all value added in mining by the crude petroleum and natural gas extraction major industry group. The relatively large number of establishments, plus the preponderance of single-establishment operating companies, indicates a competitive nature. The four largest establishments in each of the three service industries provided far less than half of the value added in each of these industries. The service industries have been included in the workably competitive sector.

NONMETALLIC MINERALS (EXCEPT FUELS) MINING

Nonmetallic minerals (except fuels) mining, the fifth and final major mining industry group, includes more four-digit SIC industries than any of the four other mining industry groups previously discussed. Many industries in this group are in either the dimension or the crushed stone group, which together included over 2,000 establishments in 1954. It is particularly difficult to classify the stone and other low-value industries because costs (especially for transportation) often localize a producer's market; this may tend to create local monopolies. On the other hand, products from other industries plus high costs may provide a highly competitive market. *Mineral Facts and Figures* states that prices are established through general supply and demand considerations in these troublesome industries.[33]

Stone.   Dimension stone industries are classified by type of stone. Although establishment size varies with the particular stone, the largest establishments dominate each industry and contribute the major portion of value added in mining. Prices vary with the type of stone, and there is no indication that the largest companies control the price level. Declining use patterns and increasing numbers of substitutes have helped to stifle demand, while heavy transportation, mining, and handling costs limit the geographical market for each quarry.

Crushed and broken stone producers face some of the same cost problems as dimension stone miners, although nonstone substitutes do not constitute as much of a threat. Most crushed stone is used in concrete and road construction, but slag and crushed gravel compete with it for the concrete market. Transportation costs are a major factor in limiting the producer's potential market. In 1960, 3 per cent of the production plants produced over 900,000 tons, or 25 per cent of total production.[34] The three stone industry groups have been included in the workably competitive sector.

Clay and Related Minerals.   The United States is self-sufficient in clay, but the clay, ceramic, and refractory minerals industry group is difficult to classify. Substitutes exist for all but the ceramic uses of clay, and about two-thirds of the industrial clays are used for ceramic purposes.[35] In 1960 the 100 leading firms supplied 15 per cent of clay production, while the remaining 85 per cent was provided by 1,300 firms.[36] More producers mined fire clay than any other specific type, but 80 per cent was captively produced in 1958. In the same year about 99 per cent of miscellaneous clay was captively produced. All of the bentonite and fuller's earth, and about 95 per cent of kaolin and ball clay, were produced by 85 companies engaged primarily in mining, milling, or otherwise preparing the material for market; these three industries have been considered workably competitive.[37] The prices of many clays are subject to negotiations, and published prices provide only a relative range of prices. Fire and miscellaneous clay prices are not published because of the heavy captive production, but have been described as relatively constant.[38]

The Feldspar Corporation produced a third of domestic feldspar in 1960.[39] Declining demand and increased use of substitutes cause overcapacity and low prices that seem rather stable. Ten companies are reported to produce 80 per cent of our domestic production, with the three leading companies providing 50 per cent.[40]

Magnesite and brucite are produced by only a few companies, and their prices are steady. In 1958 only three out of 23 magnesium compound producers mined magnesite and only one supplied brucite; magnesite totaled 10 per cent of all magnesium ores in 1958.[41] Net imports were about 5–10 per cent for magnesium compounds, and most was magnesite. Prices seem to have fluctuated during this period and to have had an upward trend.

Natural Abrasives except Sand. No concentration data were discovered for the natural abrasives, except sand, industry group. However, in 1954 only 11 operating companies produced natural abrasive stones (grindstones, pulpstones, millstones, burrstones, and sharpening stones), and 21 companies supplied natural abrasives, n.e.c. (tripoli, emery, garnet, corundum, and industrial diamonds).[42] The natural abrasive stones industry has experienced generally declining tonnage and dollar sales in recent years, but no price data were obtained. Production of each type of stone seems to be concentrated in a few regions and by very few suppliers. Natural abrasives, n.e.c., also seem to be produced under concentrated conditions. Corundum mines generally have been inactive since 1906, and it seems that only one company serves as importer and processor; the processed material is sold directly to the consumers. Emery is produced by two companies and imported in relatively small quantities by two others for the use of 45 manufacturers of emery paper and cloth. The production and consumption of industrial diamonds seem very concentrated, and most of the domestic supply is imported; prices are markedly stable and reflect concentrated conditions abroad. Five companies produced tripoli in 1960 with prices seemingly flexible. Domestic garnet was provided by five companies in 1960 and none was imported. Output of each of the industry group's products seems to be concentrated, but substitutes appear to be available for each item and essentially competitive conditions exist for the industries as a whole.

Chemical and Fertilizer Minerals. Chemical and fertilizer mineral mining also includes several four-digit industries, with both competitive and monopolistic elements. In recent years two companies are believed to have produced at least half of all barite mined in the United States, about 1,000,000 tons per year. Imports provided almost half of domestic consumption in 1956, but no stockpiling plans have been formulated. After two principal producers (Baroid Sales Division of National Lead Company and Magnet Cove Barium Company, a subsidiary of Dresser Industries), there are several others with outputs of 40,000–1,000,000 tons per year, as well as numerous smaller ones that generally supply a larger company or custom grinders.[43] Barite is not absolutely essential in every use. Barite imports showed a heavy rise between 1947 and 1958 and are very important, providing about half of domestic consumption. Prices also rose during this period, but they have been steady in recent years. The industry is included in the noncompetitive sector.

Domestic fluorspar is produced under generally competitive conditions. Imports are very important, providing half or more of our domestic consumption. In 1958 three captive plants produced a third of the acid trade finished fluorspar; one plant producing metallurgical type fluorspar was also captive.[44] In 1960 captive mines produced just under 40 per cent of domestic ore.[45] Published prices list a range within which a negotiated price is usually reached, and average prices have fluctuated moderately in recent years. Assuming that the foreign mines are not captive, the industry would seem to be competitive.

Potash, soda, and borate minerals seem to constitute a rather concentrated and captive industry. Establishments producing primarily natural potassium, sodium, or boron compounds are included in this industry. The United States is a net exporter of potassium compounds, with seven companies producing 90 per cent of our domestic output, but three of these companies have been producing only since 1951.[46] Boron minerals are produced under far more concentrated conditions, with only three companies accounting for nearly all domestic production from beds and vein deposits and from natural brine.[47] The United States accounts for nearly 95 per cent of world production. Sodium compounds, including soda ash and caustic soda, are produced under concentrated and captive conditions; prices are generally steady for long periods and a price leader seems to exist.[48] For these reasons, the potash, soda, and borate minerals industry is considered noncompetitive.

Phosphate rock seems to be mined under somewhat captive conditions, with about 30 companies mining and processing the rock in 1958.[49] This figure is slightly below the 1954 Census level. Most of the major producers also supply phosphatic fertilizer or elemental phosphorus. The United States is an exporter of phosphatic rock. The price is based on mineral content, with changes allegedly reflecting changes in the cost of fuel oil used in drying the rock. No evidence of price fixing was seen, but some price weaknesses were reported. The *1960 Mineral Facts and Figures* describes the fertilizer and phosphate industries as highly competitive; hence phosphate is included in the competitive sector.[50]

Rock salt seems to be produced under concentrated and noncompetitive conditions, with seven establishments supplying five-sixths of the total in 1954.[51] In 1958 about 68 per cent of all salt output, including brine, was captively produced by major chemical companies.[52] In addition, rock salt has a long history of identical prices and alleged collusion in its distribution. In 1958 four companies operated 12 plants to supply 50 per cent of domestic salt production, while the next nine companies operated 14 plants and supplied 33 per cent.[53] About 60 per cent of salt was produced as brine.

Sulfur is classified as a monopolistic industry. Only five companies provided all of the output in 1954, and four companies supplied 79 per cent of domestic production in 1956.[54] The United States is self-sufficient in sulfur.

Nonmetallic Minerals (except Fuels) Contract Services. The nonmetallic minerals (except fuels) contract services industry provided only about 14 per cent of the group's contract services in 1954. The remaining payments were received by similar industries in the other major mineral groups, by other mine operators in the manufacturing and wholesale trade industries, and in the nonmetallic mining industries. The four largest operating companies provide less than half of the value added in this industry, which is included in the competitive sector.[55]

Nonmetallic Minerals except Fuels. The final mining group, nonmetallic minerals except fuels, is composed of both monopolistic and competitive elements. Most gypsum is mined and processed by large, integrated companies, and about 28 per cent of our supply is imported. In 1958 there were three major companies, 10 others that only calcined or mined gypsum, and numerous small specialty producers.[56] In 1954 there were only seven medium-sized companies. United States Gypsum is the largest domestic producer, with 14 mines or quarries and 23 calcining plants in 13 states in 1957. National Gypsum Company was second with six mines and quarries and six calcining plants. These two companies also have large mines in

Nova Scotia. Gypsum faces competition from other plasters and building materials, and heavy transportation costs are a very important factor in this industry, since products are bulky, heavy, and relatively low in value. Regional resource concentration, plus heavy transportation costs, has created a large regional demand for imported gypsum. However, domestic production and imports are believed to be concentrated and noncompetitive.

Mica is imported in substantial quantities by the United States. Half of the domestic sheet mica output is produced by part-time mines, and the ten largest producers account for about 40 per cent of the domestic output.[57] Large companies have failed to produce sheet mica on a substantial scale because of the mineral's physical characteristics. Prices vary with quality, and the level is set by negotiation; the industry is believed to be workably competitive.

No data were found for native asphalts and bitumens (including gilsonite, wurtzilite, grahamite, and osokerite), but the industry included only nine producers in 1954. The small size, plus the type of products, indicates a limited and concentrated production.

Pumice and pumicite constitute a competitive industry; 85 companies in 15 western states and Hawaii produced these minerals in 1958. According to the *1960 Minerals Facts and Figures*, no small group of producers dominates the industry, whose outputs compete as a lightweight aggregate and as an abrasive.[58] Prices show a wide range and seem to fluctuate; transportation costs are important and limit the market to a few hundred miles by land. Ocean freight is much cheaper and extends the market considerably. Imports were relatively minor in 1958.

Talc, soapstone, and pyrophyllite generally are produced by different companies. In 1958 there were 37 talc, 14 soapstone, and 13 pyrophyllite producers; only three companies produced two of the three minerals.[59] Prices are negotiated by the buyer and seller and depend on the quality of the minerals. The United States is self-sufficient, and imports are almost nonexistent. The three items face competition from other materials, such as clays, as well as each other. The industry seems to be workably competitive.

There were about 80 peat producers in 1958, most of them having fewer than three employees. Total employment was about 500, with only one producer having over 100 employees.[60] Total imports equaled 83 per cent of domestic production in 1958. Retail prices of comparable domestic and imported peat are basically competitive. The industry has been included in the workably competitive sector.

The Bureau of the Census combined its data for vermiculite with those for miscellaneous nonmetallic minerals, n.e.c. The industries covered by these data are considered effectively monopolostic. There are two vermiculite producers, one being dominant. It is assumed that production occurs under concentrated conditions for the several miscellaneous minerals, which include asbestos, diatomite, natural gem stones, graphite, greensand, perlite, and Iceland spar (optical grade calcite).

IX. CLASSIFICATION OF COMMUNICATIONS AND PUBLIC UTILITIES INDUSTRIES BY COMPETITIVE STATUS

The communications and public utilities division includes three SIC major industry groups. In 1958 this division contributed $14,179 million, or 3.83 per cent, of the total national income. Most industries in this division are considered public utilities, and their effectively monopolistic operations are governmentally regulated.

TELEPHONE AND TELEGRAPH

The telephone, telegraph, and related services sector of the national income accounts is equivalent to the 1942 SIC communications major industry group 81, excluding industry group 813, radio broadcasting and television. In 1958 this sector provided $6,044 million, or 42.6 per cent, of the national income originating in the communications and public utilities division. The telephone and telegraph industry sector is regulated by state and federal authorities. Nutter considered this sector as an ineffectively regulated monopolistic industry. This designation reflected Wilcox's criticisms of telephone and telegraph regulation; some of these factors may have changed sufficiently by 1958 to warrant re-examination for recent years.[1] Wilcox's primary criticism concerned the non-state-regulated affiliates and the completely nonregulated Western Electric Company, the manufacturing subsidiary of American Telephone and Telegraph Company. Western's prices were not regulated even though it supplied almost all of AT&T's telephone equipment needs without bids. Wilcox also criticized a dual depreciation policy that allowed AT&T to adjust depreciation computations to its best interests in tax and rate matters. Several efforts by AT&T to obtain and exploit monopolistic positions in non-common-carrier communications areas, such as radio and movies, were also cited in studies of the telephone and other industries. Research by AT&T was supported by fees charged to subsidiary companies, but AT&T retained ownership of all resulting patents and charged licensing fees. Although AT&T had an FCC-regulated monopoly on international two-way communication, four companies participated in international one-way telegraph communication, and each seems to have

TABLE C-20

Percentage of National Income Originating in Industries Other than Manufacturing, Mining, Agriculture, and Trade, Classified as Monopolistic: 1939, 1954, and 1958

	1939	1954	1958
Contract construction	3.11	a	a
Banking	1.21	1.45	1.61
Insurance carriers	1.18	1.12	1.12
Pipeline transportation	0.18	a	a
Telephone and telegraph	1.39	1.45	a
Motion pictures	0.59	a	a
Radio broadcasting and television		a	0.18	0.21
Finance, n.e.c.	a	0.22	0.23

Source: Appendix C; *U.S. Income and Output, A Supplement to the Survey of Current Business, 1958*, Table I-10, pp. 130–131; *Survey of Current Business*, XLII (July 1962), Table 7, p. 21, Table A-15.

a Not classified as monopolistic for this year.

had monopoly rights in particular countries. An RCA subsidiary had about 80 per cent of the radiotelegraphy business in 1938.

The telephone and telegraph sector has been affected by several events since the Wilcox analysis. One important factor has been the emergence of the General Telephone and Telegraph Company, a strong, independent system that provides telephone service, research, and manufacturing operations. However, in 1958 the Bell system still provided about 85 per cent of the telephone business.[2] A second factor was the January 1956 consent decree in an antitrust suit brought by the Justice Department against AT&T and Western Electric.[3] The settlement limited the type of business in which the companies could participate and the kind of equipment that they could manufacture. Nonexclusive use and manufacturing licenses at little or no royalties were provided for telephone equipment, and a cost accounting system was ordered for the manufacturing subsidiary so that the parent and operating companies' equipment costs would be known. Exclusive dealerships were prohibited, as were purchase or price maintenance contracts with independent telephone companies. Royalty payments by Western Electric to its parent or affiliated companies, as well as other practices of the telephone company and its manufacturing divisions, were also prohibited.

In 1954 the National Association of Railroad and Utility Commissions (NARUC) studied the methods by which interstate and intrastate facilities were allocated in the Bell Telephone System; NARUC also studied the relationship of Western Electric's costs to the company's rate requests and profit experience.[4] The Western Union Company remains the only domestic telegraph company, but at the end of 1954 it agreed to sell its international lines. Although international service to particular areas was monopolistic, there were four cable and six radiotelegraph services operating in 1954. Rates have been determined by the FCC, which also reviews original costs and depreciation ratios for the communications industries that it regulates.

RADIO BROADCASTING AND TELEVISION

The radio broadcasting and television sector includes companies primarily engaged in the operation of radio and television stations for hire for the transmission of programs and deriving their revenues principally from advertisers or others wishing to reach the public. In 1958 this sector provided $754 million, or 5.3 per cent, of the national income originating in this division. The sector is classified as effectively monopolistic in the 1950's, even though the FCC has important regulatory powers. The federal regulation has limited the number of stations, but the regulation seems to be based on the need to maintain communications order rather than to achieve economic control, as in the other regulated industry groups. Entry and technical standards of operations are regulated by the FCC, which allocates the station frequencies and hours of operation. Networks are limited in the number of stations which they can own and operate but are unrestricted in the number of affiliates.

Nutter and Wilcox considered the radio broadcasting industry as an effectively regulated monopolistic industry, but the industry has changed greatly since 1939, and a re-examination reveals many structural and technological changes.[5] In 1938 two companies with three networks and 267 station outlets accounted for 56 per cent of total sales of radio time. In addition, contracts between networks and their outlets generally restricted the operating freedom of a station, to the network's advantage and the outlet's disadvantage. By 1958 radio broadcasting provided a lesser amount of total broadcast revenues than television. Although network radio dominance was greatly diminished, the four major network companies had transferred their dominance to television. This decline of network radio probably was hastened by the 1941 FCC regulations restricting the terms which networks could require in contracting for station affiliation. The NBC network was forced to divest itself of one of its two networks, and each interest was limited to a single AM station in any one market area.

In 1958 the three television networks and their 19 owned and operated stations received $516.7 million in total broadcasting revenues and $77.0 million in pretax income. The 495 other television stations received only

$513.3 million in total broadcasting revenues while earning $94.9 million in pretax income.[6] The television industry has been criticized for its concentrated conditions caused by network dominance and the ownership of stations by other news and entertainment media.[7] The FCC has been criticized, in turn, for allegedly encouraging this increasing concentration.

UTILITIES

The utilities: electric and gas sector of the national income accounts is derived from the electric light and power industry groups of the SIC major industry 82, heat, light, and power. In 1958 this sector provided $7,154 million, or 50.5 per cent, of the national income originating in the communications and public utility division. The local utilities and public services, n.e.c., sector is composed of the SIC major industry group 83, water and sanitary service, and the remaining industry group 823, steam heat, and power. In 1958 this sector accounted for $227 million, or 1.6 per cent, of the national income originating in the communications and public utility division.

The two national income sectors are discussed together, because all of the included industries seem to be considered public utilities in the traditional sense; a possible exception is the sanitary service industry, which might not be completely regulated. Wilcox described briefly some examples in which private utility companies were able to secure monopoly, or supralegal, profits because the state regulation was inadequate or because a holding company was not covered by the Public Utilities Holding Company Act of 1935.[8]

During the latter part of the period under consideration, the public utilities industries were still susceptible to monopolistic practices. The dangers inherent in lax state regulations were indicated by Senator Wayne Morse in 1956.[9] His testimony described the degree to which private power companies could co-ordinate their activities in order to achieve their own controversial private aims in the Pacific Northwest. Despite this possible regional breakdown in private power regulation, it appears that the situation has not deteriorated to a degree warranting an effectively monopolistic designation.

The gas industry should perhaps be classified as an ineffectively regulated public utility and possibly allocated to the monopoly group. This alternative reflects the very ineffectual natural gas price regulation by the Federal Power Commission, which was mentioned in the discussion of natural gas production. The lack of established precedents, the rapidly increasing backlog of rate increase petitions, and the ease with which rate increases have been obtained during this period—all these indicate ineffective regulation. Electric and water industry regulation has not been as severely criticized, possibly because much of it is done by the state and because public facilities are an important competitive yardstick in many areas. Also, these other utilities are much older and more securely established than the natural gas industry, and precedents and procedures have long been available for many purposes.

Statistical Measures

Three measurement problems related to this volume are described briefly below. The first and longest of the three following sections considers some of the issues involved in tying the two studies together to obtain an overview of the 1899–1958 period. The second section considers briefly some aspects of the lognormal distribution, which was not utilized in this volume. The third section provides some additional comments on the Lorenz distribution, which was applied in each study.

COMPARABILITY OF POST-1939 DATA
TO EARLIER DATA

An extension of Nutter's analysis from 1939 through 1958 requires a bridge between the two studies; this bridge is provided in the present section. The analysis could be extended through 1958 only after first establishing the comparability of data used in the two studies. The decision to extend the 1899–1939 analysis through 1958 raises questions concerning the most useful procedure available. Three alternatives are possible: (1) to follow Nutter's procedure as closely as possible, (2) to select the best method of analyzing 1958 conditions and compare these results to earlier years, and (3) to select the best means of analyzing the 1939–1958 period and compare these results to Nutter's analysis by using 1939 as a bridge year. Each alternative will be examined in turn.

Obviously it would be desirable to follow Nutter's procedure as closely as possible in order to maintain maximum comparability between the analyses. Unfortunately, this is not feasible. As indicated above, the 1899 analysis was based on national income estimates prepared by Robert Martin for the National Industrial Conference Board.[1] Nutter had to use the Martin estimates for 1899, but Department of Commerce data were utilized for his far more comprehensive study of monopoly in 1937 and 1939. The 1899–1937 evaluation was possible because he could adapt his comprehensive 1937 study to Martin's national income data for comparison with 1899.

Several considerations preclude updating this comparison by following Nutter's procedures. First, there is no recent estimate of national income based on the Martin approach or comparable to Martin's estimates for 1937 and earlier years. Second, Nutter's adjustment of manufacturing industry data involved "value-added/income-originating" ratios that were prepared by Solomon Fabricant for some earlier years but not for the current period. Third, in the absence of the necessary comparable data, estimates based on the 1937 data used by Nutter would be completely incomparable because of the length and nature of the 21-year interval. An attempt to apply the 1937 overlap ratios on an automatic basis would be equally insupportable. Consequently, direct duplication of earlier procedures is not defensible, and other methods must be considered.

A second possibility is the examination of 1958 conditions by using the best data and procedures available for this specific year. The results would then be compared to Nutter's estimates for 1937 and 1899. Obviously, this procedure involves no pretense of data or procedural comparability, and its analytical advantages are nil.

The third alternative is adopted for this study. This procedure accepts the condition that the 1899–1937 estimates cannot be updated in a precise statistical sense. Consequently, Nutter's 1937 overlap is utilized as a splice to a new series based on Department of Commerce data for 1937–1958. The comparability of data and procedures for 1958 with Nutter's results for 1937 and 1939 is described below. This procedure precludes the comparison of individual industry statistics for 1899 directly with those for 1958. It does, however, permit the separate identification of trends for 1899–1937 and 1937–1958 and the subsequent inference of the most likely overall 1899–1958 trends. This approach utilizes data and standards comparable to those for earlier years but still permits a subsequent and more detailed analysis of the 1939–1958 period.

DATA COMPARABILITY FOR PROCEDURE CHOSEN

With the selection of this procedure, the next step is an examination of the data from 1937 to 1958. In this instance, comparability of the following is required: comparability of (1) definitions of industrial groupings, (2) data for comparison of the different industrial groupings, and (3) definition and data for intragroup comparisons.

The national income estimates, used to compare industry divisions within a given year and between years, are provided by the Department of Commerce in a continuous series whose coverage of industrial divisions remained comparable after 1937. Although the intradivision definition of some major industry groups and industries varied through 1958, the changes have been identified, and the industry division data are suitable for the interyear comparisons of this study. The estimates for nonmanufacturing major industry groups were based on a single classification system and present no data comparability problems.

The third and perhaps the most difficult aspect of comparability is the provision of intradivision data that permit the comparison of industries and major industry groups between 1937 and 1958. This information is the basis for allocating national income originating within each industry division, among the three competitive classes. Examination of Appendices A–C reveals the definitions and procedures followed for the post-1939 period.

However, for manufacturing, one particular problem exists and requires special study. The concentration ratio is our first criterion for allocating national income in the manufacturing division. This ratio summarizes the structural considerations that we have associated with various classes of effective monopoly. Reclassification of industries might affect seriously the size of these concentration ratios and so influence the apparent degree of monopoly. The SIC reclassifications have affected primarily the individual industry definitions, and this has required a consolidation of some of the major industry groups, although this division was substantially unchanged.

The negligible importance of the manufacturing industries dropped from coverage since 1937 is indicated by their comparison for a common year. In 1929 the activities of these groups provided less than $\frac{1}{2}$ per cent of value added by manufacturing. Thus their omissions in some years were of negligible significance. Moreover, such omissions were balanced by the inclusion of some additional industrial activity for several census years after 1937. In some instances, industry definitions were altered to include activities previously omitted from a particular division; these portions provided an estimated $180 million of $117 billion in value added by manufacture in 1954. To assure data comparability, three complete post-1937 SIC industry additions have been deleted from the manufacturing comparisons after 1939.[2] The temporary exclusion of some industries between 1937 and 1958 had a smaller effect than the differences just mentioned.

The most difficult problems arise in major industry groups that were most radically redefined after 1939: chemicals, primary metals, machinery, and electrical machinery. In these groups many industries considered heavily concentrated in 1939 were fragmented but similarly classified in 1958 (i.e., the 1939 industries 1511 and 1517 matched the 1958 industries 3331, 3332, 3333, 3334, and 3339). Those heavily concentrated 1958 SIC industries with no distinct 1939 equivalents must necessarily be considered individually in determining the extent of effective manufacturing monopoly. In general, no significant bias caused by post-1939 SIC changes is evident.

Comparability of manufacturing product classifications is less easily determined than is comparability in manufacturing industries, although the intrayear data situation for products is similar to that met and described earlier for industries. However, the interyear evaluations of product competition are affected more seriously by the data compilation difficulties and the problems arising from changes in product definition. Unfortunately, only a few relevant product-based studies have been prepared; most of the studies in point have been prepared on an industry basis. There are three alternatives regarding the comparability of manufacturing product data: (1) to disregard the differences that might exist, (2) to abandon the use of these data in our analysis, and (3) to use the data and later delete some of the marginal products on other grounds. The third alternative has been adopted. However, most effectively monopolized products, as indicated by structural criteria, are included in effectively monopolistic industries. Thus, only a small share of the manufacturing products separately enter into the estimates of effective monopoly.

The possible effect of these changes in industry definition has been considered in studies by Harold T. Goldstein and Ralph Nelson.[3] Goldstein analyzed the changes in industry classifications and census comparability from 1929 through 1958. From his paper it is possible to determine which of the industries deemed concentrated in one year were comparable in scope for each of the years covered. Examination of these materials indicates that 77 of 122 industries considered highly concentrated in 1958 had the same coverage in 1939, while 65 of the 99 highly concentrated industries in 1939 were identically defined in 1958. This study has not been biased by introducing those industries that were comparably defined in 1939 and 1958, but the concentrated nature of other 1958 industries may reflect a very narrow post-1939 redefinition. Unfortunately, there is no certain and precise method of estimating the extent of this possible bias: for example, the bias stemming from heavily concentrated 1958 industries which were created from much broader nonconcentrated 1939 industries. Conversely, 1958 industries derived from broader but concentrated 1939 industry groups probably do not introduce a definitional bias toward concentration. The total of concentrated industries whose limits were altered during this period represents the outside limit of increased concentration due to classification changes. However, one cannot determine how many of the reclassified industries may have been concentrated under the earlier classification standards. It is apparent that declining industries were combined and eliminated as separated classes, while growing industries were broken into separate entities and new classifications established for these and new industries.[4]

Nelson utilizes Goldstein's analysis of classification changes in an attempt to determine their effects upon concentration. Nelson concludes that these effects are ambiguous when one examines unweighted frequency distributions of concentration ratios and continues:

However, for a distribution weighted by industry size, concentration increases produced by the splitting of large industries would be given greater weights than concentration declines produced by the merging of small industries. Comparisons of weighted distributions over a period of classification change would therefore show a lesser decline or greater increase in concentration than would comparisons based on an unchanging set of industry definitions.[5]

Since there is no estimate of concentration under an unchanged standard, the extent of this upward bias cannot be estimated. A comparison of classification changes indicates that the possible bias attributable to industry reclassification is relatively small for manufacturing industries and indeterminate for manufacturing products. The analysis and conclusions are subject to constraints and difficulties that led Nelson to plead: "Some general observations on the probable direction of the difference are here offered; however the conceptual and empirical obstacles are too great to warrant an attempt at a precise analysis."[6]

Comparability of data for other industry divisions involves issues of a rather different nature. In none of the nonmanufacturing major industry groups were concentration ratios used as the basis of industry reclassification. Thus the comparability problem of these groups depends upon the nature of the separate major industry group totals and the manner in which they, or portions thereof, were classified as competitive, monopolistic, or government supervised. Although the available data and the criteria used are not ideal, the nonmanufacturing major industry groups do not present significant comparability problems.

LOGNORMAL DISTRIBUTION

Since the mid-1950's, studies concerning the "extent of competition" have stressed the development and refinement of indices of structure as well as the explanation of industry structural changes over time. This is in contrast to (1) the "extent of competition" studies during the 1930's that probed the conditions of that decade and (2) the studies of the late 1940's and the early 1950's, which were primarily directed toward an overview of changes through time. However, since the mid-1950's concern has shifted to the development and refinement of measurement devices as well as to the explanation of industry structural changes over time.

One major study area has been the refinement and application of the lognormal distribution to industrial concentration analysis. Basically the lognormal distribution is "the distribution of a variate whose logarithm obeys the normal law of probability."[7] The lognormal hypothesis states that the distribution of industrial facilities can be defined by the distribution of logarithms of the companies with industries.[8] If this allegation holds true, then:

1. Changes in concentration can be evaluated by traditional tests of significance.
2. Given limited information, such as the industry's absolute concentration, one can derive estimates of the variance and the Gini coefficient.
3. One can estimate the effect of changes in one part of the distribution upon the distribution as a whole and in this way vary the hypotheses concerning the creation and expiration of companies over time.

However, these analytical advantages accrue only when there are either theoretical or empirical reasons for believing that the distribution of industrial companies or establishments is properly described by the lognormal distribution. On the other hand, the numerous and extensive creation and destruction of companies would require a very complicated assumption "to retain the lognormal distribution of the equilibrium distribution."[9] The additional complications created by the fluctuating economic and political conditions of the 1939–1958 period would seem to contribute even greater stresses to the theoretical analysis of the interaction of company "births and deaths" used to justify the lognormal distribution's application to industrial structure.

It is doubtful whether the lognormal distribution offers any greater advantages in describing concentration changes than are obtained from the more traditional concentration measures applied in this paper. The lognormal distribution is closely allied to the Lorenz distribution and thus subject to the same criticisms as the Gini coefficient. In addition, research has failed to demonstrate the unambiguous application of the lognormal measure to domestic industry distribution. Thus, use of the lognormal distribution would subject any findings to the criticism of possible inapplicability to the analysis of industrial structure. Until this applicability has been more firmly established, it seems inadvisable to utilize the lognormal distribution in the current study.

The lognormal distribution offers some interesting advantages in analyzing particular aspects of industrial structure. In this connection two recently completed studies are directly relevant because the lognormal distribution is applied as a measure of industrial concentration. Both works conclude that a qualified use of lognormal distributions may be a valuable tool of analysis in this area. Leonard W. Weiss hypothesizes that firm sizes within an industry do not increase equally proportionately but that larger firms will grow relatively faster as the dispersion of firms increases.[10] He relates these changes to an entry-exit factor that would reflect the type and degree of competition. Other things being equal, this disproportionate change might be greatest where style or model changes are the prevalent forms of competition. Although Weiss's statistical offerings supported this hypothesis, his statistical conclusions could also be explained by alternative hypotheses. William G. Shepherd's study of domestic manufacturing concentration changes also provides results inconsistent with a straight lognormal distribution.[11] His conclusions for the 1947–1958 period suggest a possible lognormal distribution that varies with the number of company births and the industry's growth rate. Shepherd feels that conglomerate mergers may have accounted for the relative stability of industry concentration between 1947 and 1958. He suggests that this explanation would also be consistent with the increased importance of large firms as providers of manufacturing activity. The additional research required to test this thesis would be directly relevant to some of the findings described earlier.

Thus, although the lognormal measure offers particular explicative opportunities, it provides no unique advantages for the more limited purposes of this study. The lognormal and its sister distributions may be useful as (1) descriptive tools of static structural analysis and (2) key variables in dynamic models of industrial development. When integrated under assumptions of a stochastic change process, these distributions may well provide new insights into the evolution of industrial structure. However, much additional developmental work remains before these new approaches and analytical tools will be ready for use in the antitrust area.

LORENZ DISTRIBUTIONS

Lorenz distributions are one of the primary analytical tools applied in Chapters 3 and 4; however, the Lorenz distribution is not a universally accepted measure of manufacturing structure.[12] Critics contend that the total number of producers may not be significant since a few sellers can dominate a market. By using Lorenz distributions, one can compare two industries with identical absolute concentration ratios and show very different degrees of relative concentration. For example, assume that the four largest companies provide 40 per cent of industrial output in both industry A and industry B. If industry A has a total of 20 companies and industry B has a total of 40 companies, A's Lorenz distribution will indicate less concentration than B's distribution, because the four largest companies would constitute a larger proportion of industry A than of industry B. Thus, a Lorenz approach may indicate a decline in concentration as small companies are eliminated, while an economist might interpret the elimination of these companies as a shift toward increased concentration.

Nevertheless, Lorenz distributions do offer two advantages when analyzing concentration for several years. First, Lorenz distributions measure an industry's relative concentration, and this is a necessary supplement to measures of absolute concentration that are concerned with one producer or a very few producers in an industry. Neither the absolute nor the relative concentration measure alone can provide an effective means of evaluating structure. An absolute concentration ratio may provide a concise measure associated with monopolistic practices. However, some issues require the consideration of changes throughout a distribution and not simply in its upper range. For example, the importance of large economic or financial interests can be evaluated only by considering changes in the distribution's other size classes. Examining broad sectors of the economy (1) provides a *prima-facie* estimate of growth of effective monopoly, and (2) may indicate some social or political consequences of a change in economic power. One should consider the dispersion, not just the uppermost tail, of an industrial distribution.

Second, Lorenz distributions are not affected by proportional size changes in the groups involved, because they are constructed from two sets of relative data. Conflicting forces may reduce the number of producers and either raise or lower their dispersion (i.e., their relative concentration). However, the chance of alternative movements and interpretations does not invalidate the use of Lorenz distributions. As in any other discipline, it would be misleading to adopt only one of several possible measures to summarize a given complex situation.

Notes

CHAPTER 1

1. See, e.g., Joseph A. Schumpeter, *Capitalism, Socialism and Democracy*, 2d ed., Harper & Brothers, New York, 1947, pp. 72–106; and John K. Galbraith, *American Capitalism: The Concept of Countervailing Power*, Houghton Mifflin Co., Boston, 1952, *passim*. For a critique of this view, see G. Warren Nutter, "Monopoly, Bigness, and Progress," *Journal of Political Economy*, December 1956, pp. 520–27.

2. The classic non-Marxian statement occurs in Arthur R. Burns, *The Decline of Competition*, McGraw-Hill, New York, 1936. Writing in 1953, one economist asserted that "virtually the whole body of received opinion—right, left, and center" accepted the fact that monopoly had increased significantly over the past half century or so (see Stanley Lebergott, "Has Monopoly Increased?" *Review of Economics and Statistics*, November 1953, p. 349).

3. The conventional distinction in economic theory between monopoly and oligopoly is analytically useful primarily because of the rigid framework of conditions other than number of sellers. Even here, the concept of absolute monopoly—a single seller of a distinct product—has little meaning. Every monopoly is a partial monopoly in the sense that the cross-elasticities of demand for its product in terms of prices of substitutes are greater than zero. The condition of oligopoly defines one limiting case, namely, that in which some cross-elasticities are infinite.

4. Most assumptions of "perfection" have meaning only in a negative sense, that is, in ruling out complicating factors that might exert an influence of only secondary importance on the phenomena being examined. Perfect (i.e., costless) mobility, for instance, cannot (and need not) be taken literally, for such an interpretation would imply continuous oscillation in the allocation of resources.

5. This, of course, is the familiar distinction between monopoly power and the exercise of that power. The statement holds even though there are no governmental or public restraints on the exercise of monopoly power, if the demand conditions refer to the relevant long run and the firm consciously and intelligently seeks to maximize profits. For instance, the calculation of demand conditions, by either direct or indirect means, incurs a cost. Many firms faced with a sloping demand curve will maximize profits by taking price as a datum, since the costs of estimating marginal revenue may exceed the gains from doing so, particularly if demand conditions change frequently.

6. Clair Wilcox, *Competition and Monopoly in American Industry*, Temporary National Economic Committee Monograph No. 21, Government Printing Office, Washington, 1940.

7. George J. Stigler, "Competition in the U.S.," *Five Lectures on Economic Problems*, Longmans, Green & Co., London, 1949.

8. Solomon Fabricant, "Is Monopoly Increasing?" *Journal of Economic History*, Winter 1953, pp. 89–94.

9. *Ibid.*, p. 93.

10. But including the more than 2 per cent classified by Stigler in the "compulsory cartel" group [our note].

11. Fabricant, *op. cit.*, p. 93.

12. Morris Adelman, "The Measurement of Industrial Concentration," *Review of Economics and Statistics*, November 1951, pp. 290–91.

13. "Four Comments on 'The Measurement of Industrial Concentration'" and "Rejoinder," *Review of Economics and Statistics*, May 1952, pp. 156–78.

14. *Ibid.*, pp. 157–58.

15. *Ibid.*, pp. 176–77.

16. Lebergott, *op. cit.*, pp. 349–51.

17. G. Warren Nutter, "Rejoinder to Mr. Lebergott," *ibid.*, pp. 352–53.

18. A summary of this work is given in the article "Industrial Concentration" in *International Encyclopedia of the Social Sciences*, Macmillan and the Free Press, New York, 1968.

19. See, e.g., P. E. Hart and S. J. Prais, "The Analysis of Business Concentration: A Statistical Approach," *Journal of the Royal Statistical Society*, Series A, 1956, pp. 150–81; Stephen Hymer and Peter Pashigian, "Firm Size and Rate of Growth," *Journal of Political Economy*, December 1962, pp. 556–69; Edwin Mansfield, "Entry, Gibrat's Law, Innovation, and the Growth of Firms," *American Economic Review*, December 1962, pp. 1023–51; R. E. Quandt, "On the Size Distribution of Firms," *American Economic Review*, June 1966, pp. 416–32; William G. Shepherd, "Trends of Concentration in American Manufacturing Industries, 1947–1958," *Review of Economics and Statistics*, May 1964, pp. 200–12; and H. A. Simon and C. P. Bonini, "The Size Distribution of Business Firms," *American Economic P view*, September 1958, pp. 607–17.

CHAPTER 2

1. Gardiner C. Means, *The Structure of the American Economy: A Report Prepared by the Industrial Section of the National Resources Committee*, Government Printing Office, Washington, 1939, Part I; W. L. Thorp and W. F. Crowder, *The Structure of Industry*, Temporary National Economic Committee Monograph No. 27, Government Printing Office, Washington, 1940; Clair Wilcox, *Competition and Monopoly in American Industry*, Temporary National Economic Committee Monograph No. 21, Government Printing Office, Washington, 1940.

2. Chapter viii is concerned with identifying market monopoly through degrees of cyclical price inflexibility. We shall not discuss this chapter. It might be mentioned that the results of a study by Crowder of the relation between concentration of output and price (and output) flexibility do not support the conclusions of Means (cf. Means, *op. cit.*, p. 152, with Thorp and Crowder, *op. cit.*, p. 360).

3. Means presented an extremely brief descriptive discussion of concentration of output in other sectors of the economy (*op. cit.*, pp. 111 and 116); Crowder gave some evidence on concentration of output in mining (Thorp and Crowder, *op. cit.*, p. 573).

4. Compare Crowder's careful statement of conclusions (Thorp and Crowder, *op. cit.*, pp. 407–12, especially the final paragraph) with the many questionable assertions by Means (see, e.g., Means, *op. cit.*, pp. 97, fourth paragraph; 116, seventh paragraph; and 152, second paragraph).

5. Means, *op. cit.*, p. 115. He qualified this statement in a footnote, saying that the concentration ratios might not differ and in "unusual circumstances" might be smaller when computed for separate products in an industry. It does not seem intuitively obvious, in the absence of specific evidence, that the ratios would be smaller only in "unusual circumstances."

6. Cf. Means's data (*ibid.*, Appendix 8) with those in Thorp and Crowder (*op. cit.*, Appendix B). The former data are for 1935; the latter for 1937. But the difference in years is probably not a sufficient explanation of the consistent difference in ratios.

7. Thorp and Crowder, *op. cit.*, p. 274.

8. *Ibid.*, pp. 420–81. The reader may find many similar examples by examination of the list of census products in those pages.

9. Means, *op. cit.*, p. 115; Thorp and Crowder, *op. cit.*, pp. 321–23.

10. All regional ratios could not be lower, but they might all be the same as the national ratio in the limiting case.

11. Evidence in the two studies is limited to common brick (see Thorp and Crowder, *op. cit.*, p. 321, n. 4).

12. *Ibid.* The national concentration ratio was 7 per cent. That for the Philadelphia area was 63 per cent. The ratios for the Los Angeles and New York City areas were so high that the data were not revealed by the *Census of Manufactures.*

13. George J. Stigler, *American Economic Review*, Supplement, June 1942, p. 7.

14. Means, *op. cit.*, pp. 112–14.

15. The first two groups are listed in Wilcox, *op. cit.*, pp. 115–18, and in Dewey Anderson et al., *Final Report of the Executive Secretary to the Temporary National Economic Committee*, Government Printing Office, Washington, 1941, pp. 11–14. The income originating in census products and in census industries should not be added together to find the extent of monopoly, for most of the former are included in the latter. The incomes originating in each group of census industries may properly be added together.

16. Manufacturing production is defined here, as elsewhere in this study, as income originating in manufacturing.

17. This extreme discrepancy is due in part to the elimination of all highly concentrated products valued at less than $10,000,000.

18. Thorp and Crowder, *op. cit.*, pp. 275–81.

19. For the 121 products, gross value was $5,801 million and value added $2,687 million; for all products, the corresponding figures were $56,843 million and $24,683 million. Products and source of data are given in Table A-2.

20. Value added for the regional industries was $3,969.2 million, while value added for all manufacturing industries was $24,692.9 million. The list of regional industries was compiled from Means, *op. cit.*, Appendix 8. The value-added data were taken from U.S. Bureau of the Census, *Statistical Abstract of the United States: 1948*, pp. 831–50.

21. Thorp and Crowder, *op. cit.*, p. 323.

22. *Ibid.*, p. 322.

23. See the generally excellent discussion of definitional problems in Wilcox, *op. cit.*, pp. 1–12, 19–20.

24. *Ibid.*, p. 20.

25. See *ibid.*, p. 208.

26. The industries are those listed in Tables A-3 through A-6 minus those in Table A-7.

27. That is, those industries mentioned only in Chapter v of the Wilcox monograph.

28. A concentration ratio is the proportion of total value of output which the four leading firms in an industry account for.

29. Since Crowder's study covered only about half of all census products, we have doubled all estimates of income originating in the census products with concentration ratios of 3/4 or larger which were not included in other industries (see Table A-6 for a list of these census products). The income data from this table were doubled when transferred to Table A-10.

The highly concentrated, but effectively competitive, industries are listed in Table A-7.

Some readers may feel that the critical concentration ratios should be lower than those which we have chosen. However, our findings indicate that the final result might not be greatly affected by lowering the critical ratios considerably. For instance, in 1939 the census industries with ratios of 2/3 or larger produced 3.8 per cent of national income, while those with ratios of 1/2 to 2/3 produced only 1.3 per cent. In event, we have actually included many industries with concentration ratios below 1/2. Those with concentration ratios below 1/2 which have been considered monopolistic (see the next note) accounted for 3.4 per cent of national income.

30. Many of the industries in Table A-5 are regionally monopolistic. All the industries in this table had national concentration ratios smaller than 1/2.

31. The figures for the workably competitive area have been residually derived. It would be worth while to measure the percentage of national income produced by industries which

were independently classified as workably competitive and to derive the percentage for monopolistic industries residually. A comparison of the two sets of results would provide a more reliable indication of the relative extent of monopoly. The results are likely to differ for at least two reasons. In the first place, computational procedures involve an essentially undeterminable error. Hence, even if the same industries were retained in the workably competitive classification, the percentage of national income independently computed as originating in those industries would almost certainly differ from the percentage residually computed. That is, for 1939 independently computed percentages of national income for competitive and monopolistic industries would most surely not sum up to 79.52. In the second place, the list of workably competitive industries determined by independent classification would probably differ from the list determined residually. Unless these two factors exactly offset each other, the results of residual and independent computation will probably differ significantly.

32. As we define the term here, nongovernmental production includes the production of governmentally supervised industries but not that of any activities which are usually included under the heading of "government" in income accounting statistics. Many of the latter activities could probably be performed by private enterprise. But any effort to single them out would meet practically insuperable conceptual and accounting problems. The term "production" refers to "income originating."

33. If railroads were also included as monopolistic, about 30 per cent of nongovernmental production would be attributable to monopolistic industries. But do most railroads really possess substantial monopolistic advantages?

34. The preceding analysis is useful, of course, only in so far as the classification of industries into groups is economically meaningful. The group classifications which we have used are those of the 1939 *Census of Manufactures*.

CHAPTER 3

1. The percentage of national income (resources) accounted for by transportation and communication fell from around 10 per cent in 1899 to approximately 8 per cent in 1939 (see Tables 2 and B-5). At the same time, railway freight ton-miles increased by about 200 per cent, railway passenger-miles by about 67 per cent; miles of telephone wire by over 3,000 per cent; and miles of telegraph wire by over 100 per cent (U.S. Bureau of the Census, *Statistical Abstract of the United States: 1948*, pp. 530, 532, 480, and 482). Of course, these figures only partly indicate the tremendous cheapening of transportation and communication. Within that period came the automobile, airplane, radio, and parcel post.

2. At the same time, cheapened transportation and communication have decreased the costs of management and of collusion. But this is a question of changes in economies of scale, which will be discussed later.

3. W. F. Ogburn et al., *Technological Trends and National Policy: Report of the Subcommittee on Technology to the National Resources Committee*, Government Printing Office, Washington, 1937, p. ix.; cf. also *ibid.*, pp. 3–6.

4. U.S. Bureau of the Census, *Statistical Abstract of the United States: 1948*, p. 896.

5. These and the following figures are based on data in Table B-5.

6. W. L. Thorp and W. F. Crowder, *The Structure of Industry*, Temporary National Economic Committee Monograph No. 27, Government Printing Office, Washington, 1940, pp. 54–97.

7. *Ibid.*, p. 56.

8. *Ibid.*, p. 54.

9. The bulge may not be uniformly greater in one curve than in another. Lorenz curves will intersect in this case, and interpretation of changes in concentration becomes somewhat ambiguous. We may safely ignore that complication in our analysis, since our objectives do not require such refinement.

10. See Table B-1.

11. Only one size class in each year is eliminated. The eliminations do not affect the 4/1 ratio of aggregate value of products (see Table B-1).

12. In light of the reduction in number of plants, the lower limit of value of products for 1904 should probably be something less than one-fourth the lower limit for 1939; for output of "surviving" plants has increased in a somewhat greater proportion than has total manufacturing output. This revision would strengthen previous conclusions, since the Lorenz curve for 1904 would exhibit a greater downward bulge relative to the curve for 1939.

13. The number covered was smaller in the censuses of 1925 and 1937 (see Table B-1).

14. See Table B-1.

15. U.S. Industrial Commission, *Reports of the Industrial Commission*, Government Printing Office, Washington. 1900–1902, Vols. I, XIII, and XIX; John Moody, *The Truth about the Trusts*, Moody Publishing Co., New York, 1904; Charles R. Van Hise, *Concentration and Control: A Solution of the Trust Problem in the United States*, The Macmillan Co., New York; Arthur S. Dewing, *Corporate Promotions and Reorganizations*, Harvard University Press, Cambridge, 1914; Harry W. Laidler, *Concentration of Control in American Industry*, Thomas Y. Crowell Co., New York, 1931.

16. These larger gaps result from two factors: (1) the much smaller number of closely substitutable products in the 1890's and (2) the less refined industrial classification, especially in official censuses, for the 1890's.

17. Nonprofit and household activities that might have been covered by national income statistics are included among workably competitive industries.

18. See Appendix B for more information on the differences between the Department of Commerce and Martin series and for an explanation of the adjustments that were made.

19. Manufacturing census products of major value with concentration ratios of 3/4 or larger are also included, as in Chapter 2.

20. The revised estimates of fraction of national income originating in 1937 in workably competitive industries and in government and in governmentally supervised industries are based on data in Tables 2, 8, and B-12.

21. See p. 25 for the division of supervised industries between competitive and monopolistic sectors.

22. In 1937 most of the effective monopoly in the transportation and communication, in our interpretation, was concentrated in communication. The two industrial areas are combined into a single industrial division because income data are not separately available for 1899. It should be noted that the only transportation industry considered competitive in 1899 is water transportation.

23. We note that, under Estimate I, 5.8 per cent of national income originated in monopolistic industries in agriculture, services, trade, and contract construction in 1937. This fraction of national income represented about 17 per cent of the combined income of those areas. An equally large fraction of national income for 1899 would represent only 12 per cent of the combined income of those areas. In view of the greater prevalence of regional markets in 1899, it may not be unreasonable to suppose that monopoly was at least two-thirds as extensive in those areas in 1899 as in 1937. Unfortunately, this conjecture can be neither substantiated nor contradicted on the basis of accessible information on conditions in 1899.

24. Recall that Estimate I includes all the industries classified as monopolistic in Chapter 2.

25. Recall that Estimate II includes only those manufacturing census industries with concentration ratios of 1/2 or larger and census products of major value with concentration ratios of 3/4 or larger.

26. See Table B-12. On the basis of Department of Commerce statistics, the proportion in 1937 is 6.7 per cent (see Table 4).

27. The rank correlation coefficients between rankings for 1899 and 1937 are 0.244 under Estimate I for 1937 and 0.452 under Estimate II for 1937. On the basis of Student's t-distribution, a correlation coefficient of 0.244 is not significant at the 30 per cent level of significance; a coefficient of 0.452 is not significant at the 5 per cent level. That is, if sixteen pairs

of numbers were selected at random, there would be a 30 per cent (5 per cent) probability of finding a correlation coefficient at least as large as 0.244 (0.452). The computation of correlation coefficients and tests of significance were performed by using formulas in George W. Snedecor, *Statistical Methods*, 4th ed., Iowa State College Press, Ames, 1946, p. 167.

CHAPTER 5

1. See Adelman, *op. cit.*, and the subsequent comments in the *Review of Economics and Statistics*, XXXIV, No. 2 (May, 1952).
2. See p. 40 for the definition of a Lorenz curve. The properties of this distribution are considered in more detail in Appendix D (pp. 228–29).
3. U.S. Department of Commerce, Bureau of the Census, *Annual Survey of Manufactures, 1951*, p. 172.
4. "Degree of inequality" cannot be precisely defined. In other words, different Lorenz curves may have the same Gini coefficient.
5. The following items were eliminated from the complete size distributions:

	Size Class (number of employees)	Number of Establishments	Value Added (million dollars)
1947	1 to 5	64,966	836
1954	1 to 5	106,960	1,554
	5 to 10	3,942	167
1958	1 to 5	105,641	1,832
	5 to 10	16,620	835

The fractions of total-value-added thus eliminated are 1.1 per cent for 1947, 1.5 per cent for 1954, and 1.9 per cent for 1958.

CHAPTER 6

1. The correlation coefficients between rankings for 1899 and 1958 are 0.398 under Estimate I for 1958 and 0.481 under Estimate II. The former is not significant at the 10 per cent level, or the latter at the 5 per cent level.

APPENDIX A

1. Many of the tables given here have been condensed from the original study by eliminating data on value and value added that can be easily found in cited sources. These data are given in appendix tables in G. W. Nutter, *The Extent of Enterprise Monopoly in the United States, 1899–1939*, The University of Chicago Press, Chicago, 1951.
2. For an extended discussion of the *Census of Manufactures*, see Solomon Fabricant, *The Output of Manufacturing Industries, 1899–1937*, National Bureau of Economic Research, New York, 1940, Appendix A.
3. See U.S. Bureau of the Census, *Census of Manufactures: 1939: Industry Classifications*, Government Printing Office, Washington, 1940.

4. See Fabricant, *op. cit.*, pp. 346–50, for more detailed evidence on the relation of these two concepts.

5. The following procedure of selection was used. Every fifth industry was chosen, the initial industry being picked "at random." The random process involved the use of tables of random numbers in R. A. Fisher and F. Yates, *Statistical Tables for Biological, Agricultural and Medical Research*, 3rd ed., Hafner Publishing Co., New York, 1948, pp. 104–9. There are six blocks of random numbers, each containing fifty rows and twenty-five columns. It was decided to pick two numbers at random from the first block, by dropping a pencil point blindly on the page, to indicate the block and row in which the number of the initial industry was to be found. The remainder found by dividing the number picked by the pencil point by 6 was to indicate the block, and the remainder found by dividing the number immediately to the right of the one picked by 50 was to indicate the row. The number on which the pencil point dropped was 68 (row 26, col. 20), 02 being the number immediately to the right (row 26, col. 21). Thus Block II, row 2, was chosen. The first number less than 55 in this row is 38 (col. 2). Therefore, the thirty-eighth industry in Table A-3—namely, "aluminum products, not elsewhere classified"—was chosen as the initial industry.

6. See Fabricant, *op. cit.*, pp. 350–57, for a more extended discussion.

7. A more thorough discussion of the nature of the data from these sources than we present below may be found in H. Barger and S. H. Schurr, *The Mining Industries, 1899–1939*, National Bureau of Economic Research, New York, 1944, Appendix B. Bureau of Mines value data by ten-year intervals over a forty-year period have been placed on a comparable industrial basis in Appendix A of that book.

8. U.S. Bureau of Agricultural Economics, *Price Spreads between Farmers and Consumers for Food Products, 1913–44*, Miscellaneous Publication No. 576, Government Printing Office, Washington, 1945.

9. *Ibid.*, p. 100. Yearly per capita consumption is not given in this source.

10. U.S. Bureau of the Census, *Statistical Abstract of the United States: 1948*, p. 9.

11. Automobile Manufacturers' Association, *Automobile Facts and Figures, 1940*, Detroit, 1940, p. 32.

12. U.S. Department of Commerce, *Survey of Current Business Supplement*, July 1947, Table 12, p. 25.

APPENDIX B

1. See note 1 in Appendix A.

2. See U.S. Bureau of the Census, *Statistical Abstract of the United States: 1948*, p. 825.

3. *Ibid.*

4. Robert F. Martin, *National Income in the United States, 1799–1938*, National Industrial Conference Board, New York, 1939.

5. U.S. Census Office, *Twelfth Census of the United States, Taken in the Year 1900: Manufactures*, Part I, Vol. VII, U.S. Census Office, Washington, 1902, p. xviii.

6. Solomon Fabricant, *The Output of Manufacturing Industries, 1899–1937*, National Bureau of Economic Research, New York, 1940, pp. 608–39.

7. *Ibid.*, p. 349.

8. See *ibid.*, p. 375.

9. See note c of Table B-7.

10. Harold Barger and S. H. Schurr, *The Mining Industries, 1899–1939: A Study of Output, Employment and Productivity*, National Bureau of Economic Research, New York, 1944, pp. 305–9.

11. Simon Kuznets, *National Income and Its Composition, 1919–1938*, Vol. II, National Bureau of Economic Research, New York, 1941, p. 472.

12. See Table A-16.   13. Kuznets, *op. cit.*, II, p. 472.

14. See text, p. 139 and Table B-7.   15. See text, pp. 48–49.

APPENDIX C

Section I

1. U.S. Executive Office of the President, Bureau of the Budget, *Standard Industrial Classification Manual*, Vol. I. *Manufacturing Industries*, Government Printing Office, Washington, 1941, p. 3.
2. Appendix A.
3. Theodore J. Kreps, "The Newspaper Industry," in *The Structure of American Industry*, ed. by Walter Adams, The Macmillan Co., New York, 1961, Chapter 15.
4. U.S. Congress, Senate, Committee on the Judiciary, Subcommittee on Antitrust and Monopoly, *Concentration Ratios in American Industry, 1958*, report prepared by the Bureau of the Census, Part II, Table 36, pp. 492–510.
5. U.S. Congress, Senate, Hearings on Economic Concentration, Part I, 1964, Senate Committee on the Judiciary, Subcommittee on Antitrust and Monopoly, testimony of Dr. John M. Blair, p. 92.

Section II

1. U.S. Executive Office of the President, Bureau of the Budget, *Standard Industrial Classification Manual*, Vol. II, Government Printing Office, Washington, 1942, p. 35.
2. *Ibid.*   3. *Ibid.*
4. Clair Wilcox, *Competition and Monopoly in American Industry*, Temporary National Economic Committee Monograph No. 21, Government Printing Office, Washington, 1940.
5. U.S. v. Paramount Pictures et al., 85 F. Supp, 881; also located in Commerce Clearing House, *Trade Cases*, 1948–1949 vol., Para. 62,473.
6. U.S. Congress, House, Committee on the Judiciary, 84th Cong., 1st Sess., May 1955, Hearings before Antitrust Subcommittee (Subcommittee #5), *Current Antitrust Problems*, part I, p. 644.
7. Commerce Clearing House, *Trade Regulation Reporter*, Vol. I, see Index.
8. U.S. Congress, House, Special Subcommittee of the Select Committee on Small Business, 86th Cong., 2nd Sess., Hearings, Part V, pp. 740–47 for Mueller's testimony. The bibliography includes other hearings and reports pertaining to the agriculture sector.
9. *Ibid.*, p. 742.
10. The Automobile Dealer Franchise Act is included in the Commerce Clearing House, *Trade Regulation Reporter*, Vol. 4.
11. Standard Stations case, 337 U.S. 293, 69 Sup. Ct. 1051; it also is located in *Trade Cases*, 1948–1949 vol., Para. 62,432.
12. This ratio was obtained in a telephone call to the offices of *Automotive Industries*, New York.
13. U.S. Federal Trade Commission, Bureau of Economics, *Economic Inquiry into Food Marketing*, Government Printing Office, Washington, 1960. This report is summarized in Commerce Clearing House, *Trade Regulation Reporter*, Vol. 3, Para. 10,367.

Section III

1. U.S. Executive Office of the President, *Standard Industrial Classification Manual*, Vol. II.
2. *Ibid.*

Section IV

1. U.S. Executive Office of the President, *Standard Industrial Classification Manual*, Vol. II.
2. U.S. Congress, House, 86th Cong., 2nd Sess., Select Committee on Small Business, Staff Report, *Banking Concentration and Small Business*, Committee print, 1960.
3. David A. Alhadeff, *Monopoly and Competition in Banking*, Bureau of Business and Economic Research, University of California, Berkeley and Los Angeles, 1954.

4. U.S. Congress, House, *op. cit.*
5. Alhadeff, *op. cit.*, Chapter XII.
6. U.S. Federal Deposit Insurance Corporation, *Annual Report, Year Ending Dec. 31, 1961*, Government Printing Office, Washington, 1962, pp. 108–11, 128–31, Tables 101, 107.
7. *Ibid.*
8. Simon Whitney, *Antitrust Policies*, The Twentieth Century Fund, Inc., New York, 1958, Vol. II, p. 381.
9. *Ibid.*   10. *Ibid.*
11. U.S. Congress, Senate, Committee on the Judiciary, 86th Cong., 2nd Sess., Report No. 1834, *The Insurance Industry, Aviation, Ocean Marine, and State Regulation*, 1960; U.S. Congress, Senate, Committee on the Judiciary, 87th Cong., 1st Sess., Report No. 831, *The Insurance Industry, Insurance Rates, Rating Organizations and State Rate Regulation*, 1961.
12. U.S. Congress, Senate, *Ocean Marine Insurance*, p. 87.
13. Health Insurance Institute, *Source Book of Health Insurance Data*, New York, 1961.

Section V

1. Wilcox, *op. cit.*, pp. 287–88.
2. *Architectural Forum*, September 1959, Vol. III, pp. 124–26.
3. Carl Brehm, "The Residential Construction Industry," in Adams, *op. cit.*, Chapter IV; U.S. Department of Labor, Bureau of Labor Statistics, *Structure of the Residential Building Industry in 1949*, Bulletin No. 1170, Government Printing Office, Washington, 1954.

Section VI

1. U.S. Department of Agriculture, *The Dairy Situation*, DS–273, August 1959, pp. 20–48.

Section VII

1. U.S. Department of Commerce, *Rationale of Federal Transportation Policy*, Ernest W. Williams, Jr. and David W. Bluestone, Government Printing Office, Washington, April 1960.
2. Thomas B. Dimmick, "Traffic and Travel Trends," 29 *Public Roads* 97, 103 (1956), quoted in D. Phillip Locklin, *Economics of Transportation*, 5th ed., Richard D. Irwin, Homewood, Ill., 1956, p. 637.
3. Public Utilities Commission of California, Transportation Division, *Report on Operations of Carriers of Property, Year 1958*, quoted in Locklin, *op. cit.*, pp. 639–40; U.S. Interstate Commerce Commission, Bureau of Transport Economics and Statistics, *Statistics of Class I, II, and III Motor Carriers, 1939–1956*, Statement No. 389 (1958), p. 24, quoted in Locklin, *op. cit.*, p. 638.
4. U.S. Interstate Commerce Commission, *Annual Report, 1946*, quoted in Locklin, *op. cit.*, p. 36.
5. H. H. Gray, "The Airlines Industry," Adams, *op. cit.*, pp. 443–85.

Section VIII

1. U.S. Department of the Interior, Bureau of Mines, *Mineral Facts and Problems*, 1960 ed., Government Printing Office, Washington, p. 404.
2. Whitney, *op. cit.*, Vol. I, p. 328.
3. U.S. Department of the Interior, *Mineral Facts*, p. 237.
4. Standard & Poor's Industry Surveys, *Metals, Lead-Zinc, Gold, etc.*, sect. 2, *Basic Analysis*, May 25, 1961, p. M100.
5. U.S. Department of the Interior, *Mineral Facts*, p. 429.
6. *Ibid.*
7. Standard & Poor's Industry Surveys, *op. cit.*, pp. M124, M125.
8. *Ibid.*, p. M125.

9. U.S. Department of the Interior, *Mineral Facts*, pp. 976, 987.

10. U.S. Department of the Interior, Bureau of Mines, *Minerals Yearbook*, 1960, Washington: Government Printing Office, 1961, p. 1211.

11. U.S. Department of the Interior, *Mineral Facts*, p. 348.

12. U.S. Department of the Interior, *Minerals Yearbook*, p. 507.

13. U.S. Department of the Interior, *Mineral Facts*, p. 16.

14. *Ibid.*, p. 23.

15. Standard & Poor's Industry Surveys, *op. cit.*, p. M135.

16. U.S. Department of the Interior, *Mineral Facts*, pp. 499–503.

17. *Ibid.*, p. 765.   18. *Ibid.*, p. 494.   19. *Ibid.*, pp. 538, 539.

20. U.S. Department of Commerce, Census Bureau, *1954 Census of Mineral Industries*, Vol. I: *Summary and Industry Statistics*, Government Printing Office, Washington, 1958, p. 10J-1.

21. *Ibid.*

22. U.S. Department of the Interior, *Mineral Facts*, p. 512.

23. U.S. Department of the Interior, *Minerals Yearbook*, p. 707.

24. U.S. Department of Commerce, *1954 Census of Minerals*, pp. 105–12.

25. U.S. Department of the Interior, *Minerals Yearbook*, p. 1119.

26. U.S. Department of the Interior, *Mineral Facts*, p. 92.

27. U.S. Department of Commerce, Census Bureau, *1958 Census of Mineral Industries*, Government Printing Office, Washington, 1962, Vol. I,

28. Whitney, *op. cit.*, Vol. II, pp. 74–81.

29. *Coal Age*, February 1962, p. 28.

30. Whitney, *op. cit.*, Vol. I, pp. 171, 172.

31. *Fortune*, Vol. IX, No. 5 (September 1959).

32. *Ibid.*

33. U.S. Department of the Interior, *Mineral Facts*, p. 809.

34. U.S. Department of the Interior, *Minerals Yearbook*, pp. 1035, 1036.

35. U.S. Department of the Interior, *Mineral Facts*, pp. 199, 205.

36. U.S. Department of the Interior, *Minerals Yearbook*, p. 355.

37. U.S. Department of the Interior, *Mineral Facts*, p. 200.

38. *Ibid.*, p. 209.

39. U.S. Department of the Interior, *Minerals Yearbook*, p. 452.

40. U.S. Department of the Interior, *Mineral Facts*, p. 284.

41. *Ibid.*, p. 483.

42. U.S. Department of Commerce, *1954 Census of Minerals*, Section 14-C.

43. U.S. Department of the Interior, *Mineral Facts*, p. 85.

44. *Ibid.*, p. 306.

45. U.S. Department of the Interior, *Minerals Yearbook*, p. 474.

46. U.S. Department of the Interior, *Mineral Facts*, p. 652.

47. *Ibid.*, p. 143.

48. *Ibid.*, pp. 746–49; *Chemical Week*, Oct. 19, 1957.

49. U.S. Department of the Interior, *Mineral Facts*, pp. 632, 633.

50. *Ibid.*, p. 640.

51. U.S. Department of Commerce, *1954 Census of Minerals*, p. 14H–26.

52. U.S. Department of the Interior, *Mineral Facts*, pp. 755–58.

53. *Ibid.*, pp. 746, 747.   54. *Ibid.*, p. 821.

55. U.S. Department of Commerce, *1954 Census of Minerals*.

56. U.S. Department of the Interior, *Mineral Facts*, p. 368.

57. *Ibid.*, p. 522.   58. *Ibid.*, p. 660.   59. *Ibid.*, p. 836.   60. *Ibid.*, p. 446.

Section IX

1. Wilcox, *op. cit.*, pp. 83–88, 98–100.

2. U.S. Federal Communications Commission, *25th Annual Report, Fiscal Year 1959*, Government Printing Office, Washington, 1959, p. 92.

3. Commerce Clearing House, *Trade Cases*, 1956 vol., Para. 68,246.

4. U.S. Federal Communications Commission, *21st Annual Report, Fiscal Year 1954–1955*, Government Printing Office, Washington, 1955, pp. 45–48.

5. Wilcox, *op. cit.*, pp. 173–76; U.S. Federal Communications Commission, *7th Annual Report, Fiscal Year 1941*, Government Printing Office, Washington, 1941, Chapter IV.

6. U.S. Federal Communications Commission, *25th Annual Report*, p. 78.

7. W. F. Hellmuth, "The Motion Picture Industry," in Adams, *op. cit.*, pp. 392–401.

8. Wilcox, *op. cit.*, pp. 93–95.

9. U.S. Congress, House, Select Committee on Small Business, Hearings, 1956.

APPENDIX D

1. See Appendices A and B for a brief description of the data and procedures employed by Nutter.

2. These were SIC (1958 ed.) industries 2025, 2141 and 3273. SIC 2027 was fluid milk pasteurizing (1947 SIC 2027) and was omitted in 1954 and 1958; SIC 2141 was tobacco stemming and redrying (1947 SIC 2141) and was omitted in 1954 and 1958; SIC 3273 was ready-mixed concrete and was omitted in 1958, the first year of its inclusion in the *Census of Manufactures*.

3. U.S. Bureau of the Census, *Historical Comparability of Census of Manufactures Industries, 1929–1958*, Bureau of the Census Working Paper No. 9, Government Printing Office, Washington, 1959; Ralph L. Nelson, *Concentration of Manufacturing Industries of the United States, A Midcentury Report*, Economic Census Study No. 2, Yale University Press, New Haven, 1963.

4. This is considered further in Appendix A.

5. Nelson, *op. cit.*, p. 58.   6. *Ibid.*, p. 57.

7. J. Aitchison and J. A. C. Brown, *The Lognormal Distribution, with Special Reference to Its Uses in Economics*, Cambridge University Press, Cambridge, England; 1957, p. 1.

8. P. E. Hart and S. J. Prais, "The Analysis of Business Concentration: A Statistical Approach," *Journal of the Royal Statistical Society*, Series A (General), 119, Part 2 (1956), pp. 150–90.

9. *Ibid.*, pp. 181–90, contains the comments of Professor Champernowne and others, as well as a reply to these comments by Hart and Prais.

10. Leonard V. Weiss "Factors in Changing Concentration," *The Review of Economics and Statistics*, XLV, No. 1 (February 1963), pp. 70–77.

11. William G. Shepherd, "Trends of Concentration in American Manufacturing Industries, 1947–1958," *The Review of Economics and Statistics*, XLVI, No. 2 (May 1964).

12. Dr. John M. Blair questions the appropriateness of Lorenz curves as measures of output concentration: "Statistical Measures of Concentration in Business, Problems of Compiling and Interpretation," *Bulletin of the Oxford University Institute of Statistics*, 18, No. 4 (November 1956). The use of Lorenz distribution is defended by P. E. Hart and S. J. Prais, *op. cit.*

Bibliography

Adams, Walter. *The Structure of the American Economy*, 3rd ed., The Macmillan Co., New York, 1961.

Adelman, Morris A. "The Measurement of Industrial Concentration," *Review of Economics and Statistics*, XXXIII, No. 4 (November 1951), 269–96, 290–93.

———, and others (C. D. Edwards, C. Stocking, E. B. George, A. A. Berle, Jr.). "Four Comments on 'The Measurement of Industrial Concentration': With a Rejoinder by Professor Adelman," *Review of Economics and Statistics*, XXXIV, No. 2 (May 1952), 156–78.

———, and others (J. N. Blair, J. Lintner, J. K. Butters). "Rejoinder" and "Further Rejoinder" to "The Measurement of Industrial Concentration: A Reply" by Blair, *Review of Economics and Statistics*, XXXIV, No. 4 (November 1952), 343–67.

Aitchison, J., and J. A. C. Brown. *The Lognormal Distribution, with Special Reference to Its Uses in Economics*, Cambridge University Press, Cambridge, England, 1957.

———. "On Criteria for Descriptions of Income Distribution," *Metroeconomics*, VI, Fase III (December 1954), 88–107.

Alhadeff, David A. *Monopoly and Competition in Banking*, The Bureau of Business and Economic Research, University of California, Berkeley and Los Angeles, 1954.

Anderson, Dewey et al. *Final Report of the Executive Secretary to the Temporary National Economic Committee*, Government Printing Office, Washington, 1941.

Architectural Forum, September 1959.

Automobile Manufacturers' Association. *Automobile Facts and Figures, 1940*, Automobile Manufacturers' Association, Detroit, 1940.

Bain, Joe S. "Price and Production Policies," in Howard S. Ellis (ed.), *A Survey of Contemporary Economics*, Blakiston Co., Philadelphia, 1948.

Barger, Harold, and S. H. Schurr. *The Mining Industries, 1899–1939:*

A Study of Output, Employment and Productivity, National Bureau of Economic Research, New York, 1944.

Beal, George Max, and Henry N. Bakken. *Fluid Milk Marketing*, Mimir Publishers, Madison, Wisc., 1956.

Berle, A. A., Jr. "Four Comments on 'The Measurement of Industrial Concentration,'" *Review of Economics and Statistics*, May 1952, 172–74.

Blair, John M. "Statistical Measures of Concentration in Business, Problems of Compiling and Interpretation," *Bulletin of the Oxford University Institute of Statistics*, 18, No. 4 (November 1956).

Bogen, Jules. *The Competitive Position of Commercial Banks*, New York University Graduate School of Business Administration, New York, 1959.

Burns, Arthur R. *The Decline of Competition*, McGraw-Hill Book Co., New York, 1936.

"Can Soda Ash Soak Up Excess Caustic Soda?" *Chemical Week*, Oct. 19, 1957.

Coal Age, February 1962.

Commerce Clearing House. *Trade Cases*, 1948–1949 Vol., 1956 Vol., Commerce Clearing House, New York.

———. *Trade Regulation Reporter*, Vols. 1, 3, and 4, Commerce Clearing House, New York, 1958.

Dewing, Arthur S. *Corporate Promotions and Reorganizations*, Harvard University Press, Cambridge, 1914.

Edwards, C. D. "Four Comments on 'The Measurement of Industrial Concentration,'" *Review of Economics and Statistics*, May 1952, 156–61.

Fabricant, Solomon. *The Output of Manufacturing Industries, 1899–1937*, National Bureau of Economic Research, New York, 1940.

———. "Is Monopoly Increasing?" *Journal of Economic History*, Winter 1953, 89–94.

Fisher, R. A., and F. Yates. *Statistical Tables for Biological, Agricultural, and Medical Research*, 3rd ed., Hafner Publishing Co., New York, 1948.

Fortune, LX, No. 5 (September 1959).

Galbraith, John K. *American Capitalism: The Concept of Countervailing Power*, Houghton Mifflin Co., Boston, 1952.

———. "Monopoly and the Concentration of Economic Power," in Howard S. Ellis (ed.), *A Survey of Contemporary Economics*, Blakiston Co., Philadelphia, 1948.

George, E. B. "Four Comments on 'The Measurement of Industrial Concentration,'" *Review of Economics and Statistics*, May 1952, 168–72.

Hart, P. E., and S. J. Prais. "The Analysis of Business Concentration: A Statistical Approach," *Journal of the Royal Statistical Society*, Series A, 1956, 150–81; Series A (General), Vol. 119, Part 2, 1956, 150–90.

Hayek, F. K. *The Road to Serfdom*, The University of Chicago Press, Chicago, 1944.

Health Insurance Institute. *Source Book of Health Insurance Data*, Health Insurance Institute, New York, 1961.

Hymer, Stephen, and Peter Pashigian. "Firm Size and Rate of Growth," *Journal of Political Economy*, December 1962, 556–69.

Jewkes, John. *Ordeal by Planning*, The Macmillan Co., New York, 1948.

Kayson, Carl, and Donald F. Turner. *Antitrust Policy, an Economic and Legal Analysis*, Harvard University Press, Cambridge, Mass., 1959.

Kuznets, Simon. *National Income and Its Composition, 1919–1938*, Vol. II, National Bureau of Economic Research, New York, 1941.

Labor Research Association. *Monopoly in the United States*, International Publishers, New York, 1942.

Laidler, Harry W. *Concentration of Control in American Industry*, Thomas Y. Crowell Co., New York, 1931.

Lebergott, Stanley. "Has Monopoly Increased?" *Review of Economics and Statistics*, November 1953, 349–51.

Lent, George E. *The Changing Structure of Commercial Banking*, Dartmouth College, Hanover, N.H., 1960.

Lerner, Abba. "The Concept of Monopoly and the Measurement of Monopoly Power," *Review of Economic Studies*, I (June 1934), 157–75.

Lewis, W. Arthur. *Monopoly in British Industry*, Fabian Research Series No. 91, Fabian Publications, Ltd., London, 1945.

Locklin, D. Philip. *Economics of Transportation*, 5th ed., Richard D. Irwin, Homewood, Ill., 1960.

Mansfield, Edwin. "Entry, Gibrat's Law, Innovation, and the Growth of Firms," *American Economic Review*, December 1962, 1023–51.

Martin, Robert F. *National Income in the United States, 1799–1938*, National Industrial Conference Board, New York, 1939.

Mason, Edward S. *Economic Concentration and the Monopoly Problem*, Harvard University Press, Cambridge, Mass., 1957.

Means, Gardiner C. *The Structure of the American Economy: A Report Prepared by the Industrial Section of the National Resources Committee*, Part I, Government Printing Office, Washington, 1939.

Moody, John. *The Truth about the Trusts*, Moody Publishing Co., New York, 1904.

Nadler, Marcus, and Jules Bogen. *The Bank Holding Company*, New York University Graduate School of Business, New York, 1959.

Nelson, Ralph L. *Concentration of Manufacturing Industries of the United States, A Midcentury Report*, Economic Census Studies, No. 2, Yale University Press, New Haven, 1963.

Nutter, G. Warren. *The Extent of Enterprise Monopoly in the United States, 1899–1939*, The University of Chicago Press, Chicago, 1951.

———. "Industrial Concentration," *International Encyclopedia of the Social Sciences*, Macmillan and the Free Press, New York, 1968.

———. "Monopoly, Bigness, and Progress," *Journal of Political Economy*, December 1956, 520–27.

———. "Rejoinder to Mr. Lebergott," *Review of Economics and Statistics*, November 1953, 352–53.

Ogburn, W. F., et al. *Technological Trends and National Policy: Report of the Subcommittee on Technology to the National Resources Committee*, Government Printing Office, Washington, 1937.

Pashigian, Peter Bedros. *The Distribution of Automobiles and Economic Analysis of the Franchise System* (a 1960 winner of the Ford Foundation Doctoral Dissertation Series), Prentice-Hall, Englewood Cliffs, N.J., 1961.

Quandt, R. E. "On the Size Distribution of Firms," *American Economic Review*, June 1966, 416–32.

Schumpeter, Joseph A. *Capitalism, Socialism and Democracy*, 2nd ed., Harper & Brothers, New York, 1947.

Shepherd, William G. "Trends of Concentration in American Manufacturing Industries, 1947–1958," *Review of Economics and Statistics*, XLVI, No. 2 (May 1964), 200–12.

Simon, H. A., and C. P. Bonini. "The Size Distribution of Business Firms," *American Economic Review*, September 1958, 607–17.

Simons, Henry C. *Economic Policy for a Free Society*, The University of Chicago Press, Chicago, 1948.

Slater, Charles C. *Economic Changes in the Baking Industry* (published for the American Bakers Association as a supplement to *Baking in America*, Northwestern University Press, Evanston, Ill., 1956), American Bakers Association, Chicago, 1958.

Snedecor, George W. *Statistical Methods*, 4th ed., Iowa State College Press, Ames, 1946.

Standard & Poor. *Standard & Poor's Industry Surveys: Metals, Lead-Zinc, Gold, etc.*, Sect. 2. *Basic Analysis*, May 25, 1961.

Stigler, George J. "The Case against Big Business," *Fortune*, XLVII, No. 5 (May 1952), 123, 158–67.

———. "Competition in the U.S.," *Five Lectures on Economic Problems*, Longmans, Green & Co., London, 1949.

———. "The Extent and Bases of Monopoly," *American Economic Review*, XXXII (Suppl., June 1942), 1–22.

———. *Five Lectures on Economic Problems*, Longmans, Green & Co., London, 1949.

Stocking, G. W. "Four Comments on 'The Measurement of Industrial Concentration,'" *Review of Economics and Statistics*, May 1952, 161–68.

Tarshis, Lorie. *The Elements of Economics*, Houghton Mifflin Co., Boston, 1947.

Thorp, Willard L., and Walter F. Crowder. *The Structure of Industry*, Temporary National Economic Committee Monograph No. 27, Government Printing Office, Washington, 1941.

U.S. Bureau of Agricultural Economics. *Price Spreads between Farmers and Consumers for Food Products: 1913–44*, Miscellaneous Publication No. 576, Government Printing Office, Washington, 1945.

U.S. Bureau of the Census. *Abstract of the Census of Manufactures: 1914*, Government Printing Office, Washington, 1917.

———. *Abstract of the Census of Manfactures: 1919*, Government Printing Office, Washington, 1923.

———. *Biennial Census of Manufactures: 1921*, Government Printing Office, Washington, 1924.

———. *Biennial Census of Manufactures: 1923*, Government Printing Office, Washington, 1926.

———. *Biennial Census of Manufactures: 1925*, Government Printing Office, Washington, 1928.

———. *Biennial Census of Manufactures: 1937*, Part I, Government Printing Office, Washington, 1939.

———. *Census of Manufactures: 1905*, Part I, Government Printing Office, Washington, 1907.

———. *Census of Manufactures: 1909*, Government Printing Office, Washington, 1912.

———. *Census of Manufactures: 1939: Industry Classifications*, Government Printing Office, Washington, 1940.

———. *Census of Manufactures: 1954*, Government Printing Office, Washington, 1957.

———. *Census of Manufactures: 1958*, Government Printing Office, Washington, 1961.

———. *Census of Mineral Industries: 1954, Summary and Industry Statistics*, Vol. I, Government Printing Office, Washington, 1958.

———. *Census of Mineral Industries, 1958; Summary and Industry Statistics*, Vol. I, Government Printing Office, Washington 1962.

———. *Historical Comparability of Census of Manufactures Industries, 1929–1958*, Bureau of the Census Working Paper No. 9, Government Printing Office, Washington, 1959.

———. *Mines and Quarries: 1902*, Government Printing Office, Washington 1905.

————. *Sixteenth Census of the United States: 1940; Manufactures: 1939*, Vols. I and II, Government Printing Office, Washington, 1942.

————. *Sixteenth Census of the United States: 1940; Mineral Industries: 1939*, Vol. I, Government Printing Office, Washington, 1942.

————. *Statistical Abstract of the United States: 1923*, Government Printing Office, Washington, 1923.

————. *Statistical Abstract of the United States: 1932*, Government Printing Office, Washington, 1932.

————. *Statistical Abstract of the United States: 1940*, Government Printing Office, Washington, 1940.

————. *Statistical Abstract of the United States: 1946*, Government Printing Office, Washington, 1946.

————. *Statistical Abstract of the United States: 1948*, Government Printing Office, Washington, 1948.

U.S. Census Office. *Twelfth Census of the United States, Taken in the Year 1900: Manufactures*, 4 Parts, Government Printing Office, Washington, 1902.

U.S. Comptroller of the Currency. *Annual Report*, Government Printing Office, Washington, 1960.

U.S. Congress, House. Committee on Interstate and Foreign Commerce. *Hearings: Automobile Labeling*, 84th Cong., 1st Sess., May 28, 1955, Government Printing Office, Washington, 1955.

————. Committee on Interstate and Foreign Commerce. *Hearings: Automobile Marketing Legislation*, 84th Cong., 1st and 2nd Sess., July 1955, April and May 1956, Government Printing Office, Washington, 1956.

————. Committee on Interstate and Foreign Commerce. *Agency Hearings*, 85th Cong., 1st Sess., February and March 1957, Government Printing Office, Washington, 1957.

————. Committee on Interstate and Foreign Commerce. *Hearings: Independent Regulatory Agencies Legislation*, 86th Cong., 2nd Sess., March and April 1960, Government Printing Office, Washington, 1960.

————. Committee on the Judiciary. *Hearings: Bank Mergers*, 84th Cong., 1st Sess., 1955, Government Printing Office, Washington, 1955.

————. Committee on the Judiciary, Antitrust Subcommittee. Subcommittee No. 5, *Hearings: Current Antitrust Problems*, Part I, 84th Cong., 1st Sess., May–June 1955, 3 vols., Government Printing Office, Washington, 1955.

————. Committee on Small Business. *United States versus Economic Concentration and Monopoly: An Investigation of the Effectiveness of the Government's Efforts to Combat Economic Concentration. A Staff Report to the Monopoly Subcommittee, Pursuant to H. R. 64*, 79th Cong., Government Printing Office, Washington, 1941.

————. Select Committee on Small Business. *Banking Concentration and*

Small Business, Staff Report, Committee Print, 86th Cong., 2nd Sess., 1960, Government Printing Office, Washington, 1960.

———. Select Committee on Small Business. *Hearings: The Organization and Procedures of the Federal Regulatory Commissions and Agencies and Their Effect on Small Business.* 84th Cong., 1st Sess., 1955–1956, Government Printing Office, Washington, 1956.

———. Select Committee on Small Business. *The Organization and Procedures of the Federal Regulatory Commissions,* Report of Subcommittee No. 1 to Select Committee on Regulatory Agencies and Commissions, 84th Cong., 2nd Sess., December 1956, Government Printing Office, Washington, 1956.

———. Select Committee on Small Business. *Price Discrimination in Dairy Products: Hearings Pursuant to H. R. 56,* Parts 1 and 2, 85th Cong., 1st and 2nd Sess., 1957 and 1958, Government Printing Office, Washington, 1958.

———. Select Committee on Small Business. *Small Business Problems in the Dairy Industry,* Report No. 2231, 88th Cong., 2nd Sess., 1960. Government Printing Office, Washington, 1960.

U.S. Congress, Senate. Committee on Commerce. *National Transportation Policy,* Report No. 445, 87th Cong., 1st Sess., 1961. Government Printing Office, Washington, 1961.

———. Committee on Government Operations. *Agency Reorganization Plans of 1961,* 87th Cong., 1st Sess., June 1961, Government Printing Office, Washington, 1961.

———. Committee on Interstate and Foreign Commerce. *Hearings: Automobile Marketing Practices: Finance and Insurance,* 85th Cong., 1st Sess., March 1957, Government Printing Office, Washington, 1957.

———. Committee on the Judiciary. *Concentration in American Industry,* Report of the Subcommittee on Antitrust and Monopoly to the Committee on the Judiciary, Pursuant to S. R. 57, 85th Cong., 1st Sess., 1957. Government Printing Office, Washington, 1957.

———. Committee on the Judiciary. *Concentration Ratios in American Industry, 1958,* Report prepared by the Bureau of the Census for the Subcommittee on Antitrust and Monopoly of the Committee on the Judiciary together with Industrial Views, Committee Print, Part 1, 87th Cong., 2nd Sess., 1962, Government Printing Office, Washington, 1962.

———. Committee on the Judiciary. *Corporate Mergers and Acquisitions,* Report No. 132, 85th Cong., 1st Sess., 1957. Government Printing Office, Washington, 1957.

———. Committee on the Judiciary. *The Insurance Industry, Aviation, Ocean Marine, and State Regulation,* Report No. 1834, 86th Cong., 2nd Sess., 1960, Government Printing Office, Washington, 1960.

————. Committee on the Judiciary. *The Insurance Industry, Insurance Rates, Rating Organizations and State Regulation*, Report No. 831, 87th Cong., 1st Sess., 1961, Government Printing Office, Washington, 1961.

————. Committee on the Judiciary, Subcommittee on Administrative Practices and Procedure. *Report on Regulatory Agencies to the President Elect (the Landis Report)*, 86th Cong., 2nd Sess., December 1960, Government Printing Office, Washington, 1960.

U.S. Department of Agriculture. *The Dairy Situation*, DS–273, August 1959, Government Printing Office, Washington, 1959.

U.S. Department of Commerce, Office of Business Economics. *Business Statistics, a Supplement to the Survey of Current Business*, 1959 ed., Government Printing Office, Washington, 1959.

————. *National Income, a Supplement to the Survey of Current Business*, 1954 ed., Government Printing Office, Washington, 1954.

————. "National Income and Product Statistics of the United States: 1929–46," *Survey of Current Business Supplement*, July 1947, Government Printing Office, Washington, 1947.

————. Ernest Williams, Jr., and W. Bluestone. *Rationale of Federal Transportation Policy*, Government Printing Office, Washington, 1960.

————. *Survey of Current Business*, XI, No. 7 (July 1960), Government Printing Office, Washington, 1960.

————. *U.S. Income and Output, a Supplement to the Survey of Current Business*, 1959 ed., Government Printing Office, Washington, 1959.

U.S. Department of the Interior, Bureau of Mines. *Mineral Facts and Problems*, 1960 ed., Government Printing Office, Washington, 1960.

————. *Minerals Yearbook, 1960*, Government Printing Office, Washington, 1961.

U.S. Department of Labor, Bureau of Labor Statistics. *Structure of the Residential Building Industry in 1949*, Bulletin No. 1170, Government Printing Office, Washington, 1954.

U.S. Executive Office of the President, Bureau of the Budget, *Standard Industrial Classfication*, Government Printing Office, Washington, 1942.

U.S. Federal Communications Commission. *7th Annual Report, Fiscal Year 1941*, Government Printing Office, Washington, 1941.

————. *21st Annual Report, Fiscal Year 1954–1955*, Government Printing Office, Washington, 1955.

————. *25th Annual Report, Fiscal Year 1959*, Government Printing Office, Washington, 1959.

U.S. Federal Deposit Insurance Corporation. *Annual Report, Year Ended December 31, 1961*, Government Printing Office, Washington, 1962.

U.S. Federal Trade Commission, Bureau of Economics. *Economic Inquiry into Food Marketing*, Government Printing Office, Washington, 1960.

U.S. Industrial Commission. *Reports of the Industrial Commission*, Vols. I, XIII, and XIX, Government Printing Office, Washington, 1900–1902.

Van Hise, Charles R. *Concentration and Control, a Solution of the Trust Problem in the United States*, The Macmillan Co., New York, 1914.

Weiss, Leonard V. "Factors in Changing Concentration," *Review of Economics and Statistics*, XLV, No. 1 (February 1963), 70–77.

Whitney, Simon. *Antitrust Policies*, 2 vols., The Twentieth Century Fund, New York, 1958.

Wilcox, Clair. *Competition and Monopoly in American Industry*, Temporary National Economic Committee Monograph No. 21, Government Printing Office, Washington, 1940.

Williams, Ernest, Jr. *Economics of Transportation*, rev. ed., Harper Bros., New York, 1959.

———, and W. Bluestone. *Rationale of Federal Transportation Policy*, U.S. Department of Commerce, Government Printing Office, Washington, 1960.

Index